OXFORD THEOLOGICAL MONOGRAPHS

Oxford Theological Monographs

THE ENGLISH SEPARATIST TRADITION
By B. R. WHITE. 1971

THE PRINCIPLE OF RESERVE IN THE WRITINGS OF
JOHN HENRY NEWMAN
By R. C. SELBY. 1975

GELASIAN SACRAMENTARIES OF THE 8TH CENTURY
By M. B. MORETON. 1975

THREE MONOPHYSITE CHRISTOLOGIES
By R. C. CHESNUT. 1976

RITUALISM AND POLITICS IN VICTORIAN BRITAIN
By J. BENTLEY. 1978

THE ONTOLOGY OF PAUL TILLICH
By A. THATCHER. 1978

BECOMING AND BEING
By C. E. GUNTON. 1978

CALVIN AND ENGLISH CALVINISM TO 1649

R. T. KENDALL

OXFORD UNIVERSITY PRESS

1979

Oxford University Press, Walton Street, Oxford OX2 6DP

OXFORD LONDON GLASGOW
NEW YORK TORONTO MELBOURNE WELLINGTON
KUALA LUMPUR SINGAPORE HONG KONG TOKYO
DELHI BOMBAY CALCUTTA MADRAS KARACHI
NAIROBI DAR ES SALAAM CAPE TOWN

Published in the United States by
Oxford University Press, New York

British Library Cataloguing in Publication Data
Kendall, R. T.
  Calvin and English Calvinism to 1649
  – (Oxford theological monographs)
  1. Calvinism – England – History
  I. Title
  230′.4′2   BX9480.G7   79-40669
ISBN 0-19-826716-9

Printed in Great Britain
at the University Press, Oxford
by Eric Buckley
Printer to the University

To my Father
my best teacher

PREFACE

THIS book is my D.Phil. thesis which I submitted to the Theology Faculty Board of Oxford in 1976 under the title 'The Nature of Saving Faith from William Perkins (d. 1602) to the Westminster Assembly (1643-1649)'. I regret that it has not been practicable to include the charts of Theodore Beza and William Perkins in the Appendix. They make no real contribution to the argument, however, only that they visually demonstrate Perkins's dependence upon Beza's system.

There are dogmatic questions raised by this book which I do not answer, for this is a piece of historical theology not dogmatic theology. I have not argued whether Calvin or anyone else is on the side of Scripture. My method has been to follow what each man actually says (and does not say) and raise the questions which their own assumptions call for. I have received sufficient feedback already from a good number of people who have read or have heard about the thesis to anticipate one or two burning questions this book raises. It was therefore a temptation to add one or two things to my original work, but I have resisted this. These queries do not relate directly to the general argument but to some implications regarding Calvin's teaching on the atonement and also certain statements by Calvin himself which, some thought, support a different view. Regarding the latter, I had in fact faced these, and I am satisfied that what I have shown about Calvin's position will stand. I do aspire to treat this subject fully some day.

There are also non-dogmatic issues that I have had to pass by. It was necessary to put a limit on the general period, the people treated, and other subject matter which these men raised (e.g. ecclesiological). This book may well have begun with Augustine, Thomas Aquinas, or most certainly Martin Luther. Moreover, at least one hundred worthy men should be included between William Tyndale and Samuel Rutherford. I have chosen the most prominent and influential men of their day and from these have drawn only the tip of the iceberg. Furthermore, the story does not end with the Westminster Confession of Faith or Catechisms. I should be most gratified if this book encourages scholars to show how subsequent divines fit into the broader picture I have begun to paint, especially men like John Bunyan, John Owen, Andrew Fuller, and Jonathan Edwards.

This book traces the doctrine of faith from Calvin to Perkins to the Westminster Assembly in order to discuss in what sense Westminster theology may be regarded as the theological legacy of Calvin and/or Perkins. The main argument will begin when Perkins's doctrine of faith is set in the context of his Continental and English precursors. It was necessary to bring in Arminius as well as the Antinomian controversy, for without these cross-currents there probably never would have been a Westminster Confession of Faith. But I was not expecting the interesting subsidiary discovery I came on to.

My great surprise, however, was my major conclusion, for I had long held (and published) that Westminster theology was that of John Calvin, or at least the logical extension of his thought. My research led me to a different view, but one which has not retarded my appreciation either for Calvin himself or those who are commonly called 'Calvinists'. Whether Perkins and his followers ought properly to be called Calvinists I will leave for the reader finally to judge, but I suspect that calling the Perkins tradition *English* Calvinism will be acceptable in any case.

I turn now to my debts. I suppose it is a good thing if a research student thinks his own supervisor is the best, but I will always believe that mine really was. I will never cease to be thankful that Dr B. R. White, Principal of Regent's Park College, was assigned to me by the Faculty Board. When I came up to Oxford in 1973 my sights were set on doing John Owen's view of the priestly work of Christ, a subject suggested to me by Dr J. I. Packer. Assuming that I was fairly well acquainted with Owen, Dr White put me on to Owen's pre-history (beginning with Tyndale) so that my treatment of Owen would be in a historical context. The result (which neither he nor I anticipated) was that I never got to John Owen.

Apart from my supervisor those who have contributed to this book would make a list exceedingly long. I owe an incalculable debt to Dr J. I. Packer, who saw me as often as I needed him when he was Associate Principal of Trinity College, Bristol. I also frequently consulted with Dr D. Martyn Lloyd-Jones, always my beloved friend but now one of my predecessors at Westminster Chapel. I wish to thank my examiners, Dr T. H. L. Parker and Dr B. R. Worden, who made my *viva* a productive hour. Dr Parker has since given me a good deal of his time. I am especially grateful to Dr John S. Macquarrie, Lady Margaret Professor of Divinity at Oxford, for his encouragement. A good number of others have read my thesis, but I am most obliged to Elizabeth Catherwood of London, and Dr N. B. Magruder of Louisville, Kentucky. All the above have provided most helpful comments, but this book, presented to the reader with almost no changes at all, should not be taken as an endorsement by any of these.

I want to thank the three American professors who encouraged me to come to Oxford: Dr Eric Rust and Dr Dale Moody of Southern Baptist Theological Seminary, Louisville, Kentucky, and Dr William J. Morison of the University of Louisville. I owe a debt to other professors at my old seminary, among them Dr W. Morgan Patterson (now at Golden Gate Baptist Theological Seminary, Mill Valley, California), who gave me a fresh appreciation for church history, and Dr James Leo Garrett (now at Baylor University, Waco, Texas), who first taught me to think theologically in terms of historical development.

I owe a most profound debt to Dr and Mrs James H. Milby, now living in Brentwood, Tennessee, who stood by me faithfully during my three years in Oxford with their prayers and financial support.

My research led me to Holland (Dordrecht, and The Hague), Noyon, France, and Geneva. But in the end all I needed for this book was on deposit either at the Bodleian Library, Oxford, or the British Museum, London. I express appreciation to both of these great libraries but especially to those in Duke Humphrey in the Bodleian.

Working with the people of Oxford University Press has been a particularly pleasant experience.

Finally, my greatest debt of all is to my wife and two children. They supported me unselfishly during those years in which the Bodleian saw more of me than they did. But this brings me to yet another surprise which has come to us since being over here, and this surpasses all. We have chosen to remain in Britain. None of us had the remotest thought of making our Mother Country a permanent home, especially as the traffic has flowed largely westward since 1620 with ever increasing speed. But in the year of my country's two hundredth birthday our Bicentennial gesture was to remain in that land which, with the help of the central figures of this book, gave America her soul.

London
1979

CONTENTS

Contents

INTRODUCTION

In 1589, when the Protestant ecclesiological controversy in the England of Elizabeth I was at its height, William Perkins published his first major work, *A Treatise tending vnto a declaration whether a man be in the estate of damnation or in the estate of grace: and if he be in the first, how he may in time come out of it: if in the second, how he maie discerne it, and perseuere in the same to the end.*[1] This treatise inaugurated a new era in English theology. Perkins's writings generally emphasize soteriology not ecclesiology, and *Whether a Man* particularly assumes a doctrine of faith, however refined or modified by his followers, which was given credal sanction by the Westminster Assembly (1643–9). Although his *magnum opus*[2] is more systematic, the 1589 treatise graphically sets forward the central issue of my own book.

This book is concerned with the nature of 'saving' faith (which only God's elect possess) as opposed to 'temporary' faith (which the reprobate, or non-elect, may have). The fundamental concern in the theology of Perkins and his followers centres on the question, How can one know he is elect and not reprobate? The doctrine of double predestination[3] is an assumption in the Perkins tradition. Hence their doctrine of faith is developed in the context that all men are eternally predestined either to election or reprobation, salvation or destruction, heaven or hell.

It has been generally assumed that William Perkins and his followers were followers of the Genevan reformer John Calvin and that the theology embraced in the Westminster Confession of Faith was true Calvinism, or, at least, the logical extension of his thought.[4]

---

[1] Hereinafter called *Whether a Man*. This was his first book to achieve wide popularity. See *infra*, p. 53 n. 2, for references to Perkins's works to be used below.

[2] *Armilla Aurea* (1590), translated as *A Golden Chaine* (1591).

[3] This is the belief that God foreordained a certain number of men to salvation (the elect) and a certain number of men to perdition (the reprobate); this number can neither be increased nor diminished by anything men can do.

[4] The same could be said for the Synod of Dordrecht (Dort) (1618–19) which championed the famous Five Points of Calvinism (popularly recalled by the acrostic TULIP): total depravity, unconditional election, limited atonement, irresistible grace, and perseverance of the saints. J. I. Packer says that the Synod of Dort formula of limited atonement states what Calvin 'would have said had he faced the Arminian thesis'. 'Calvin the Theologian', *John Calvin* (Abingdon, 1966), 151. Limited atonement is the belief that Christ died for the elect only.

2   *Introduction*

B. B. Warfield claims that there is nothing in the Westminster
Confession 'which is not to be found expressly set forth in the
writings' of John Calvin.[1] This assumption has been accepted rather
uncritically by most theologians and historians generally and the
rank and file of Presbyterians and Baptists particularly.[2] While
Presbyterians trace their theological roots to the Westminster
Confession, the majority of Baptists trace theirs at least to the
Second London Confession (1677) which followed the Westminster Confession almost verbatim save for statements relating
to ecclesiology.[3] Reformed churches generally look to the Belgic
Confession (1561) via the Synod of Dort for their theological
beginnings.[4] In a word: a good number of Protestant bodies in the
Western world are in some way indebted either to the Westminster
Confession or the Synod of Dort for much of their theological
heritage.

This book attempts in part to reassess the assumption that
Calvin's soteriology was faithfully upheld by the venerable divines
who drew up the Westminster Confession and the Shorter and
Larger catechisms. The present book is not the first to claim that
Calvin held that Christ died for all men. Moise Amyraut (1596–
1644) apparently thought he was but following Calvin when he
insisted that Christ died for all men.[5] The Scottish theologian
William Cunningham (d. 1861) granted that uncertainty concerning
Calvin's real position had at times emerged, but concluded: 'no

[1] B. B. Warfield, *Studies in Theology* (1932), 148. Cf. A. A. Hodge, *The Atonement*
(1868), 357–67; and William Cunningham, *The Reformers and the Theology of the
Reformation* (1862), 397.
[2] Frank S. Mead, *Handbook of Denominations in the United States* (Nashville,
1975), 217, when referring to Calvin's influence upon Presbyterianism, states that
Calvin's 'system' may be 'summarized in 5 main points' by which he means those
described above on p. 1 n. 4. Mead also refers to 'Particular, or Calvinistic, Baptist
churches'. Ibid. 37. Particular Baptists were so named for their belief in 'particular
redemption', a term used interchangeably with limited atonement.
[3] Most Baptists in existence today, including the Southern Baptist Convention
(membership approximately 13 million), stem from the Particular Baptists of the
seventeenth century. A very small minority of Baptists, including the General
Baptists in America (membership approximately 70,000), are traceable to 'Arminian
Baptists'. See my 'The Rise and Demise of Calvinism in the Southern Baptist
Convention' (unpublished MA thesis, University of Louisville, 1973).
[4] John A. Leith, *Creeds of the Churches* (Richmond, 1973), 127ff. The Savoy
Declaration (1658), the first major confession of Congregationalism, followed the
Westminster Confession almost verbatim save for ecclesiological matters.
[5] Brian G. Armstrong, *Calvinism and the Amyraut Heresy: Protestant Scholasti-
cism and Humanism in Seventeenth-Century France* (Madison, 1969), 130–60.

sufficient evidence has been brought forward that Calvin held that Christ died for all men, or for the whole world.'[1]

Calvin's doctrine of atonement, however, is not the subject of this book. A definitive study on this is yet to be written. What follows is a study of the nature of saving faith in William Perkins and his followers against the context of what Calvin believed concerning faith. Calvin's doctrine of atonement comes into the picture because of its inseparable connection with his understanding of assurance. The author hopes to make a contribution by throwing some light on (1) the relation between saving faith and Christ's death and intercession in Calvin's theology; (2) the relation of faith to Christ's death in the theology of Theodore Beza; (3) Perkins's apparent dependence on Beza and certain Heidelberg theologians of the sixteenth century; (4) the way in which voluntarism (faith as an act of the will in contrast to a passive persuasion in the mind) gained ascendancy in the Perkins tradition; (5) the vacillating fate of the doctrine of temporary faith among those whose thought was shaped by the Perkins tradition.

The main questions upon which this study will centre may be briefly summarized: (1) whether the 'seat' of faith is located in the understanding or in man's will; (2) whether faith precedes repentance in the *ordo salutis* (or vice versa); (3) whether assurance of salvation may be enjoyed by a 'direct' act of faith or if such assurance must be delayed until a 'reflex' act of faith comes; (4) what is the ground of assurance; and (5) what place a doctrine of temporary faith has in a theology that makes one's sanctification or repentance the ground of assurance.

Our method will be to trace the doctrine of faith from William Perkins through his most prominent followers to the Westminster Assembly and to make an assessment whether Westminster theology may be regarded as the theological legacy of the Perkins tradition.[2] The main argument will begin when Perkins's doctrine of faith is set in the context of his Continental and English precursors. Perkins's leading followers will be examined up to and including the Antinomian controversies (in America and England) which preceded the Westminster Assembly. An interesting subsidiary feature emerges in the study: it shows the surprising degree of reciprocity

---

[1] Cunningham, op. cit. 397.

[2] 'Westminster theology' in this book refers to the nature of saving faith in the three main documents that issued from the Westminster Assembly, viz. the Confession of Faith, the Larger Catechism, and the Shorter Catechism.

that exists between Westminster theology and the doctrine of faith in Jacobus Arminius.

There appears to be no study comparable to that proposed above.[1] This is remarkable indeed considering the fact that the documents which issued from the Westminster Assembly are reckoned to be among the most influential in the history of Protestantism. The nearest study to that proposed in this book is Norman Pettit, *The Heart Prepared* (New Haven, 1966), which deals with the doctrine of preparation for grace in the general period of this book. Although Pettit's study does not terminate with the Westminster Assembly (nor does he treat it), his work cannot go unnoticed since many of the divines to be examined below are treated by him. The doctrine of preparation, moreover, is essentially connected to their doctrine of faith. Pettit's book proceeds from a fundamental mistake, and consequently presents an incorrect interpretation of many of his writers. Pettit seems not to understand the inseparable connection between preparation for grace and assurance of salvation in the theology of those he studies. It will be demonstrated below that preparation for faith is tantamount to assurance of election. Pettit's misapprehension appears to be owing largely to his failure to grasp the nature of the doctrine of reprobation in the divines he treats. He speaks of whether one is 'thoroughly reprobate or perhaps somewhere between reprobation and regeneration'.[2] None of the English divines in his book would talk like this since they assumed that reprobation is appointed and fixed by God's eternal decree; only the elect, never the reprobate, could be regenerated.[3] Pettit does not appear to realize that it was

[1] T. F. Torrance, *The School of Faith* (1959), deals with the catechisms of the Westminster Assembly in the light of some earlier ones but does not attempt to get at the historical roots of Westminster theology, much less trace the historical development prior to it.

[2] Norman Pettit, *The Heart Prepared*, 61. Cf. 65, where Pettit speaks of 'the line where reprobation left off and regeneration began' and progressing 'from reprobation to regeneration'. This error is repeated on p. 218 in his book.

[3] Pettit seems to confuse 'damnation' with 'reprobation'. As will be seen below, 'damnation' is the state to which both the reprobate *and* the elect are born; the elect come out of it but the reprobate cannot. While all the reprobate are born into the state of damnation, not all who are born into the state of damnation are reprobate. Reprobation in any case is not a dynamic state, as though one could come out of it. Pettit's treating Henry Bullinger and not Beza (or the Heidelberg theologians) may be why he misses this. Pettit assumes Bullinger was the chief Continental influence on these divines. Bullinger's influence in fact was probably only marginally felt in England after the emergence of Perkins's writings. Bullinger's *Decades* were never reprinted after *Whether a Man* emerged from the press.

the doctrine of predestination, particularly the doctrine of reprobation, that lay behind the need for a doctrine of preparation in the first place. These divines were pastors who faced people who had immense fears that they might be reprobate, not elect. The very idea of preparation emerged as a rationale by which anxious souls could determine as soon as possible that they were not eternally damned. For this reason, then, being prepared also meant being assured that God was savingly at work in them. Pettit does not deal with the doctrine of assurance, a subject he could not have avoided had he seen the fundamental implications of the reformed doctrine of predestination.

Preparation for faith, in so far as it will be an issue in this book, may be simply understood as the process by which a man becomes willing to believe. This process is to be seen largely as a function of God's Law and is either that which may be included *in* the regeneration process but prior to faith, or prior both to regeneration and faith. Regeneration may be defined as the gift of saving life which characterizes the elect alone, never the reprobate. In other words, to know that one is regenerate is to know one is elected to salvation.

It is now necessary to turn to other definitions of terms. It is common to refer to the main figures of this book as 'Puritans'. While all would likely agree that 'it is difficult to find a common denominator'[1] of 'Puritanism', scholars nevertheless retain the term. Basil Hall, who does not accept the term uncritically, attempts to solve the problem by limiting 'Puritanism' to those 'serious' people in the Church of England before 1642 'who desired some modifications in Church government'.[2] This conclusion is reached following his contention that 'it is surely reasonable for historians to use a word as it was used by those who made it'.[3] If so, it is surely reasonable to drop the term for those who rejected it. Perkins rejected it and called it a 'vile' term.[4] But Hall lists Perkins with those he claims 'were Puritans in fact',[5] even though Perkins never published a word calling for modifications in Church government nor does he suggest any kind of Church government at all.

Davies refers to 'Puritans' generally to denote those who saw the

---

[1] G. K. Clark, *The English Inheritance* (1950), 103.

[2] Basil Hall, 'Puritanism: the Problem of Definition', *Studies in Church History* (1965), ii. 289.

[3] Ibid. 287.

[4] *Workes*, iii. 15.

[5] Hall, op. cit. 293.

Church as 'incomplete'.[1] Sasek takes the same line but admits his
definition 'creates graver problems than it resolves'.[2] It seems then
that if one accepts the term 'Puritan' one must, if consistent, either
readjust the definition to fit one man at a time, or, if dealing with a
tradition, begin with one definition and end up with another.[3]
Trinterud tries to resolve the issue by offering three categories of
'Puritanism',[4] and Porter suggests four.[5]

Recent studies in the period of this thesis have been dominated by
literary, historical, and sociological interests; theologians have
lagged behind. From the various theological studies since Perry
Miller's works, few surprises have emerged. A fresh start is therefore
called for, and this book will commence by laying aside the
traditional term. While there is merit in calling some of the divines
of this book 'Puritans', the present study regards the term generally
as not very useful.

Hence this book will adopt a term that objectively depicts the
theological thrust of its central figures. The fundamental concern of
these divines is the knowledge of saving faith; this concern is
heightened by the fact that their soteriology is thoroughly *predestinarian*. The person who listened to their sermons would
naturally be afraid he might be one of those that God predestined to
Hell, and 'which was his fate he did not know and the suspense
tortured him'.[6]

It is crucial to grasp Perkins's doctrine of the temporary faith of
the reprobate. While a rigid predestinarianism was not new to
English theology, Perkins's doctrine and use of the notion of
temporary faith—the central idea in *Whether a Man*—was. *Whether
a Man* actually begins with the assumption of the inalterable decree

[1] Horton Davies, *The Worship of the English Puritans* (Glasgow, 1948), 1.

[2] L. A. Sasek, *The Literary Temperament of the English Puritans* (Louisiana, 1961),
15f.

[3] This is precisely what J. F. H. New does. *Anglicans and Puritans* (1964), 3. He
also curiously states 'we know whom we mean' by the 'Puritans' (ibid. 3). Cf. William
Haller, *The Rise of Puritanism* (New York, 1957), 3ff.; G. H. and K. George, *The
Protestant Mind of the English Reformation* (Princeton, 1961), 406; Christopher Hill,
Society and Puritanism in Pre-Revolutionary England (1969), 15-30. These studies
further illustrate the dilemma one faces with this term.

[4] L. J. Trinterud (ed.), *Elizabethan Puritanism* (New York, 1971), 10ff.; (1) the
original, anti-vestment party; (2) the passive-resistance party (in which he puts
Perkins); and (3) the Presbyterians.

[5] H. C. Porter, *Puritanism in Tudor England* (1970), 9ff.; (1) the English
Separatists; (2) the 'evangelical Puritans' (in which he puts Perkins); (3) the radical
dissenters; and (4) Presbyterians.

[6] R. G. Usher, *Reconstruction of the English Church* (1900), i. 79.

of reprobation. Its comprehensive title is given as a warning to professing Christians to examine themselves lest they happen to possess but a temporary faith—a lofty position to which the reprobate, though doomed from the start, may attain. In his preface Perkins cites the Parable of the Sower (Luke 8: 4-15) and urges his readers to consider that a man 'may seeme both unto himselfe and to the Church of God to bee a true professour of the Gospel, and yet indeede be none'. One may have the 'certaine fruites' that a true child of God has, be 'perswaded in a generall and confused manner', and still be unregenerate because a definite number of such are so predestined from eternity. *Whether a Man* opens with 'Certaine Propositions declaring how farre a man may goe in the profession of the Gospell, and yet be a wicked man and a Reprobate'.[1]

Behind his reference to 'how farre' a reprobate may go is Perkins's view that the non-elect may excel, though damned all the while, in the 'certaine fruites' of the elect; this comes about by what he calls an *ineffectual* calling, a term he borrows from Beza.[2] The ineffectual calling of the non-elect is none the less so powerful that the subject manifests all the appearances—to himself and others—of the elect: such as zeal, good works, even sanctification The pastoral implications of such a teaching are enormous. A sincere Christian could well fear he was but reprobate.[3]

The doctrine of temporary faith became the embarrassment, if not the scandal, of English Calvinism. The followers of Perkins claimed less and less for it so that it eventually presented no threat at all to the believer; William Ames gave its virtual demise a systematic sanction. This teaching seems to have begun with Calvin himself and to have been perpetuated especially by Perkins. Neither Calvin nor Perkins apologizes for a teaching that may seem to some as pastorally insensitive. This teaching depicts God as giving the reprobate, whom He never intends to draw effectually, but a 'taste' of His grace. Indeed, in the preface to *Whether a Man* Perkins claims that this temporary faith 'proceedeth from the holy Ghost, but yet it is not sufficient to make them sound professors'. These men teach this doctrine simply because they find it in Scripture; to them it explains such passages as Matthew 7: 21-3, Hebrews 6: 4-6, and the Parable of the Sower.

---

[1] *Workes*, i. 356.

[2] Cf. *infra*, p. 36 n. 1. This is precisely the point which Pettit, op. cit., fails to grasp.

[3] Cf. *infra*, pp. 126 ff. There is little doubt that anxiety such as Mrs Drake underwent was intensified, if not caused, by the idea of temporary faith.

The thesis in *Whether a Man* is that a man may think himself regenerate when he is not, but a truly regenerate man 'maie discerne' that he is. In this connection Perkins employs 2 Peter 1: 10 ('Give diligence to make your calling and election sure: for if ye do these things, ye shall never fall'), a verse he sees as the chief mandate for preaching generally as well as the formula by which Christians particularly may prove to themselves that they have been the object of an *effectual* calling. The verse 2 Peter 1: 10 may be safely called the biblical banner for the Perkins tradition; it stands out in bold relief on the title-page of *Whether a Man* and heads the list of Scriptures printed on the title-pages of his other works.

It is Perkins's conviction, then, that the regenerate man may discern that he has the knowledge of *saving* faith, or assurance of election. Such knowledge Perkins calls 'experimental'.[1] The testimony of the Spirit is given by 'an experiment' that is not conjectural but 'an infallible certenty of the pardon of sinne'.[2] Perkins believes that 2 Peter 1: 10 is to be related to one's conscience.[3] The conscience itself, he believes, takes effect in a man's mind by a process of syllogistic reasoning. Conscience pronounces judgement 'by a kinde of reasoning or disputing, called a practicall syllogisme'.[4] By the 'practicall syllogisme of the holy Ghost'[5] one may not only have 'experimentall certentie of the truth of the Bible'[6] but know 'hee is in the number of the elect'.[7]

This study will refer to Perkins and his followers as 'experimental predestinarians'. These men hold in common the belief that 2 Peter 1: 10 is God's command and man's formula for proving to himself his own predestination to salvation.[8] The proof is grounded upon experimental knowledge derived through the 'practical syllogism'.[9] The practical syllogism will be understood in this book as drawing a conclusion by reflecting upon oneself. The practical syllogism, although not always called this by each of Perkins's followers, is none the less consistently employed as an accurate instrument or mirror by which one certifies to himself his own election. Beza seems not to have used the term, but anticipates its function when he claims that we must conclude that we are elected by beginning 'at the sanctification which we feele in ourselves'.[10] Perkins himself

---

[1] *Workes*, i. 621.   [2] Ibid. 534.   [3] Ibid. 510.   [4] Ibid. 529.
[5] Ibid. ii. 322.   [6] Ibid. i. 476.   [7] Ibid. 540.   [8] Ibid. iii. *382.
[9] This may be a term of Ursinus's coinage. Cf. *infra*, p. 40 n. 12. Thus when Niesel puts the question whether or not the practical syllogism is in Calvin, he apparently reads Ursinus's idea back on to Calvin's theology. Cf. *infra*, p. 28 n. 7.
[10] *Infra*, p. 33 n. 1.

used the practical syllogism in two ways: by reflecting upon the fact of having believed, or reflecting upon the appearances of sanctification or repentance in oneself.

The term 'experimental' will be used rather than 'experiential' to describe these predestinarians, for two reasons. First, it is *their* word. Secondly, the word 'experimental' contains a useful ambiguity since it refers to experience but also to testing a hypothesis by an experiment. The experimental predestinarians put this proposition to a test: 'whether a man be in the state of damnation or in the state of grace.' Perkins states the hypothesis: 'Every one that believes is the child of God.' The test is: 'But I doe beleeve.' The conclusion follows: 'therefore I am the child of God.'[1] This will be seen often in this book as assurance by the reflex act (another term for the practical syllogism). Thus the method of achieving assurance of salvation is to scrutinize the claim of faith in oneself; if found to be true, the conclusion follows that one has *saving* faith.

'There are two kinds of knowledge,' John Calvin says; the 'knowledge of faith, and what they call experimental knowledge.'[2] These two kinds of knowledge are a chief concern of this book.

---

[1] *Workes*, i. 541.
[2] J. Calvin, *Comm.* Zech. 2: 9. Cf. *infra*, p. 13 n. 1.

PART ONE
THE REFORMERS

1

JOHN CALVIN'S DOCTRINE OF FAITH

FUNDAMENTAL to the doctrine of faith in John Calvin (1509-64) is his belief that Christ died indiscriminately for all men.[1] Equally crucial, however, is his conviction that, until faith is given, 'all that He has suffered and done for the salvation of the human race remains useless and of no value for us'.[2]

Calvin stresses the death of Christ in connection with assurance of salvation, but places the origin of saving faith in the intercessory work of Christ at the Father's right hand. While Christ *died* for all,[3]

[1] This assertion will be developed below. This study will draw from Calvin's *Institutes of the Christian Religion* (Library of Christian Classics, 1961). Calvin's Old Testament commentary references are from the Calvin Translation Society (Edinburgh, 1847-53); New Testament commentary references are from those edited by D. W. and T. F. Torrance (Edinburgh, 1959-72). Latin citations are from the corresponding sources in *Ioannis Calvini Opera* (Brunswick and Berlin, 1863-1900) (Corpus Reformatorum edition).

[2] *Inst.* III. i. 1. This significant statement of Calvin at the beginning of Book III in the *Institutes* assumes that the question of the scope of the atonement is beyond controversy. His treatment of the atonement is found largely in Book II, *passim*. Had Calvin directly addressed the question, For whom did Christ die?, obviously the matter would have been cleared once for all in his own day. To Calvin the Scriptures alone say all that is needed, therefore he does not always comment directly on a Scripture which to him is stated plainly, as in the case of Christ dying for 'all' or the 'world'. He generally leaves verses like these alone, but never does he explain, for example, that 'all' does not mean *all* or 'world' does not mean the *world*, as those after him tended to do. It would appear then that, when he casually refers to 'the salvation of the human race' at the beginning of Book III, it was a foregone conclusion that such was taken for granted in Book II. He appears also to assume the same thing in his definition of faith (*infra*, p. 18 n. 8), when he says that faith is founded on the 'freely given promise in Christ'.

[3] *Comm.* Isa. 53: 12 and *Comm.* Heb. 9: 28. Both verses use the word 'many'. Calvin in both places stresses that the 'many' for whom Christ died really means 'all'. In both places he also refers to Rom. 5: 15 which mentions 'many'; but it too means 'all', Calvin says. This view of Calvin's breaks with Luther's. Luther holds that 'Christ did not die for absolutely all', but for 'many', meaning the elect. *Luther: Lectures on Romans* (Library of Christian Classics, 1961), 252. 'The word *many*', Calvin says, 'does not mean a part of the world only, but the whole human race'. *Comm.* Mark 14: 24. It is 'incontestable that Christ came for the expiation of the sins of the whole world'. *Concerning the Eternal Predestination of God* (1961) (hereinafter called *Predestination*), 148. 'And when he says *the sin of the world* he extends this kindness indiscriminately to the whole human race.' *Comm.* John 1: 29. 'Christ

'He does not pray for all', Calvin claims.[1] Had not Christ died for *all*, we could have no assurance that *our* sins have been expiated in God's sight.

> For since He necessarily hates sin, how shall we be convinced that He loves us until those sins for which He is justly angry with us have been expiated? Thus before we can have any feeling of His fatherly kindness, the blood of Christ must intercede to reconcile God to us.[2]

This statement reveals why Calvin feels so strongly about a universal expiation by Christ's death; Christ's death is that to which we look because it is the 'pledge' that God loves us. Calvin does not direct us to God's secret decree; it is 'Christ alone' to Whom 'faith ought to look'.[3] For 'we are to learn to fix our eyes on the death of Christ, whenever our salvation is concerned'.[4]

Had Christ died only for those whom God had chosen by His secret decree, then, it would obviously cease to be a pledge to all. But 'our Lord Jesus suffered for all and there is neither great nor small who is not inexcusable to-day, for we can obtain salvation in Him'.[5] This is why 'no worse injury can be done to Him than not to believe the Gospel'.[6] John 3: 16 says God so loved the 'world', which is 'a general term, both to invite indiscriminately all to share in life and to cut off every excuse from unbelievers.'[7] When Calvin took pen in hand to refute the Decrees of the Council of Trent point

suffered for the sins of the world, and is offered by the goodness of God without distinction to all men.' *Comm. Rom.* 5: 18.

[1] *Sermons on Isaiah's Prophecy of the Death and Passion of Christ* (1956) (hereinafter called *Sermons of Isaiah's Prophecy*), 145. Cf. *Comm.* Isa. 53: 12. In both of these places Calvin refers to Christ's prayer in John 17, a prayer Calvin thinks applies to the elect only. Cf. *Comm.* John 17: 9. What Calvin does *not* do is to link the scope of Christ's intercessory prayer to Christ's death, as those after him tended to do.   [2] *Comm.* John 3: 16.

[3] *Comm.* John 3: 16. Cf. *Comm.* John 15: 9: 'For he who seeks to be loved by God without the Mediator gets imbrangled in a labyrinth in which he will find neither the right path or the way out. We should therefore direct our gaze to Christ, in whom will be found the pledge of the divine love.'

[4] *Comm. Rom.* 5: 11.

[5] *Sermons on Isaiah's Prophecy*, 141. 'For God commends to us the salvation of all men without exception, even as Christ suffered for the sins of the whole world.' *Comm. Gal.* 5: 12.

[6] *Comm.* John 3: 33.

[7] *Comm.* John 3: 16. When Calvin comments on John 12: 46 ('I am come a light into the world'), he says: 'The universal particle seems to have been put in deliberately, partly that all believers without exception might enjoy this benefit in common and partly to show that unbelievers perish in darkness because they flee from the light of their own accord.' *Comm.* John 12: 46.

by point in *Acta synodi tridentinae: cum antidoto* (1547), he stated that he had no comment on that decree which affirmed that Christ died for all men.[1]

On the other hand, while Christ died for all and is offered to all, 'yet not all receive Him', Calvin acknowledges.[2] But there is an explanation for this: God's eternal predestination. It is 'plain that it comes to pass by God's bidding' that salvation comes to some 'while others are barred from access to it'.

We shall never be clearly persuaded, as we ought to be, that our salvation flows from the wellspring of God's free mercy until we come to know His eternal election, which illumines God's grace by this contrast: that He does not indiscriminately adopt all into the hope of salvation but gives to some what He denies to others.[3]

That some do not believe is to be traced to God's predestination, then, which is His 'eternal decree, by which He compacted with Himself what He willed to become of each man'. Thus 'eternal life is foreordained for some, eternal damnation for others'.[4]

The decree of election, however, is not rendered effectual by the death of Christ. For if that were true, it follows that (1) Christ obviously did not die for the whole world after all, or (2) since He died for all, all are elected. In other words, if the decree of election is rendered effectual by Christ's death, those for whom Christ died *must* be saved.[5] Calvin, however, thinks that Christ died for all and yet all are not saved.[6] As to the objection Beza might

[1] *Ioannis Calvini Opera*, op. cit. vii. 371 ff.

[2] *Comm.* Rom. 5: 18. [3] *Inst.* III. xxi. 1.

[4] Ibid. III. xxi. 5. The methodological arrangement of the *Institutes* is noteworthy. The doctrine of predestination is inserted in III. xxi, or nearly at the end of Calvin's long discussion of God, Christ, and Faith. Predestination 'by no means determines' Calvin's system; he employs the doctrine of predestination after he raises the question 'how this differentiation [viz. why some believe and others do not] comes about. J. K. S. Reid, Introduction, *Predestination*, 9, 11. It is noteworthy also that Calvin says men are 'drawn from a corrupt mass' (*massa corrupta*). *Inst.* III. xxiii. 3. He says nothing more, and in any case prohibits speculation beyond what is given in Scripture. Ibid. III. xxi. 1-2.

[5] As will be seen below, this is precisely the view that lies behind Beza's position. François Wendel errs when he connects Calvin's doctrine of election to Christ's death. Wendel says that Christ's death in Calvin's theology renders 'election effectual'. *Calvin* (1969), 231 f.

[6] Indeed, St. Paul 'clearly proves the stupidity of the argument of certain interpreters who maintain that all are elected without distinction, because the doctrine of salvation is universal, and because God invites all men to Himself without distinction (*promiscue*). The general nature of the promises does not alone and of itself make salvation common to all. Rather, the peculiar revelation which the prophet has mentioned restricts it to the elect.' *Comm.* Rom. 10: 16.

raise,[1] that if some perish for whom Christ died then God would be demanding double payment, Calvin has this answer: they are 'doubly culpable'.

Unbelievers who turn away from Him and who deprive themselves of Him by their malice are to-day doubly culpable. For how will they excuse their ingratitude in not receiving the blessing in which they could share by faith?[2]

Calvin insists that the death of Christ is not to be regarded 'from its external act but from the power of the Spirit'.[3] The issue, he argues, is not 'how great' the power of Christ's death is, or 'what efficacy it has in itself, but to whom He gives Himself to be enjoyed'.[4] 'Outwardly He shed His blood, but inwardly and spiritually He brought cleansing. In short, He died on earth, but the power and efficacy of His death came from heaven.'[5] This then is why Calvin says that all which Christ did on the cross 'remains useless and of no value' until we believe.[6]

The decree of election, then, is not rendered effectual in Christ's death but in His ascension and intercession at the Father's right hand. The ascension was the event that 'opened the way into the Heavenly Kingdom, which had been closed through Adam'.[7]

---

[1] Cf. *infra*, p. 31 n. 5.

[2] *Sermons on Isaiah's Prophecy*, 141. There is a formula that is often raised by proponents of a doctrine of limited atonement that purports to align their teaching with the universalistic passages of Scripture: Christ died *sufficiently* for *all* but *effectually* for the *elect*. Ursinus (examined, below) upheld this formula as it was held by Thomas Aquinas and Peter Lombard. *The Summe*, 300. It was also followed by Luther's teacher John Staupitz (d. 1524). See J. Staupitz, 'Eternal Predestination and Its Execution in Time', *Forerunners of the Reformation* (1967), 192. Calvin takes note of this way of handling the problem—'the common solution' that has 'prevailed in the schools'—raises it twice, and rejects it both times. *Predestination*, 148. *Comm.* 1 John 2: 2. Calvin could, however, allow for the truth of the formula since only the elect savingly believe. But that he does not accept the formula appears to be why he could say, 'it is no small matter to have the soules perish which wer bought by the blood of Christ. *Sermons of M. John Calvin, on the Epistles of S. Paule to Timothie and Titus* (1579), 817. Calvin's treatment of Heb. 9: 15 follows the same view. This Scripture might be taken to uphold a limited atonement. Luther understands 'the called' therein to refer to the elect. *Luther's Works* (1963), xxix. 214. Calvin notes: 'Some take *the called* in the sense of the elect; in my judgment wrongly.' *Comm.* Heb. 9: 15.

[3] *Comm.* Heb. 9: 14. 'Though Christ offered a visible sacrifice, it is spiritually . . . that we must reckon it in order to take hold of its reward and fruits.' *Comm.* Matt. 27: 51.

[4] *Predestination*, 149.

[5] *Comm.* Heb. 8: 4.

[6] *Inst.* III. i. 1.

[7] Ibid. II. xvi. 16.

For, having entered a sanctuary not made with hands, He appears before the Father's face as our constant advocate and intercessor. Thus he turns the Father's eyes to his own righteousness to avert His gaze from our sins.[1]

While Christ died for all, 'He Himself declares that He does not *pray* for all the world'; such intercession is for the elect only.[2] Calvin makes Christ's intercession analogous to the high priest in the Old Testament who went behind the veil into the holy of holies but not without blood. This Calvin calls 'the ratification of the atonement'—that which makes the atonement 'take effect'.[3]

For, as in the ancient Law the priest, who 'never entered without blood', at the same time interceded for the people; so what was there shadowed out is fulfilled in Christ. . . . First, He offered the sacrifice of His body, and shed His blood, that He might endure the punishment which was due to us; and secondly, in order that the atonement might take effect, He performed the office of an advocate, and interceded for all who embraced this sacrifice by faith; as is evident from that prayer . . . 'I pray not for these only, but for all who shall believe on me through their word.'[4]

Therefore Christ the priest 'has entered heaven through His own body because He now sits on the right hand of the Father'.[5] This act, then, carries out the decree of election.[6]

Calvin's position, despite his saying Christ's death for all makes all inexcusable, still requires that one be among the number of the elect to be saved. His view does not allow that the number of the elect could be either increased or diminished. It therefore raises the question whether or not Christ is interceding for us in particular. Calvin, however, anticipates the question and seems to believe that none need have the slightest anxiety about this. 'If we then belong to their number', that is, those who are elected and for whom Christ has prayed, 'let us be fully persuaded that Christ has suffered for

[1] Ibid. [2] *Sermons on Isaiah's Prophecy*, 145 (my italics).
[3] *Comm.* Isa. 53: 12. [4] Ibid. [5] *Comm.* Heb. 9: 11.
[6] Without the 'power and intercession of the Mediator', Calvin asserts that 'you have no hope of salvation, you are all lost in your sins'. *Sermons on Isaiah's Prophecy*, 144. This significant (and crucial) point in Calvin's theology seems to have been overlooked by a number of scholars. Wilhelm Niesel, *The Theology of Calvin* (1956), deals at length with Christ the mediator in Calvin's thought, but misses the significance of Calvin's view of Christ's intercession at the Father's right hand. Essentially the same may be said for J. F. Jansen, *Calvin's Doctrine of the Work of Christ* (1956); A. Dakin, *Calvinism* (1940); A. M. Hunter, *The Teaching of Calvin* (Glasgow, 1920); and M. P. Hoogland, *Calvin's Perspective on the Exaltation of Christ* (Kampden, 1966). Paul Van Buren, *Christ in our Place* (Edinburgh, 1957), 89–91, gives attention to Christ's intercession but concludes (with no evidence) that Calvin's position is that Christ prays for those for whom He died: 'all'.

us'.[1] It is therefore his view that since Christ died for all, there is no problem left save that of sheer unbelief in the Word of God itself. Thus, consistent with his view that faith looks to Christ alone, Calvin points us to the death of Christ, not that which is hidden from us.

The 'secret plan of God, which lay hidden, is brought to light' by faith.[2] That the shedding of Christ's blood 'may not be nullified, our souls are cleansed by the secret watering of the Spirit'.[3] The ascended Christ 'sits on high' that He may 'quicken us to spiritual life'.[4] Christ gives the Spirit to the elect, 'to each man in a certain proportion, and not to every man alike, but as He Himself thinks good'.[5]

What the elect are given, then, is a 'measure' of faith out of Christ's infinite bounty.[6] This measure of faith is none the less fully assuring in its 'first and principal parts'. 'When first even the least drop of faith is instilled in our minds, we begin to contemplate God's face, peaceful and calm and gracious towards us. We see Him afar off, but so clearly as to know we are not at all deceived.'[7] Calvin defines faith as 'a firm and certain knowledge of God's benevolence toward us, founded upon the truth of the *freely given promise in Christ*, both revealed to our minds and sealed upon our hearts through the Holy Spirit'.[8]

Yet Calvin holds that all faith is 'implicit' because it is given in measure. 'We certainly admit that so long as we dwell as strangers in the world there is such a thing as implicit faith; not only because

---

[1] *Comm.* Isa. 53: 12. All that Calvin believes regarding the universality of Christ's death is mirrored in his teaching concerning the sacraments. The visible symbol of baptism is 'ratified' by faith (*Comm.* Rom. 6: 4), as feasting on Christ in the bread and wine is made effectual by faith. *Inst.* IV. xvii. 5. As Christ is offered to all indiscriminately but not all receive Him so the sacraments 'are also offered to the wicked, who, however, do not find God more favorable but rather incur a heavier condemnation'. Indeed, 'just as Christ is offered and held forth by the Father to all unto salvation, yet not all acknowledge and receive Him' in the sacrament. *Inst.* IV. xiv. 7. Thus as Christ is the 'pledge' or 'mirror' of Divine love (*Comm.* John 15: 9), so are the sacraments likewise to be understood; 'we may call them mirrors in which we may contemplate the riches of God's grace, which He lavishes upon us'. *Inst.* IV. xiv. 6. Therefore, as the believer is not directed to Christ's hidden intercession but only His open death, so the believer is directed to gaze at the 'pledge' of His grace in the sacraments.

[2] *Inst.* III. xxiv. 3   [3] Ibid. III. i. 1.

[4] Ibid. II. xvi. 16.

[5] *Sermons on the Epistle to the Ephesians* (1975), 342.

[6] Cf. *Comm.* Eph. 4: 7 and *Comm.* Rom. 12: 3.

[7] *Inst.* III. ii. 19.   [8] Ibid. III. ii. 7 (my italics).

many things are as yet hidden from us, but because surrounded by many clouds of errors we do not comprehend everything'.[1] Calvin also calls implicit faith a 'preparation of faith' (*fidei praeparatio*).[2] This is not to be confused with preparation *for* faith; he means that the knowledge of faith, although true, and assuring, is yet inarticulate.[3] It is none the less 'graced with the title "faith"; yet it was only the beginning of faith'.[4]

In any case, faith is the product of the secret 'testimony of the Holy Spirit'.[5] And it is 'Christ's office' to give life, 'but only to the elect'.[6] The 'grace of the Spirit' moreover 'is a mirror' in which we see Christ.[7] Faith to Calvin then is not only the ultimate consequence of election but the immediate result of the simultaneous work of Christ at the Father's right hand and the internal testimony of the Spirit.

The position which Calvin wants pre-eminently to establish (and fundamentally assumes) is that faith is *knowledge*. Calvin notes some biblical synonyms for faith, all simple nouns, such as 'recognition' (*agnitio*) and 'knowledge' (*scientia*).[8] He describes faith as illumination (*illuminatio*),[9] knowledge as opposed to the submission of our feeling (*cognitio, non sensus nostri submissio*),[10] certainty (*certitudino*),[11] a firm conviction (*solida persuasio*),[12] assurance (*securitas*),[13] firm assurance (*solida securitas*),[14] and full assurance (*plena securitas*).[15]

What stands out in these descriptions is the given, intellectual, passive, and assuring nature of faith. What is absent is a need for gathering faith, voluntarism, faith as man's act, and faith that must await experimental knowledge to verify its presence. Faith is 'something merely passive, bringing nothing of ours to the recovering of God's favour but receiving from Christ that which we lack'.[16]

---

[1] Ibid. III. ii. 4.   [2] Ibid. III. ii. 5.   [3] Ibid. III. ii. 4.
[4] Ibid. III. ii. 5. Calvin is attacking the Roman Catholic view of implicit faith—assent to the teachings of the Church—which he thinks bedecks men with 'grossest ignorance'. Ibid. III. ii. 2.
[5] Ibid. III. i. 1. Cf. III. i. 4: 'Faith is the principal work of the Holy Spirit.'
[6] *Comm.* John 17: 3.
[7] *Comm.* John 16. 16. Cf. *Comm.* John 15: 26: 'The inward and secret testimony of the Spirit' functions 'to testify of Christ'. It should be noted that the Spirit is 'secret' and therefore not an emotional feeling, as it were; it is that which focuses objectively on Christ.
[8] *Inst.* III. ii. 14.   [9] Ibid. III. i. 4.   [10] Ibid. III. ii. 2.
[11] Ibid. III. ii. 6.   [12] Ibid. III. ii. 16.
[13] Ibid.   [14] Ibid.
[15] Ibid. III. ii. 22.   [16] Ibid. III. xiii. 5.

It is but the 'instrument (*instrumentum*) for receiving righteousness',[1] a 'kind of vessel' (*quasi vasi*),[2] which transmits the knowledge of our justification: 'a passive work, so to say, to which no reward can be paid'.[3] God justifies us by 'the intercession of Christ',[4] and that intercession, in turn, brings us to the apprehension of God's mercy.[5] Faith to Calvin may be described as merely witnessing what God has already done in Christ.

What is peculiar to the elect then is conversion by an act of God. Conversion is necessary because man's nature is fallen; the image of God in man is 'not totally annihilated and destroyed' but still 'so corrupted that what ever remains is frightful deformity'.[6] Through Adam's fall the image of God in man was 'obliterated' and Adam's offspring consequently were immersed in the 'most filthy plagues, blindness, impotence, impurity, vanity, and injustice'.[7] The result is the 'works of the flesh' in man;[8] terms such as 'flesh', 'nature', 'natural', and 'sin' are used interchangeably in Calvin's thought to depict the natural order as opposed to that which is supernatural: the regenerate. This he calls the 'gift' of a 'special illumination, not a common endowment of nature'.[9] For man's 'nature' is corrupt; his 'supernatural gifts' were 'stripped from him'.[10] There is nothing 'supernatural' in man; there is *nature* only, for 'all qualities belonging to the blessed life of the soul have been extinguished from him, until he recovers them through the grace of regeneration'.[11]

In order to know God man must be given a 'new' will. The will in man's nature 'did not perish, but was bound to wicked desires that it cannot strive after the right'.[12] The issue, Calvin thinks, is not whether man by his nature will seek God but whether 'he discern good by right reason; that knowing it he choose it; that having chosen it he follow it'. Calvin concludes: 'much as man desires to follow what is good, still he does not follow it.' No man 'aspires' to eternal blessedness but by the 'impulsion' of the Holy Spirit.[13] 'Paul's saying would not make sense,' Calvin argues, 'that "it is God who is at work to will in us", if any will preceded the grace of the Spirit' (*siqua voluntas praecederet Spiritus gratiam*).[14] Calvin exclaims: 'Away then with all that "preparation" which many babble about!'[15]

---

[1] *Inst.* III. xi. 7.   [2] Ibid.   [3] *Comm.* John 6: 29.   [4] *Inst.* III. xi. 3.
[5] Ibid. III. xiv. 17. 'We are received into grace by God out of sheer mercy', which 'comes about by Christ's intercession and is apprehended by faith'.
[6] Ibid. I. xv. 4.   [7] Ibid. II. i. 5.   [8] Ibid. II. i. 8.
[9] Ibid. II. ii. 20.   [10] Ibid. II. ii. 12.   [11] Ibid.   [12] Ibid.
[13] Ibid. II. ii. 26.   [14] Ibid. II. ii. 27.   [15] Ibid.

Conversion therefore is supernatural; it is above nature. God does not co-operate with nature; He supplants nature with a new will and does this by effacing nature. God does not aid the will already in nature; He gives man a new will outside nature. It is not nature, or flesh, or the will, that is merely 'strengthened'; conversion means a new will altogether. Our natural will is abolished— 'effaced'.

If, therefore, a stone is transformed into flesh when God converts us to zeal for the right, whatever is of our own will is effaced. What takes its place is wholly from God. I say the will is effaced (*voluntatem dico aboleri*).[1]

Fundamental to Calvin's doctrine of conversion then is that (1) the natural will is extinguished and (2) God substitutes for it a good one from Himself.[2] Calvin himself claims to have experienced a 'sudden conversion'.[3]

TEMPORARY FAITH

While the natural man cannot aspire to blessedness prior to regeneration, the Spirit of God does work in the natural order, distributing 'most excellent benefits' for the good of mankind. Calvin reasons that 'it is no wonder' that 'the knowledge that is most excellent in human life is said to be communicated to us through the Spirit of God'.[4] However, the Spirit's working in the natural order is apart from His effectual creation of faith in the elect; these benefits are to be distinguished from the 'Spirit of sanctification' in believers.[5] It is interesting that Calvin never uses the adjectives 'secret' or 'internal' with reference to the Spirit's working in the natural order. Yet the ability to do 'physics, dialectic, mathematics, and other like disciplines', though in the unregenerate, comes from the Spirit; it is the 'general grace of God'.[6] Such grace 'can conceive and produce a *Summa Theologica*, a *Mass in B Minor*, a King's

---

[1] Ibid. II. iii. 6.

[2] Ibid. II. iii. 7. If God *aids* our weak will, 'then something would be left to us. But since God 'makes' the will, the good in it is thus placed 'outside' us. Ibid. II. iii. 9.

[3] Preface, *Comm.* Psalms. T. H. L. Parker, *John Calvin* (1975), 163, interprets *subita conversione* as 'unexpected conversion', further amplifying the given and passive nature of conversion to Calvin.

[4] *Inst.* II. ii. 16.   [5] Ibid.

[6] This is sometimes called 'common grace'. Cf. Herman Bavinck, 'Calvin and Common Grace', *Calvin and the Reformation* (New York, 1909).

College Chapel, or a Hamlet. But it cannot break through the realm of the mystery of God.'[1]

Calvin goes beyond this, however. Without meaning the secret work of the Holy Spirit in regeneration or merely (for example) the ability to do mathematics, Calvin explicitly propounds a 'special grace' of God within 'common nature'.[2] This is operative in the reprobate; it is called 'a transitory faith'.[3] This concept poses the chief pastoral problem in Calvin's theology, and in the experimental predestinarian tradition.

Calvin espouses the possibility of temporary faith for two reasons: 'it is evident from the teaching of Scripture and daily experience'.[4] Regrettably, he seems not to have anticipated the dilemma this teaching could create. Much less could he have known that a tradition would emerge that would incorporate his teaching and try to solve the problem it raises by a voluntaristic doctrine of faith. His own effort to solve the problem is less than satisfactory; had he fully perceived the pastoral implications he raised he might have shown how his own doctrine of faith could be retained without appealing to man's will as the ultimate ground of assurance.[5] Never does Calvin appeal to man's desire to believe as the proof of saving faith, yet he comes short of any concrete counsel to a weak believer who may wonder if his faith is but temporary.

It should be pointed out, moreover, that the treatment of temporary faith in the *Institutes* comes in the context of Calvin's discussion of the scholastic teaching of 'formed' and 'unformed' faith, a distinction he calls 'worthless'.[6] Calvin argues that true faith 'can in no wise be separated from a devout disposition'.[7] It follows for him that 'unformed' faith 'does not deserve to be called faith'.[8] He calls it faith after all, however, since some are said 'to believe for a while' (Luke 8: 13).[9] From this he proceeds to attribute faith to the reprobate.

---

[1] T. H. L. Parker, *The Doctrine of the Knowledge of God* (1952), 112.

[2] *Inst.* II. ii. 17. Calvin depicts King Saul (1 Sam. 10) as one who has such special grace but who is not regenerate. Cf. *Inst.* III. ii. 12.

[3] Ibid. III. ii. 11. Calvin uses *temporalis fides* and *fide caduca ad tempus*.

[4] Ibid. III. ii. 12.

[5] As will be seen below, the *will* or *desire* to believe is seen by experimental predestinarians as that which is a sure sign of *saving* faith.

[6] *Inst.* III. ii. 8. This teaching is that an 'unformed' faith—mere assent to Scripture—may not be 'formed', i.e. supplemented by love and piety, but it is still a valid faith.

[7] Ibid. [8] Ibid. III. ii. 10. [9] Ibid.

Calvin, however, is not entirely insensitive to the problem.

I know that to attribute faith to the reprobate seems hard to some, when Paul declares it the result of election. Yet this difficulty is easily solved. For . . . experience shows that the reprobate are sometimes affected by almost the same feeling as the elect, so that even in their own judgment they do not in any way differ from the elect.[1]

Calvin thinks it 'not at all absurd' that the reprobate should have 'a taste of the heavenly gifts—and Christ, (Hebrews 6: 4-5), that they may be 'more convicted and inexcusable'.[2] That these are doomed by God's predestination obviously does not keep Calvin from considering them inexcusable.[3] The reprobate at any rate 'never receive anything but a confused awareness of grace, so that they grasp a shadow rather than the firm body of it'. This is the consequence of a 'lower working of the Spirit' (*inferior Spiritus operatio*),[4] which seems to be what would later be termed an 'ineffectual' calling.[5]

Calvin has said two things here that will bear further examination: first, the reprobate may have 'almost the same feeling as the elect'; secondly, this is 'but a confused awareness of grace'. He goes on to say that the reprobate 'believe that God is merciful toward them, for they receive the gift of reconciliation, although confusedly and not distinctly enough'. Moreover, they seem 'to have a beginning of faith in common' with the elect.[6]

Calvin recognizes the obvious objection that a true believer could suspect his own faith to be but that of the reprobate:

I reply: although there is a great likeness and affinity between God's elect and those who are given a transitory faith, yet only in the elect does that confidence flourish which Paul extols, that they loudly proclaim Abba, Father.[7]

This answer may satisfy the one who enjoys such a confidence. But to the poor soul who does not have it, such an answer could add to

---

[1] Ibid. III. ii. 11. [2] Ibid. Cf. *Comm.* Heb. 6: 4.
[3] 'I know that many greatly dislike this doctrine—that some are rejected, and that yet no cause can be found in themselves why they thus remain disapproved by God. But there is here need of docility and of a meek spirit, to which Paul also exhorts us, when he says, "O man, who art thou who answerest against God?"' *Comm.* Mal. 1: 2-6.
[4] *Inst.* III. ii. 11. [5] *Infra*, p. 36 n. 1; p. 68 n. 2.
[6] *Inst.* III. ii. 11. Cf. *Comm.* Matt. 13: 20. 'They themselves think that they have a true faith.' Though 'not born again' they have 'some elements of godliness'. *Comm.* Luke 17: 13. [7] Ibid.

his frustration. For Calvin must know that a true believer can become discouraged and imagine his 'implicit' faith to be but that 'confused awareness' which a reprobate may have. And if the reprobate may experience 'almost the same feeling as the elect', there is no way to know finally what the reprobate experiences. Furthermore, if the reprobate may believe that God is merciful towards them, how can *we* be sure our believing the same thing is any different from theirs? How can we be so sure that our 'beginning of faith' is saving and is not the 'beginning of faith' which the reprobate seem to have?

If Calvin had specifically addressed these vital questions, he might have shown why a voluntaristic approach is not the right one when confronting such a dilemma; his failure to address these questions may, in part, lie behind the emergence of a system that would bear his name but be substantially different from his own. In any case, one thing in this connection which Calvin does make clear is that the reprobate's temporary flourishing comes to an end sooner or later.[1]

However, Calvin possibly thinks his theology as a whole does answer these questions. For even if the reprobate experience 'almost the same feelings as the elect', Calvin warns against looking to one's feelings in any case. Indeed, the one thing above all else which Calvin emphasizes is that we must never look to ourselves for assurance.

There are two points in Calvin's doctrine of faith that are relevant. First, saving faith in the elect is indestructible.[2] The apostasy in Hebrews 6: 4–6 refers to the reprobate with temporary faith, and in any case the true believer 'who violates the second table of the Law, or who in his ignorance transgresses the first is not guilty of this rebellion'.[3] The second point is that when Calvin uses

---

[1] Those with 'temporary faith' have 'a promise of faithfulness at the outset', and 'embrace the Gospel greedily, but soon after fall away'. *Comm.* Matt. 13: 20. They eventually 'hasten the death to which they were appointed'. *Comm.* Matt. 15: 13. Such a falling is when one 'forsakes the Word of God, who extinguishes its light, who denies himself the taste of the heavenly gift, and who gives up partaking of the Spirit. This is complete renunciation of God.' *Comm.* Heb. 6: 4.

[2] *Inst.* III. ii, *passim.* Cf. ibid. III. xxii. 7: 'Christ does not allow any of those whom He has once for all engrafted into His body to perish . . . the intrinsic cause of this is in Himself.' 'There is no doubt, when Christ prays for all the elect, that He implores for them the same thing as He did for Peter, that their faith may never fail.' Ibid. III. xxiv. 6.

[3] *Comm.* Heb. 6: 4. Cf. *Inst.* III. iii. 23: 'the Novationists interpret "lapsing" to mean the act of a man who, taught by the law of the Lord not to steal or fornicate, does not abstain from theft or fornication. On the contrary, I affirm . . . it is not any particular failing that is here expressed.'

the word *faith* he means assurance of saving faith, salvation, eternal life, or election.[1] The later distinction between faith and assurance seems never to have entered Calvin's mind. Assurance to Calvin comes by what would later be called the *direct* act of faith.

Calvin's doctrine of assurance may be put in one sentence. Appealing to Ephesians 1: 4, he says:

> But if we have been chosen in Him, we shall not find assurance of our election in ourselves; and not even in God the Father, if we conceive Him as severed from His Son. Christ, then, is the mirror wherein we must, and without self-deception may, contemplate our own election.[2]

That which Calvin does not do, then, is to urge men to make their calling and election sure to themselves. He thinks Christ's death is a sufficient pledge and merely seeing Him is assuring. Never does he employ 2 Peter 1: 10 in connection with seeking assurance of salvation. He regards 2 Peter generally as an encouragement 'to make proof' of one's calling 'by godly living'[3] and 2 Peter 1: 10 particularly as an argument that our election is to be 'confirmed' by 'a good conscience and an upright life'.[4] It should be noted moreover that Calvin does not link this verse to the conscience in terms of deducing assurance of salvation.

> This assurance of which Peter speaks should not, in my opinion, be referred to conscience, as though the faithful acknowledged themselves before God to be elect and called. I take it simply of the fact itself, that calling is shown to be confirmed by a holy life.[5]

Two reasons why Calvin interprets 2 Peter 1: 10 in this way may be suggested. First, since believers have assurance already, any further exhortation to them to seek assurance would be redundant. Secondly, since there may be a 'great likeness and affinity' between God's elect and the reprobate with temporary faith, appealing to one's good works, conscience, or feeling as the ground of assurance would give no comfort when it is known that the reprobate too may have 'almost the same feeling'. Calvin consistently urges men not to look to themselves.

---

[1] His very definition of faith encompasses this. Cf. Ibid. III. ii. 16, 19, 28, 40. Those who do fall never had 'the heartfelt trust in which certainty of election has'. Ibid. III. xxiv. 7.

[2] Ibid. III. xxiv. 5.

[3] *Comm.* 2 Pet., preface.

[4] *Comm.* 2 Pet. 1: 10. Cf. *Inst.* III. vi. 1 and III. xv. 8.

[5] Ibid.

Indeed, 'if you contemplate yourself, that is sure damnation'.[1]
For if men begin to judge whether they are regenerate 'by good
works, nothing will be more uncertain or more feeble'. For if works
be 'judged of themselves, by their imperfection they will no less
declare God's wrath than by their incomplete purity they testify to
His benevolence'.[2] Moreover, 'when the Christian looks at himself
he can only have grounds for anxiety, indeed despair'.[3] We should
not seek assurance by 'conjecture', for faith corresponds 'to a simple
and free promise'; hence 'no place for doubting is left'.[4]

It is vital to Calvin's doctrine of faith that men are to take no
comfort from the 'fruits' of regeneration 'unless they *first* apprehend
God's goodness, sealed by nothing else than the certainty of the
promise'.[5] Behind this assertion lies Calvin's conviction that faith
must precede repentance in the *ordo salutis*.

Now it ought to be a fact beyond controversy that repentance not only
constantly follows faith, but is also born of faith. . . . There are some,
however, who suppose that repentance precedes faith, rather than flows
from it, or is produced by it as fruit from a tree. Such persons have never
known the power of repentance, and are moved to feel this way by an
unduly slight argument.[6]

The reason Calvin feels so strongly about this is because he thinks 'a
man cannot apply himself seriously to repentance without knowing
himself to belong to God'. Moreover 'no one is truly persuaded that
he belongs to God unless he has first recognized God's grace'.[7]

Calvin's position on this further rules out any preparation for
faith on man's part. For we cannot turn to God or do anything that
pertains to obedience until first we have been *given* faith. But not
only that; there is nothing in Calvin's doctrine that suggests, even in
the process of regeneration, that man must be prepared at all—
including by the work of the Law prior to faith. He allows that the
Law *can* have the effect of preparing men 'to seek what previously
they did not realize they lacked', but this assertion comes in the
context of a discussion that suggests such is but an accidental effect
of the Law.[8]

---

[1] *Inst.* III. ii. 24.   [2] Ibid. III. xiv. 19.
[3] *Comm.* I Cor. I: 9.   [4] *Inst.* III. ii. 38.
[5] Ibid. III. xiv. 19 (my italics).   [6] Ibid. III. iii. I.

[7] Ibid. III. iii. 2. Repentance is 'the true turning of our life to God, a turning that
arises from a pure and earnest fear of Him; and it consists in the mortification of our
flesh and of the old man, and in the vivification of the Spirit'. Ibid. III. iii. 5.

[8] Ibid. II. vii. 11.

Calvin holds that the Law has three uses: (1) it shows the righteousness that is acceptable to God;[1] (2) it restrains by fear of punishment those who have no care of justice;[2] (3) it applies to believers—its 'principal use'.[3] It is in the second use that Calvin mentions that the Law, which serves as a 'bridle', can have the effect of showing man his need. But never does he hint that this effect is necesssary before faith.

Calvin's teaching on faith and repentance in the *ordo salutis* mirrors his theology of the covenant of grace as a whole. As faith precedes repentance in the *ordo salutis*, Grace precedes Law in the history of redemption. As faith corresponds to the freely given promise and repentance refers to our obedience, Calvin likewise holds that the Old Testament is founded on grace and that the Law was given afterwards for the purpose of obedience. Had Calvin held that repentance precedes faith in the *ordo salutis* it would not be surprising to find a covenant of works preceding the covenant of grace mirrored in his theology of the covenant. But there is no trace of the idea in Calvin that God initially made a covenant of works with man and later instituted the covenant of grace, a view that became orthodox in the experimental predestinarian tradition.

Calvin recognizes there are differences between the two Testaments,[4] but his stress is on the similarity between the two.[5] Those in the Old 'participated in the same inheritance and hoped for a common salvation with us by the grace of the same Mediator'.[6] Indeed, 'the covenant made with all the patriarchs is so much like ours in substance and reality that the two are actually one and the same'.[7] For 'the Old Testament was established upon the free mercy of God, and was confirmed by Christ's intercession'.[8] The Law then was 'not devoid of reference to Christ'; it was 'added' four hundred years after Abraham's death to keep Israel in readiness until His coming.[9] This is why the 'principal use' of the Law is for believers (in both Testaments); it is the 'best instrument for them to learn

---

[1] Ibid. II. vii. 6.   [2] Ibid. II. vii. 10.   [3] Ibid. II. vii. 12.

[4] Ibid. II. xi, *passim*. They are: (1) the Old stresses the 'earthly' benefits, the New the 'heavenly'; (2) the Old shows the 'image' of truth, the New the 'substance'; (3) the Old is 'literal', the New 'spiritual'; (4) the Old was one of 'bondage', the New 'freedom'; (5) the Old refers to one nation, the New to all nations.

[5] Ibid. II. x, *passim*. See editor's comments, II. x. i, n. 1.

[6] Ibid. II. x. 1. 'Calvin applies the principle "by Christ alone" not only to his own time and to the exclusion of salvation by works, but to all ages.' Parker, *Knowledge of God*, 67.

[7] *Inst.* II. x. 2. Cf. *Comm.* Acts 15: 9.

[8] *Inst.* II. x. 4.   [9] Ibid. II. vii. 1.

more thoroughly each day the nature of the Lord's will'.[1] Thus repentance, which follows faith, is increased as it reflects 'the standard of God's law'.[2] The object of regeneration then is 'to manifest in the life of believers a harmony and agreement between God's righteousness and their obedience, and thus confirm' their adoption.[3]

To the degree that our obedience confirms our adoption, 'experimental knowledge' may give 'subsidiary aid to its confirmation'.[4] But such 'fruits' can only give comfort 'a posteriori'.[5] 'Love', then, may serve as an 'inferior' aid, a 'prop to our faith'.[6] But even in the context of this concession Calvin hastens to add that none should conclude from this that 'we must look to our works for our assurance to be firm'.[7]

Behind all that has been stated above lies Calvin's conviction that the 'seat' of faith is in the 'heart'.[8] While the natural will is 'effaced' in conversion, what belongs in man 'remains entire'.[9] By 'heart' Calvin means the mind. When he says that faith is 'not in the head' he means that it is not merely a 'bare idea';[10] by faith one is 'convinced by a firm conviction'.[11] By heart, then, he means a fully persuaded mind.[12]

Therefore if we want to know we are in the number of the elect, we must be *persuaded* that Christ died for us. We know this by a direct act of faith. This is why Calvin can affirm: 'If Pighius asks how I know I am elect, I answer that Christ is more than a thousand testimonies to me.'[13]

---

[1] *Inst.* II. vii. 12.

[2] Ibid. III. iii. 16. Repentance is never perfect in this life, however. Ibid. III. iii. 10–14.

[3] Ibid. III. vi. 1.   [4] *Comm.* Josh. 3: 10.

[5] *Inst.* III. xiv. 19.   [6] *Comm.* 1 John 3: 19.

[7] Ibid. Niesel, op. cit., makes the point that it is 'impossible to assert' that Calvin teaches the practical syllogism (176); rather, he warns against it (181).

[8] *Comm.* Rom. 10: 10.   [9] *Inst.* II. iii. 6.

[10] *Comm.* Rom. 10: 10.   [11] *Inst.* III. ii. 16.

[12] The 'heart' is often used 'for the mind itself, which is the intellectual faculty of the soul'. *Comm.* Deut. 29: 4. Cf. *Comm.* John 12: 40. This is why Calvin says 'the commencement of faith is knowledge; its completion is a firm and steady conviction'. *Comm.* Eph. 1: 13. Cf. *Inst.* III. ii. 36.

[13] *Predestination*, 130.

2

THEODORE BEZA AND
THE HEIDELBERG THEOLOGIANS

FUNDAMENTAL to the doctrine of faith in Theodore Beza (1519–1605), Calvin's successor in Geneva, is his belief that Christ died for the elect only.[1] Beza's doctrine of a limited atonement makes Christ's death that to which the decree of election has particular reference and that which makes the elect's salvation efficacious.[2] It must therefore be argued that, as a result of this soteriological position, Beza's doctrine (1) inhibits the believer from looking directly to Christ's death for assurance; (2) precipitates an implicit distinction between faith and assurance; (3) tends to put repentance before faith in the *ordo salutis*; and (4) plants the seed of voluntarism in the doctrine of faith. In a word: Beza's doctrine requires the use of the practical syllogism in order for one to be persuaded he is one of those for whom Christ died.

While a strong doctrine of predestination tends to characterize the soteriology of Calvin's leading contemporaries in the Reformed tradition on the Continent,[3] it appears that Beza was the first of

---

[1] This will be developed below. The study will draw from several writings of Beza. *A briefe and piththie summe of the christian faith* (1565? (Bodl. Tanner 126); every other page numbered consecutively; page 1a follows page 1 in references below). Hereinafter called *Briefe and Pithie*, this reached six editions (1563 to 1589). *A Little Catechisme* (1578). *A Booke of Christian Questions and answeares* (1578; every other page numbered consecutively). Hereinafter called *Questions and Answers*; five editions (1572 to 1586). *A Briefe Declaration of the chiefe points of Christian religion set forth in a Table* (1613). Hereinafter called *Briefe Declaration*, this was published in 1575, but under the title *The Treasvre of Trueth* in 1576 and 1581. *A Discourse, of the true and visible Markes of the Catholique Churche* (1582). Hereinafter called *Visible Markes*. *Sermon vpon the Three First Chapters of the Canticle of Canticles* (1587). Hereinafter called *Canticles*. Beza's other works are largely irrelevant for this study. Latin references are from *Confessio Christianae Fidei* (1575) (translated as *Briefe and Pithie*) and *Qvaestionum et Responsionem Libellus* (1577) (translated as *Questions and Answers*).

[2] This would not be true with Beza's teaching only but with that of anyone who holds to the classical doctrine of limited atonement. In a word: those for whom Christ died must necessarily be saved; those for whom He did not die must necessarily be damned.

[3] For example, Martin Bucer (1491–1551) and Peter Martyr (1500–62) hold views that make the number of the elect fixed and predetermined. Bucer says

these to make the doctrine of predestination central to his system. Taking his cue from Romans 9 generally and St. Paul's discussion of the 'lump' particularly,[1] Beza devises a system that later became known as supralapsarianism.[2] He raises the question whether the term 'lump' means 'the created and corrupted mankinde, whereout of God ordineth some to honour and some to dishonour?' and concludes:

There is no doute but God taketh both ye sorts out of the same lump, ordeining them to contrary endes. Yet doo I say and playnely avouth, that Paule in the same similitude, mounteth up to the said soverain ordinance whereunto even the very creation of mankinde is submitted in order of causes, and therefore much lesse dooth the Apostle put the foreseene corruption of mankinde before it. For firste by the terme Lump (*massae*), there is manyfestly betokened a substance as yet unshapen (*materia adhuc rudis*), and onely prepared to woorke uppon afterwarde. Againe in likening God to a Potter, and mankinde to a lumpe of clay whereof vessels are to bee made afterworde, out of all doubte the Apostle betokeneth the first creation of men. Furthermore hee shoulde speake unproperly, to say, that vessels of wrath are made of that lumpe. For if that lumpe betokened men corrupted: then were they vessels of dishonour already, and the potter shoulde not bee saide to make them, other than such as they had them selves already.[3]

Thus while Calvin says men are chosen from a 'corrupt mass', Beza argues that the elect—and reprobate—are predestined from a mass 'yet unshapen'.

'foreknowledge, predestination and election are at this point one and the same thing'. There is 'even a predestination of the wicked' but this may be called '"reprobation" instead'. *Common Places of Martin Bucer* (Abingdon, 1972), 96-7. Martyr's treatment suggests a semantic difference; 'predestination' refers to 'saints onlie' while 'the reprobate are not predestinate' since sin is the only cause of reprobation. *The Common Places of the most famous and renowned Divine Doctor Peter Martyr* (1583), Part 3, 8-11. A more dynamic view of predestination, however, is that of Henry Bullinger (1504-75). In the *Decades* he says that predestination is God's decree 'either to save or destroy men', but does not state clearly the basis on which the decree is made. God has decreed 'to save all, how many soever have communion and fellowship with Christ' and 'to destroy or condemn all, how many soever have no part' in Christ. Bullinger moreover laments that 'many verily, curiously and contentiously enough' dispute the 'points' of predestination, which endangers God's glory and 'the salvation of souls'. *The Decades of Henry Bullinger*, Parker Society (1848-51), iv. 185 ff.

[1] Rom. 9: 23: 'Hath not the potter power over the clay, of the same lump to make one vessel unto honour, and another unto dishonour?'

[2] This term apparently emerged near the time of the Synod of Dort (1618-19). Cf. Carl Bangs, *Arminius* (Nashville, 1973), 67.

[3] *Questions and Answers*, 84 f.

Supralapsarianism, then, is the position that the decrees of election and reprobation have logical priority over the decree of both Creation and the Fall; predestination thus refers to the destinies of men not yet created, much less fallen. While Beza can claim that the reprobate were predestined because of 'corruption, lack of faith, & iniquitie', he contends that God executed a 'condemnation' towards the reprobate, though predestined prior to the Fall.[1] Man was created in a 'ryght state' but 'chaungeable'; the Fall of man issued in this 'just hatred' towards the reprobate.[2]

Beza logically works out his system so that Jesus Christ is the Redeemer of the elect; the reprobate have no Redeemer according to this scheme—neither to begin nor to end with. The elect have the Redeemer, before Creation or the Fall. Jesus Christ is the 'onely mediator between God and his elect eternally ordained'. God sent Christ 'to save his electe and chosen by him'.[3] 'Gods whole wrath', however, was 'utterly inflamed against all the sinnes of all the chosen; even til satisfaction were made to the full', such being paid by Christ.[4]

The only hope of salvation then is not only that one is chosen from eternity (for Calvin's theology also posits this) but that one is among those who have been offered the Redeemer. If the knowledge that Christ died for us can be obtained, we may be certain we will not perish; for God will not demand double payment for sin. This inference for Beza is the remedy by which Satan's assaults upon the elect are answered:

Thou saiest Sathan that god is the perfectly righteous and revenger of all iniquitie. I doe confesse, but I will joygne thereto an other property of Justice which thou haste left out, that is, for as much as god is righteous he is content with one payment.[5]

Indeed God is righteous and 'will not be payde double, and Jesus Christe god and man hath by one obedience made satisfaction to the infinite magistye of God'. Thus 'it followeth that my iniquities can

---

[1] *Briefe Declaration*, 13f. This teaching is an assumption in Chapters I–IV of *Briefe Declaration*.

[2] Ibid. 15–22.

[3] *Briefe and Pithie*, 3–4. 'With one only offering and sacrifice of him self should sanctifie all the elect . . . And to the intent thys remedy should not be founde and ordeyned in vayne, the Lord God determined to give this his sonne with all things appertayning to salvation, to them whome hee had determined in himself to choose: and on the other side, to give them unto his sonne.' *Briefe Declaration*, 30 ff.

[4] *Questions and Answers*, 7.   [5] *Briefe and Pithie*, 21.

no more fraye nor trouble me, my accountes and dettes beinge
assuredly rased and wyped out by the precious bloud of Jesus Christ
which was made accursed for me, dyinge righteous for the un-
righteous'.[1]

It will be recalled that Calvin holds that the issue with regard to
Christ's death is not the efficacy in itself but to whom Christ gives
Himself to be enjoyed.[2] But Beza, by positing the Redeemer for the
elect only, makes His death efficacious in itself. Since God will not
demand double payment, those for whom Christ died *must* be saved.
Had Christ died for all, according to the value Beza places on
Christ's death, all would be saved.

Moreover, while Calvin says Christ is the mirror in Whom we
contemplate our election, Beza understands Ephesians 1: 4 not only
in terms of the elect's having been given the Redeemer in eternity
but suggests their salvation was an accomplished fact before they are
grafted into Christ in time.

The beginning of our salvatyon commeth of God, who first chose us in
Christ ere we were born, yet and ere ever the foundacions of the world wer
laid and also firste loveth us in the time of our beeing born, when as yet we
bee not geven unto Christe & graffed into him in verye deede, but are too be
geven and graffed.[3]

What Beza does not do is to make Christ the mirror of our
election. While he maintains God will not demand double payment
'—so that the elect's salvation is assured—the inevitable conclusion
is that we cannot directly participate in this assurance. We have no
pledge, as it were, that *we* are elected; for we have no way of
knowing whether we are one of those for whom Christ died. Had
Christ died for all, we could freely know we are elected. But Beza
has told us Christ died for the elect. This makes trusting Christ's
death presumptuous, if not dangerous: we could be putting our
trust in One who did not die for us and therefore be damned. Thus
we can no more trust Christ's death by a direct act of faith than we
can infallibly project that we are among the number chosen from
eternity: for the number of the elect and the number for whom
Christ died are one and the same. The ground of assurance, then,
must be sought elsewhere than in Christ.

Beza knows this. He works out his theology with this in mind and
comes up with the solution: we look inside ourselves. We cannot

---

[1] *Briefe and Pithie*, 21a.   [2] *Supra*, p. 16 n. 4.
[3] *Questions and Answers*, 34 (irreg. pagination).

ascend to God's eternal counsel but we can see whether He is at work in us.

Nowe when Sathan putteth us in doubt of our election, we maye not searche first the resolution in the eternall counsell of god whose majesty we cannot comprehende, but on the contrarye we must beginne at the sanctifi- cation which we feele in our selves . . . forasmuch as our sanctification from whence proceedeth good works, is a certaine effect (*effectum*) of the faith or rather of Jesus Christ dwelling in us by faith.[1]

Beza directs us not to Christ but to ourselves; we do not begin with Him but with the effects, which points us back, as it were, to the decree of election. Thus, while Calvin thinks looking to ourselves leads to anxiety, or sure damnation, Beza thinks otherwise. Sancti- fication, or good works, is the infallible proof of saving faith. 'Behold now both the effects, which if we feele working in us, the conclusion is infallible, that we have faith, and consequently Jesus Christ is in us unto eternal life as is aforesaid.'[2]

Thus Beza resorts to the practical syllogism. It therefore pre- cipitates a distinction between faith and assurance and paves the way for what the writers in this tradition will term the reflex act. For the *knowledge* of faith is the 'conclusion' deduced by the effects. It is as though Beza says: all who have the effects have faith; but I have the effects, therefore (the infallible conclusion) I have faith. Indeed, Beza asserts that one should 'conclude with himself I am in Jesus Christ by faith, and therefore I cannot perishe, but am sure of my salvation'.[3] It seems then that it is not faith which assures but the conclusion that proves faith is there.

This implicit distinction between faith and assurance is further seen by Beza's insistence that we must 'apply' Christ to ourselves. Consistent with his doctrine of limited atonement, Beza states that it is hardly enough to believe that 'Jesus Christ came to save synners'; rather one must 'particularlye applye' Christ 'to himself', the promise of his salvation.[4] When Beza calls faith 'a certaine know- ledge'[5] he sounds very much like Calvin. But there is a real difference, and Beza cannot let this definition end there; this knowledge is 'asserteyned' in the heart by appropriating the 'pro-

---

[1] *Briefe and Pithie*, 36a, 37.

[2] Ibid. 26 (irreg. pagination).

[3] Ibid. 24. Beza asks: 'But whereby may a man know whether he have faith or no?', and answers: 'By good workes.' *A Little Catechisme*, 5th sect., q. 1.

[4] *Briefe and Pithie*, 24.

[5] Ibid. 15a.

mise' of salvation.[1] Calvin calls faith a persuasion; Beza says one must 'persuade himself certainly'.[2]

Behind Beza's assertion that faith is to be ascertained by applying the promise lies a voluntaristic doctrine of faith. The seed of voluntarism is found in these lines:

> Q. And they which have this fayth, are they saved?
> A. Yea of necessitie, for god hath given his sonne to the ende that every one which beleveth in him, should have life everlasting: and he is not a lyer.[3]

This assertion seems to assume that faith is something which is rewarded. For what Beza does not do is to point men to Christ; he points men instead to faith. If they conclude they have faith, then they may conclude that they have Christ. To Calvin, looking to Christ *is* faith; Calvin could point men directly to Christ since Christ died for all. Beza begins not with Christ but with faith; faith, if found, is rewarded with salvation in Christ but this salvation comes to the believer indirectly. This manner of knowing whether one has Christ is later called the indirect act of faith or the reflex act. At any rate it is the essence of the practical syllogism.

It is this which also implies that faith is an act of the will, although Beza falls short of putting it like this. Had he clearly stated that faith is an act of the will, no doubt Perkins after him would have followed on this point as he tended to do on all else which Beza teaches. But all which William Ames would later correct is embedded in the teaching of Theodore Beza. Beza simply does not make clear what Ames later makes clear indeed.

This is not to suggest that Beza thinks that man takes the initiative in his salvation. Beza believes the very opposite. That a man believes at all—indeed, that his will is moved to seek after God—is only to be explained in terms of God's enabling grace.[4] Beza simply wants to place the knowledge of faith within reach of any anxious enquirer. Thus the will is presupposed in faith in Beza's scheme. This is clearly implied by the inference that God obliges

---

[1] *Briefe and Pithie*, 15a. Cf. *Questions and Answers*, 23 f.: true faith is 'a stedfast assent of the mind' whereby 'eche man applieth particularly to himselfe, the promise of everlasting life in Christ'.

[2] *Briefe and Pithie*, 189 f. Beza also defines faith as 'a certaine perswasion and assurance, which every true christian man *oughte to have*, that God the Father loveth him, for Jesus Christ his sons sake'. *A Little Catechisme*, 4th sec., q. 3 (my italics). But that faith needs verification 'by good workes' tends to make Beza's claim that faith is assurance suspicious. This is perhaps why he says one 'oughte to have' it.

[3] Ibid., q. 6.   [4] Ibid. q. 5.

Himself to act when we come forward with faith. This thinking is to be contrasted with Calvin's point that faith is something to which no reward can be paid.[1] Calvin's statement means that the knowledge Christ is ours is passively given; Beza's statement means that faith is that which *binds* Him Who 'is not a lyer'. Beza's thinking also coheres well with the doctrine of faith that lies behind the covenant theology of the Heidelberg divines. The crucial point is that it is not Christ Himself who is offered; it is rather the condition that is offered, viz. to whoever meets it by proving to himself that he has faith.

Such appropriation is not a simple matter in Beza's teaching. Beza depicts conversion as a composite of two works of grace: a 'first grace' (faith) and a 'second grace' (sanctification). The first grace is rendered void, however, if it is not ratified by the second. It is the second grace which assures, for the first grace may not persevere.

That the first grace is effectuall, it is to bee imputed to Gods second grace, for wee should straytwaies fall from the first, if there followed not another immediately after, to make the former effectuall, and so must yee proceede on still from grace to grace.[2]

That we 'use' the first grace well 'wee may thanke the second grace for it'.[3] What Beza means is that 'the causes of a thing cannot bee workinge in very deede, unless the effects of it come foorth together with it'.[4] The effects—sanctification—joined with the cause constitute saving faith. Beza's implicit voluntarism emerges: through the first grace 'we may wil'; through the second 'we do wil in deede'.[5]

Beza describes sanctification and repentance in much the same way.[6] It may be seen therefore how he reverses Calvin's order of faith and repentance. Beza does not specifically say that faith follows repentance, however. But by making the knowledge of saving faith subject to the second grace (sanctification) he reverses the order Calvin intends. For Calvin insists we cannot truly repent until we are first assured of God's grace. Beza delays assurance until the 'effects' are there; thus a change of life precedes the assurance that we have faith indeed.[7]

---

[1] *Supra*, p. 20 n. 3.   [2] *Questions and Answers*, 31.
[3] Ibid. 31a.   [4] Ibid. 34f.   [5] Ibid. 30a.
[6] *Briefe and Pithie*, 25f., 190; *A Little Catechisme*, 6th sect., q. 3 and 10th sect., q. 6; *Canticles*, 23f.; *Questions and Answers*, 45ff.
[7] 'A most assured faith' comes 'by this repentance of which I spake, I meane a true assurance of conscience'. *Canticles*, 23f.

When Beza makes sanctification the ground of assurance he puts the knowledge of faith within reach of anyone who wills to be godly—save for one thing: he retains the doctrine of temporary faith. This doctrine poses serious problems for a theology which posits that one must verify his faith by good works. Beza none the less holds that reprobates are sometimes affected with a 'callying ineffectuall', which is but a temporary or general faith.[1] Those with such are 'most miserable of all', since they

climbe a degree higher, that their fall might bee more grievous: for they are raised so high by some gift of grace, that they are a little mooved with some taste of the heavenly gift: so that for the time they seeme to have received the seed, and to be planted in the Church of God, and also shew the way of salvation to others.[2]

The unregenerate may have 'the appearances of vertues, ordinarilie called Moral vertues'. But such are different from 'the works of the children of God governed by the spirit of regeneration'.[3] Beza, however, does not state what the differences are. The knowledge of divinity moreover, which must be produced by God's Spirit, is 'also common to many reprobates'.[4] The natural reason 'that is in any man unregenerated, dooth oftentimes strive against his lustes',[5] and the wicked can have 'sorrow of sin'.[6] These depictions of the possibilities of temporary faith are mild when compared with those seen below in Perkins. But Beza's propounding an ineffectual calling of the reprobate keeps a concept alive that hardly seems appropriate to a teaching that also makes good works the ground of assurance. From Beza's descriptions we may fear that our good works are but the moral virtues of the unregenerate. Our sanctification can give little comfort when we know the reprobate too may be 'raised so high by some gift of grace' that he seems to be regenerate. But Beza claims that from sanctification 'we gather fayth'; he concludes: the sanctified man 'is of necessitye chosen'.[7] If 'the effects' are there, 'consequently our election' is proved, 'as the lyfe of the body is perceived by feeling and mooving'.[8]

---

[1] *Briefe Declaration*, 39.   [2] Ibid. 40.   [3] *Canticles*, 269.
[4] *Visible Markes*, unpaginated.   [5] *Questions and Answers*, 47.
[6] *Canticles*, 309. 'Wee must put a great difference betweene that sort of waking which is proper to Gods elect, and which proceedeth from his meere grace . . . and that waking & good morrow of sinne which the wicked have, which leadeth such as are reprobate into despaire . . . as is to be seene in that horrible example of Judas the traitor.' Ibid.
[7] *Questions and Answers*, 87a.   [8] Ibid. 87.

Beza's final solution is that we persevere in holiness.

Quest. But the garlond is geven to those onely that holde out.
Ans. I graunt so. And therefore whoseoever is elected craveth perseverance & obtaineth it.[1]

It is not surprising then that Beza appeals to 2 Peter 1: 10 in connection with assurance of election based on a good conscience.

For this cause Saint Peter admonishes us to make our vocation & election sure by good workes. Not that they be the cause of our vocation & election . . . But forasmuch as good workes bring testimonie to our conscience that Jesu Christ dwelleth in us, & consequently we cannot perishe, being elected to salvation.[2]

'Good works' are those which 'God hath commanded' in the Law.[3]

Beza believes, moreover, that the role of the Law in conversion is vitally important. While Calvin notes the differences between the Old and New Testaments, he emphasizes the continuity between the two. Beza does not disavow the continuity but stresses the difference. Indeed, 'the ignorance of this distinction between the law and the gospell is one of the principall causes & rootes of all the abuses' which have corrupted Christianity.[4] The significant divergence from Calvin on this matter is that Beza stresses the role of the Law in preparation for faith. The 'fyrste' use of the Law is to show our sins, 'make us sory, and to humble and throw downe our selves to the uttermost. It also kindles 'the first poynt of repentaunce'.[5] As 'the colour of blacke is never better sette forthe then when whyte is sette by it, so the spirite of God *beginneth* by the preachyng of the lawe'.[6]

The question whether faith precedes repentance or vice versa in the *ordo salutis* emerges from Beza's discussion of the role of the Law in conversion. If the Law is to be preached *first* for the purpose of producing a change in us, repentance is inevitably implied; hence repentance precedes faith. Beza claims that the Spirit works through the Law, but he does not say at what point regeneration begins. He does say that having 'true Repentance' is 'a good way to bee prepared to receive pardon'.[7] It is the Law which produces 'the first poynct of repentance'. Thus Beza not only reverses the order Calvin

---

[1] Ibid. 88a.
[2] *Briefe and Pithie*, 37 f. Beza describes 'three temptations' by which Satan assaults the saints. The ultimate comfort (if not remedy) which Beza provides is that we know we have faith by 'her effectes and workes'. Ibid. 24 f.
[3] *A Little Catechisme,* 5th sect., q. 2.
[4] *Briefe and Pithie*, 50 (irreg. pagination).
[5] Ibid. 54a.   [6] Ibid. 53a (my italics).   [7] *Canticles,* 422.

intends by delaying assurance until a change is present but comes very close indeed to putting repentance before faith in the *ordo salutis* by stressing the role of the Law in conversion.

It seems then that Beza's doctrine of faith substantially diverges from that of Calvin; the difference is not quantitative but qualitative.[1] The origin of this departure is linked to Beza's doctrine of limited atonement; when Christ is not held forth to all men as the immediate ground of assurance, the result is not only introspection on our part but a need to assure ourselves upon the very grounds Calvin warns against.

THE HEIDELBERG THEOLOGIANS

When the Palatinate Reformation needed to define its faith, Frederick III turned to the faculty of theology at Heidelberg. On this faculty were Zacharias Ursinus (1534–83), Kaspar Olevianus (1536–87), and Girolamo Zanchius (1516–90). In 1563 the Heidelberg Catechism was drawn up by Ursinus and Olevianus.[2] It was translated and published in England in 1572, and went into at least eight editions by 1619. Ursinus also wrote a commentary on the catechism that was widely read in England.[3] Some writings of Olevianus[4] and Zanchius[5] were also read in England.

The significant contribution of the Heidelberg theologians is their

---

[1] Cf. J. S. Bray, *Theodore Beza's Doctrine of Predestination* (Niewkoop, 1975). Bray sees Beza as 'a transitional figure who bridged the gap' between Calvin and 'Reformed orthodoxy' (142). Bray does not treat Reformed orthodoxy (save for some secondary sources) and his grasp of Calvin never moves beyond Wendel, *Calvin* (thirty-five references) or E. A. Dowey, *The Knowledge of God in Calvin's Theology* (New York, 1965) (twenty-eight references). He claims that the difference between Calvin and Beza is 'subtle' (85), 'quantitative, not qualitative' (111). Bray thinks Beza was forced to defend Calvin's system (129) and implies that Beza's way of doing it was the only way it could be done. He never comes to grips with Calvin himself, nor does he attempt to understand those on the other side of the 'bridge'. Had he done so he would have seen that Beza is not merely a bridge but the architect of a system fundamentally different from Calvin's.

[2] Emile G. Léonard, *A History of Protestantism* (1967), ii. 13.

[3] *The summe of christian religion* (eight editions between 1587 and 1633). Hereinafter called *The Summe* (1633).

[4] *An Exposition of the Symbole of the Apostles* (1581). The original Latin treatise was written in 1576; hereinafter called *Symbole*.

[5] *H. Zanchius His Confession of Christian Religion* (Cambridge, 1599). The original Latin treatise was written in 1585; hereinafter called *Confession*. In 1595 Perkins published *A Case of Conscience* and appended to it his translation of a treatise by Zanchius under the title 'A Briefe Discourse taken ovt of the writings of H. Zanchius'. Perkins, *Workes*, i. 429–38. Hereinafter called 'Discourse'.

federal theology:[1] the motif known as the covenant of works and the covenant of grace. This emerges as 'covenant of works' and 'covenant of faith' in *The Summe*.[2] Ursinus presents this as an assumption not an innovation. His almost casual reference to this is in his defence of the perseverance of the saints:

When as He judgeth according to the Gospel, that is not according to the covenant of workes, as our own obedience, which should satisfie the law, but according to the covenant of faith, or the righteousness applied unto us by faith . . .[3]

Ursinus defines the covenant of God:

A mutuall promise and agreement between God and men, whereby God giveth men assurance, that He will be gracious and favourable to them, remit their sinnes, bestow new righteousness, his holy Spirit, and life eternall for and by his Sonne our Mediatour: and on the other side, men binde themselves to Faith and Repentance; that is, to receive this so great a benfit with true Faith, and to yeeld true Obedience unto God.[4]

Olevianus develops his theology within the context of the covenant: such rests not on our merit but 'in faith alone'.[5] God deals with His elect by a covenant 'because there is no apter forme or meeter way of doing it'.[6] By this God promises 'to binde himselfe unto us that are repentant and beleeve in him'.[7]

Ursinus says there is one covenant in 'substance and matter, but two in Circumstances'.[8] In the Old Covenant men were bound to the obedience of 'the whole Mosaicall Law, Morall, Ceremonial, and Civill'. The New 'bindeth us only to the Morall or Spirituall Law, and to the use of the Sacraments'.[9] We partake of the New Covenant by faith, which is engendered by the Gospel. But 'this order' must be observed:

First, the Law is to be proposed, that thence wee may know our misery. Then, that we may not despaire after our misery is knowne unto us, the Gospel is to be taught . . . [which] showeth unto us the manner how we are

---

[1] Cf. Latin *foedus*: 'covenant'.

[2] *The Summe*, 94. Wolfgang Musculus (1497–1563) suggests a similar motif when he speaks of a 'generall' covenant (to all men) and a 'speciall & everlasting' covenant (to the elect). The latter is based upon the 'condition' of faith. *Common places of Christian Religion, gathered by Wolfgangus Musculus* (1563), 121 f. The idea is also suggested in Bullinger: God 'by a certaine league hath joined Himself to mankind, and that He hath most straitly bound Himself to the faithful, and the faithful to Himself'. *Decades* (PS), iii. 330.

[3] *The Summe*, 94.   [4] Ibid. 124.   [5] *Symbole*, 55.   [6] Ibid. 52.
[7] Ibid. 52 f.   [8] *The Summe*, 125   [9] Ibid. 127.

to repent. Thirdly, that after we attaine unto our delivery, we wexe not careless and wanton, the Law is to be taughte againe, that it may be the levell, squire, and rule of our life and actions.[1]

Zanchius too stresses the role of the Law, the 'meanes' by which we 'might bee prepared more and more for the receiving of Christ'.[2] The Law shows men their duty and sinfulness and produces 'a greater and earnester desire of the promised Saviour'; by it men become 'disposed and prepared to take holde of Christ by faith'.[3] The Gospel requires that we (1) desire to have 'all our affections chaunged'; (2) embrace Christ by faith 'without any wavering' so that we believe our sins are pardoned; and (3) we 'labour by all meanes, to observe whatsoever Christ hath commaunded'.[4] The Law requires perfect obedience; the Gospel requires faith, but such as 'cannot bee without true repentance'.[5]

Ursinus defines faith as 'a certaine knowledge, whereby I surely assent' to God's Word, and 'an assured trust' of remission of sins.[6] Justifying faith is 'seated' in 'the will and heart of man'.[7] Ursinus does not say what he means by 'heart', but the thrust of his theology suggests that he means affections. As to what faith is, 'no man truly understandeth, but hee who hath it' since he who believes 'knoweth that he doth believe'.[8] The 'security' that we are saved consists in the testimony of the Spirit and 'the effects of true faith, which we perceive to be in us', namely, 'true repentance, and a constant purpose of believing, and obeying God according to all his precepts'.[9] For out of the 'earnest desire of performing obedience' arises 'our assurance of our true faith'.[10]

While Ursinus defines faith as 'a certaine knowledge' it must be noted he also claims that 'a good conscience is a certaine knowledge, that wee have faith'.[11] The conscience is 'nothing else' but 'a Practicall Syllogisme' in the mind.[12] It seems that a good conscience, then, is the ground of assurance for Ursinus.

Ursinus says there are four kinds of faith: historical, temporary, faith of miracles, and justifying faith.[13] Historical faith is but 'bare

---

[1] *The Summe*, 128.   [2] *Confession*, 47.   [3] Ibid. 51.
[4] Ibid. 94.   [5] Ibid. 96.   [6] *The Summe*, 133.
[7] Ibid. 136. Zanchius says there are two kinds of 'actions' of faith: one in the understanding, another in the will. *Confession*, 327.
[8] *The Summe*, 137. Zanchius says, 'let every one of us to make an assumption by himself in his mind: But I am of the faithfull: for I finde in my selfe that I truly beleeve.' 'Discourse', 430.
[9] *The Summe*, 32–3.   [10] Ibid. 33   [11] Ibid. 95.
[12] Ibid. 39.   [13] Ibid. 134.

knowledge of what God has done (which the devils have)'.[1] Temporary faith is 'to assent unto the doctrine of the Church, together with profession and joy therein, though not true, and unfeigned'. This comes from some cause other than 'a lively sense' of God's grace and without the 'application of the promise' to oneself.[2] The faith of miracles is a gift of revelation whereby one may be able to predict a certain event, to be able to cast out devils, and work miracles.[3] Justifying faith is the aforementioned 'certaine knowledge'.

Perkins will repeat these kinds of faith, combining the first three with Beza's concept of an ineffectual calling of the reprobate. It will be seen below that Perkins appears to draw largely from Beza but also from these Heidelberg divines; these mix well for they have in common a doctrine of faith that makes sanctification the ground of assurance. Ursinus espouses a limited atonement;[4] all stress the practical syllogism. Zanchius claims that if one concludes that he believes, 'even God himselfe' concludes 'for thee, that thou art predestinate to eternall life'.[5]

The Heidelberg divines also hold in common with Beza that the Law goes before the Gospel in preparing men to faith. That this tends to reverse Calvin's order of faith and repentance has been noted. Ursinus moreover stresses 2 Peter 1: 10 as the formula by which we are to know our election.[6] Zanchius interprets 2 Peter 1: 10 the same way.[7] Olevianus claims that 'new obedience' is 'an undoubted testimony' of saving faith.[8]

The Heidelberg divines, then, have in common with Beza a qualitatively different doctrine of faith from that of John Calvin.

---

[1] Ibid.   [2] Ibid. 134-5.   [3] Ibid. 135-6.

[4] Christ died 'only for the elect' and 'not for the world'. The 'many' (e.g. Heb. 9: 28) means the elect, not all. John 17: 9 refers to the number for whom Christ died. Ibid. 298 ff.   [5] 'Discourse', 430.

[6] *The Summe*, 513.   [7] 'Discourse', 437.   [8] *Symbole*, 244 f.

3

SOME ENGLISH PRECURSORS
OF PERKINS

WHILE the shape of Perkins's theology is most akin to that of Beza and the Heidelberg theologians,[1] the experimental predestinarian tradition has theological roots in England as well. In *Whether a Man* Perkins inserts 'A Dialogve of the State of a Christian man, gathered here and there out of the sweet and sauorie writings of Master Tindall and Master Bradford'.[2] While this treatise does not make clear exactly what Perkins finds appealing in these reformers, their writings indicate a doctrine of faith that anticipates much of what is to be found in Perkins.

WILLIAM TYNDALE (d. 1536)

William Tyndale has a distinctive covenant theology, not one that speaks of a covenant of works and a covenant of grace but one which parallels what the Heidelberg divines put forward in their federal theology. Tyndale's is a 'promise and conditional-covenant' motif.[3] He seems to have developed the details of this after his debate with Thomas More (d. 1535), and it was apparently employed as a 'defence against the charge of antinomianism'.[4]

'Where thou findest a promise', Tyndale says, 'there must thou understand a covenant.'[5]

All the good promises which are made us throughout all the scripture . . . are all made us on this condition and covenant on our party, that we hence forth love the law of God, to walk therein, and to do it, and fashion our lives thereafter. . . . there is no promises made him, but to them only that promise to keep the law.[6]

---

[1] This will be developed below.

[2] *Workes*, i. 381 ff.

[3] L. J. Trinterud, 'A Reappraisal of William Tyndale's Debt to Martin Luther', *CH* (1962), 39.

[4] William Clebsch, *England's Earliest Protestants 1520–1535* (1964), 115.

[5] *Doctrinal Treatises* (PS), 470.

[6] *Expositions* (PS) 6.

For 'none of us can be received to grace but upon a condition to keep the law'.[1]

Tyndale's doctrine of assurance is based on keeping the Law. Grace will not 'continue any longer', he claims, than the 'purpose' to keep the Law 'lasteth'. If we break the Law, 'we must sue for a new pardon; and have a new fight against sin, hell, and desperation, ere we can come to a quiet faith again'.[2]

Tyndale distinguishes between true faith and a 'feigned faith', that which does not issue in a love for God's law.[3] The latter he also calls a 'story faith'[4] and a 'historical faith'.[5] Assurance of saving faith comes by obedience to the Law. He regards 2 Peter 1: 10 as being a mandate to godly living, which, in turn, assures us of our being chosen.[6]

JOHN BRADFORD (d. 1555)

John Bradford has a strong doctrine of predestination, one that was put in writing owing to his encounter with some anti-predestinarian separatists in the King's Bench prison. 'The effects of salvation they so mingle with the cause', he laments.[7] Bradford also claims that 'Christ's death is sufficient for all, but effectual to none but to the elect only'. Since Christ 'prayed not' for all (John 17: 9) it follows for Bradford that 'for whom He "prayed not", for them He died not'.[8]

Bradford has a pastoral concern that transcends his defence of his predestinarian theology. He delights in assuring others of their election. None of God's chosen will perish, he writes to a distressed soul, 'of which number I know you are'.[9] If God 'had not chosen you (as most certainly he hath), he would not have so called you'. For 'your thankfulnesse and worthiness are fruits and effects of your election'. Yet such effects will be 'much more fruitful and effectual, by how much you waver not'.[10]

Bradford also places repentance before predestination in order of concerns.

But, if you feel not this faith, then know that predestination is too high a matter for you to be disputers of it, until you have been better scholars in the school-house of repentance and justification, which is the grammar

[1] *Doctrinal Treatises*, 7. [2] Ibid.
[3] *Answer to More* (PS). 70, 106, 199. [4] Ibid. 197.
[5] *Expositions*, 146. [6] Ibid. 193.
[7] *The Writings of John Bradford* (PS), ii. 170f. [8] Ibid. i. 320.
[9] Ibid. ii. 109. [10] Ibid. 113–14.

school, wherein we must be conversant and learned, before we go to the university of God's most holy predestination . . .[1]

Bradford describes repentance as sorrowing for sin, a trust of pardon, and 'a purpose to amend, or conversion to a new life'.[2] Bradford's view of the covenant, however, hardly agrees with Tyndale's. God's covenant 'dependeth and hangeth upon God's own goodness' and 'not on our obedience or worthiness in any point', Bradford claims, 'for then should we never be certain'.[3]

LAURENCE CHADERTON (1537–1640)

Laurence Chaderton was Perkins's tutor at Christ's College, Cambridge.[4] He was among the first to confront Peter Baro (d. 1599), 'an Arminian *avant la lettre*'.[5] He also introduced the thought of Peter Ramus (d. 1572) to Cambridge.[6] Chaderton published little, however, and what survives under his name gives but a hint of his theology.[7]

Chaderton's sermon at Paul's Cross is based on Matthew 7: 21–3, a text that is sometimes taken to depict temporary faith. He labels the figures of the text 'counterfeit and hypocritical professors' known by their 'external confession of Christ'.[8] These have an 'outward shewe' but are void of 'inwarde synceritie and true beliefe'. True Christians are contrasted with those who work their salvation 'securely, coldely, and carelessly, and not in fear and trembling'. Chaderton urges us to examine ourselves 'that we may see whether we doe truely stand in the grace of God or no'. To be careless means that our works 'neither are, nor can be unto us the pledges and seales of our salvation'. Chaderton concludes his sermon by noting 'how farre' it is that 'sinners and ungodly men may resemble the deare children of God, and yet be voyd of the graces of regeneration'.[9]

---

[1] *The Writings of John Bradford* (PS), ii. 134.   [2] Ibid. i. 45.

[3] Ibid. ii. 153.   [4] Ian Breward (ed.), *William Perkins* (Abingdon, 1970), 3.

[5] H. C. Porter, *Reformation and Reaction in Tudor Cambridge* (Cambridge, 1958), 281, 378.

[6] W. S. Howell, *Logic and Rhetoric in England, 1500–1700* (Princeton, 1956), 150 ff.

[7] Two sermons survive: *An Excellent and godly sermon preached at Paules Crosse* (1578, 1580). Hereinafter called *Godly Sermon* (1580). *A Fruitful sermon* (four editions, 1584 to 1618).

[8] *Godly Sermon*, unpaginated.

[9] Chaderton's other sermon takes its text from Rom. 12: 3–8. He stresses pastoral duties and urges that a pastor 'Feede, feede, feed'. Preaching must be based 'partly by the fear of gods judgments, & partly by the love of his mercies'. The wicked are to be exhorted to repentance by having laid before them 'the eternall and severe judgements and curses of God'. *A Fruitful sermon* (1589), 57–8.

RICHARD GREENHAM (d. 1594)

Richard Greenham was the first English divine to deal at length with 'afflicted consciences'. Fuller says Greenham's 'masterpiece was comforting wounded consciences', and that he was 'an instrument of good to many, who came to him with weeping eyes, and went from him with cheerful souls'.[1]

Greenham matriculated at Pembroke College, Cambridge, in 1559, and was a Fellow there from 1566 to 1570. He was rector at Dry Drayton, five miles from Cambridge, from 1571 to 1591. He was the first pastor of prominence and influence of the experimental predestinarian mould, and was a patriarchal figure in the tradition itself. There is no conclusive evidence that he influenced Perkins, but Perkins could not have been unaware of Greenham's ministry. Greenham frequently came into Cambridge to preach, exerting an influence among the students.[2]

'The first thing required in a Christian', Greenham believes, is 'that he be able to trie himself and his estate before God, whether he be in the faith or no.'[3] To put it another way: the first thing one must learn from God's word is 'to make a right and sound entrance to our salvation'. This process is begun by obtaining 'the true understanding of the Law' so that we may be 'persuaded of the greatnes of our sinnes, and the misery due to the same'. This he calls the 'right sight' of our sins.[4] Greenham is concerned lest one seek justification by passing over the essential function of the Law so as 'to avoyde the wound of conscience'. Therefore he urges, 'Let us first labour to know sinne, then to sorrow for sinne', without which we cannot 'feele our sinnes in Christ forgiven'.[5]

The whole of Greenham's soteriology is summed up in this: the 'Law is to prepare, the Gospell is to follow after'.[6] While the Law is that which 'commaundeth all good, and forbiddeth all evill', the Gospel 'containeth the free promises of God made unto us in Jesus Christ, without any respect of our deservings'.[7] While the Law provides no ability to perform the Gospel, the Gospel through the power of the Spirit enables us to do good.[8]

---

[1] Thomas Fuller, *The Church History of Britain* (Oxford, 1845), v. 192.

[2] M. M. Knappen, *Tudor Puritanism* (Chicago, 1970), 382. Greenham's writings were published posthumously. His *Workes* (nearly 900 folio pages), first published in 1599, reached its sixth edition by 1612.

[3] *Workes* (1612), 229f. [4] Ibid. 72.

[5] Ibid. 105. [6] Ibid. 59.

[7] Ibid. 72. [8] Ibid. 88.

However, before the elect are regenerated it is sometimes necessary that the Lord sends 'crosses, sometimes povertie, sometime
sicknes, sometime reproach, sometime a troubled minde, sometime
private miserie, and sometimes a publike calamitie . . . before they
be humbled'.[1] Greenham laments about preachers who glibly say to
distressed people, 'Why are you heavie my brother? why are you so
cast down my sister? Be of good cheer: take it not so grievously.
What is there that you should feare? God is mercifull, Christ is a
Saviour.' These are 'speeches of love', Greenham retorts, but do as
much good 'as if they should pour cold water into their bosomes'.
What such people need, he asserts, is to be cast down even further.
These speeches of love merely 'over heale the conscience, and abate
some present grief' but momentarily. Such premature consolation
causes the malady to grow 'sorer'.[2]

Greenham says there are two kinds of faith: a general faith and a
particular faith. The former is 'whereby I believe God to be true in
all his workes',[3] or merely being assured that God is 'such a one as
his word prescribeth'.[4] One must have a general faith before he can
have a particular faith,[5] the latter being 'applying things to our
selves'.[6] This particular faith is either (1) 'whereby I believe God to
be just in his threatnings, and so am made penitent' or (2) when 'I
believe him to bee mercifull in his promises, and so come to
repentance'.[7] True faith Greenham defines as 'a true perswasion of
the mercies of God merited by our Lord Jesus Christ'.[8]

Greenham's definition of faith suggests Calvin's, as also when
Greenham says this faith is to be contrasted with 'a lighter & lesser
worke of the spirit, which may be quenched'—an 'inferiour' work
which may be 'taken away'. But Greenham's statement above that
we must *apply* the promise suggests that he is combining both
Calvin and Beza. In any case, the 'inferiour' work of the Spirit he
relates to Hebrews 6: 4-6 and the Parable of the Sower. This work
of the Spirit is like lightning which gives no certain light and 'doth
not continue any time'. The very possibility of such a work means
'we must take heede that we never quench any grace or gift that God
bestoweth upon us'.[9]

Greenham claims there is a difference between having the Spirit
and knowing one has Him. One may 'know' he has the Holy Spirit
(1) if when he falls he retains his former hatred of sin; (2) if sorrow

---

[1] *Workes* (1612), 232.   [2] Ibid. 106.   [3] Ibid. 88.
[4] Ibid. 51.   [5] Ibid. 176.   [6] Ibid. 51.
[7] Ibid. 88.   [8] Ibid. 81.   [9] Ibid. 246.

increases with sins; (3) 'if thou grow in godly care' in preventing further sins; and (4) if, after one falls, he is careful to redeem that which was lost by the same fall.[1]

The emphasis upon the need for holiness of life is a prominent strain in Greenham's writings. We apprehend Christ 'dying for our sinnes when we feele sinne dye in us', he says.[2] Although good works do not justify, 'they that doe no good workes, declare that they neither are justified nor sanctified . . . therefore cannot be saved'.[3] He lists fifteen 'Sweete and sure signes of Election, to them that are brought low'. Greenham places a premium on being 'brought low'; the signs mainly describe one who has a hatred of sin, a meekness of spirit, a desire to glorify God, a purpose to leave his offences, and a delight in the flourishing of the Church.[4]

Greenham's way of comforting the afflicted conscience is to ensure that one is 'brought low' and afflicted indeed, then to assure men of their election if their supreme aim is godly living.

[1] Ibid. 245.   [2] Ibid. 68.   [3] Ibid. 87.   [4] Ibid. 208f.

PART TWO

WILLIAM PERKINS'S DOCTRINE OF FAITH

4

WILLIAM PERKINS'S
DOCTRINE OF FAITH

WILLIAM PERKINS (1558-1602) is to be seen as the fountain-head
of the experimental predestinarian tradition. This is not because he
was an original thinker but because he was the first powerful figure
in his day to synthesize several strands of thought into a popular
predestinarian system—one which revolves around 2 Peter 1: 10 as
the way we prove our election to ourselves. It will be argued
moreover that Perkins's scheme is preponderantly Theodore Beza's,
and that the incorporation of the federal theology of the Heidelberg
theologians into Beza's system constitutes a good match; but that
the injection of Calvin's doctrine of faith into it does not.

William Perkins was born in Marston Jabbet, Warwickshire, in
1558. He enrolled as a pensioner in June 1577 at Christ's College,
Cambridge. His tutor was Laurence Chaderton. He received the BA
in 1581, the MA in 1584, and was elected that year to a Fellowship
at Christ's. Towards the end of 1584 he was appointed lecturer at
Great St. Andrews. His sermons 'were not so plain, but the piously
learned did admire them; nor so learned, but the plain did
understand them'. He 'used to pronounce the word *Damn* with such
an Emphasis, as left a dolefull Echo in his auditors ears a good while
after'.[1]

Perkins seems not to have used the pulpit at St. Andrews for any
purpose other than preaching the Gospel. But he reportedly was
summoned before the Vice-Chancellor of Cambridge University in
January 1587 to answer charges about a sermon he preached in the
college chapel. He allegedly said that kneeling to receive communion was superstitious, as well as the administration of the
elements to himself by the presiding minister. He seems to have cleared
himself of these charges, but stated that in things indifferent one

---

[1] Samuel Clarke, *The Marrow of Ecclesiastical History* (1675), 415. 'The Scholar
could heare no learneder, the Townsman plainer Sermons.' Thomas Fuller, *Abel
Redivivus* (1651), 434.

must go as far as he can from idolatry, supporting this stance upon the authority of Bucer, Calvin, and John Jewell.[1]

In any case, Perkins did not face the discipline of the university authorities again. This encounter over ecclesiological intricacies may have helped him refine his calling. His career thereafter, not to mention his writings, show clearly that he believed 'there were more fundamental issues than contentions about the details of liturgy'.[2] When pressed by some about the lawfulness of subscription, 'he declined to manifest his opinion therein'. He was 'glad to enjoy his own quiet, and to leave others to the liberty of their own consciences'.[3] Indeed, Perkins's 'first love' was 'continuing his paines in the Church of Saint Andrewes';[4] for 'all held Perkins for a prophet— I mean for a painful dispenser of God's will in his word'.[5] In *Whether a Man* Perkins laments about those who were preoccupied with non-soteriological matters. Such 'crie out for discipline, their whole talke is of it', but 'as for the law of God, and the promises of the Gospel, they little regard'.[6]

Perkins married on 2 July 1595, and therefore had to resign his Fellowship. Samuel Ward (d. 1643) wrote in his diary on 5 July: 'Good Lord, graunt that now after Mr. Pirkins departure ther follow no ruyne to the colledg.'[7] The marriage produced seven children, three of whom died in childhood and one of whom was born posthumously.[8] After several weeks of intense suffering of the stone, Perkins died on 22 October 1602.

By the end of the sixteenth century Perkins had replaced the combined names of Calvin and Beza[9] as one of the most popular

---

[1] Ian Breward (ed.), *The Work of William Perkins* (Abingdon, 1970), 4–5. This is the most recent scholarly treatment of Perkins. It treats Perkins's theology in a very general way, dealing minimally with his doctrine of faith. Its strength is in Perkins's biography.

[2] Ibid. 6.

[3] Fuller, *Church History*, v. 170.

[4] Fuller, *Redivivus*, 435.

[5] Fuller, *Church History*, v. 171.

[6] *Workes*, i. 409.

[7] M. M. Knappen (ed.), *Two Elizabethan Diaries* (1933), 109.

[8] Breward, op. cit. 13.

[9] By 1600 there were no less than ninety editions of Calvin's works published in England (including repeated issues of sermons, commentaries, and the *Institutes*): twenty-seven from 1570 to 1580; thirty-two from 1580 to 1590; six from 1590 to 1600. There were fifteen editions of the *Institutes* (twelve of these from 1574 to 1587). Beza's various works reached fifty-six editions (including repeated issues) by 1600: thirty-eight from 1570 to 1580; seven between 1590 and 1600.

authors of religious works in England.[1] Some of these were already being translated into other languages. After his death, Perkins's works were printed in Switzerland, Germany, Holland, France, Bohemia, Ireland, and Hungary, plus translations into Spanish and Welsh published in London.[2] Between 1600 and 1608 three one-volume editions of Perkins's collected works were issued. After 1608 the collected works constituted three folio volumes (totalling over 2,500 pages) which reached eight printings by 1635, alongside repeated editions of other single treatises.[3]

On the whole, Perkins's treatises are essentially soteriological in nature. Never once does he refer to elders, deacons, and Church courts which had been stressed in the classical movement. Perkins was once involved in the trial of some ministers who were connected with the classical movement, but only as a witness for the prosecution.[4] While it is not unusual for Perkins to be called 'the greatest of the sixteenth-century Puritan theologians',[5] or 'the prince of the puritan theologians',[6] to stereotype him in this

---

[1] Perkins witnessed seventy-six editions (including repeated issues) during his lifetime, seventy-one of which came after 1590.

[2] Breward, op. cit. xi. See ibid. 613–32 for a complete list of Perkins's works.

[3] This study will draw from *The Workes of that Famovs and VVorthy minister of Christ in the Vniversitie of Cambridge, Mr. William Perkins* (referred to here as *Workes*): volume i (1608), volumes ii and iii (1609). Note: some editions of the *Workes* vary in pagination. It does not seem useful to list all of Perkins's individual treatises (totalling forty-seven); nearly all are relevant but many overlap in pertinent material. The most useful for the present study are, from volume i: 'Foundation of Christian Religion' (Perkins's catechism; nineteen editions from 1590 to 1647); 'A Golden Chaine' (nine editions from 1590 to 1614 (apart from *Armilla Aurea*: eight editions from 1590 to 1614)); 'An Exposition of the Symbole or Creed' (seven editions from 1595 to 1631); 'Whether a Man' (eight editions from 1589 to 1619); 'A Case of Conscience' (five editions from 1592 to 1597); 'Two Treatises' (on repentance and the warfare between flesh and spirit; seven editions from 1593 to 1632); 'A Discourse of Conscience' (1596, 1597); 'A Reformed Catholike' (six editions from 1597 to 1634); 'A Graine of Musterd-seede' (eight editions from 1597 to 1630). From volume ii: 'The Whole Treatise of the Cases of Conscience' (twelve editions from 1606 to 1651); 'A Commentarie on the Five First Chapters of the Epistle to the Galatians' (1604, 1617); 'A Christian and Plaine Treatise of Predestination' (1606; translated from *De Praedestinationis Modo et Ordine*, which Arminius read (and answered), five editions from 1598 to 1613); 'The Arte of Prophecying' (1607). From volume iii: 'A Godly and Learned Exposition of Christs Sermon on the Mount' (1608, 1611); 'A Clovd of Faithfvll Witnesses' (three editions, 1607 to 1622). Note: the pagination of volume iii begins anew after 'Sermon on the Mount'; the second set of pagination is marked *.

[4] Breward, op. cit. 10. Cf. Collinson, *The Elizabethan Puritan Movement*, 403 ff.

[5] Horton Davies, *Worship and Theology in England* (1970), 424.

[6] Collinson, op. cit. 125.

way tends to overlook the fact that he saw himself as being in the mainstream of the Church of England, which he often defended.[1] He says,

our owne Churches in England hold, beleeve, and maintaine, and preach the true faith, that is, the ancient doctrine of salvation by Christ, taught and published by the Prophets and Apostles, as the booke of the Articles of faith agreed upon in open Parliament doth fully shew.[2]

Not unlike John Jewell (d. 1571) who appealed to the Church Fathers against Rome,[3] Perkins attacked the papists on the one side and separatists on the other.[4] Augustine heads the list in order of frequency of quotation (no less than 588 references, either by name or work cited), followed by Chrysostom (with 129), Jerome (120), Ambrose (105), Tertullian (81), Cyprian (64), and Basil (49).[5] Perkins was 'the first of the Cambridge best-selling authors', making his postumous publications 'almost a local industry' for some.[6]

On the other hand, Perkins's theology does indeed indicate a different emphasis when contrasted with a divine like Jewell. Perkins devoted himself primarily to showing men that they must, and how they can, make their calling and election sure to themselves. This concern evolved to a series of 'cases' of conscience. In 1592, with 2 Peter 1: 10 imprinted on the title-page, came *A Case of Conscience, the Greatest that ever was: how a man may know whether he be the childe of God, or no.* This was Perkins's ultimate concern.

The systematic treatment of Perkins's theology as a whole, however, is *A Golden Chaine.* The title-page discloses his aim, not to mention his agreement with another theologian:

[1] *Workes,* iii. 65, 264, *286, *389, *425, *574. Perkins does not defend the episcopacy as such, however. Collinson, op. cit., does not place Perkins in the classical movement.

[2] *Workes,* i. 313.

[3] *The Works of John Jewell* (PS), *passim,* especially in his reply to Thomas Harding (d. 1572). Cf. S. L. Greenslade, *The English Reformers and the Fathers of the Church* (Oxford, 1960), 18.

[4] *Workes,* iii. 65, 264, *574.

[5] He cites Robert Bellarmine (d. 1621) chiefly as the papist authority when attacking Rome (seventy-seven times), and cites Aquinus thirty-six times, although sometimes to support his own position.

[6] Porter, *Reformation,* 267. By contrast, Richard Hooker (d. 1600), *Of the lawes of ecclesiasticall politie* (1593), did not sell well at first, and never rivalled Perkins's works in popularity before 1640.

A GOLDEN CHAINE:
or,
THE DESCRIPTION OF THEOLOGIE:
Containing the order of the causes of Saluation and
Damnation, according to Gods word. A view whereof is to be seene
in the Table annexed
Hereunto is adioyned the order which M. Theodore Beza
vsed in comforting afflicted consciences.

The 'Table annexed' is indeed 'the order which M. Theodore Beza used' and is vividly reproduced by Perkins, whose annexed chart— 'an ocular Catechisme to them which can not read'—is an embellishment, but not an alteration, of Beza's chart.

The most obvious feature of *A Golden Chaine* is the centrality of the doctrine of double predestination. Perkins argues over the order of the decrees; his is a supralapsarian system. *A Golden Chaine* carries the *ordo salutis* from the eternal decrees to the final consummation of all things, with the unfolding of the execution of those decrees concerning the elect and reprobate placed in between. In the treatise Arminius will read, Perkins claims to defend '(as they call it) the Calvinists doctrine'.[1] That Perkins could make this claim is sufficient proof that Calvin's true position was already beginning to be misunderstood in Perkins's day. Perkins appears to think that Beza's view is essentially Calvin's.

God's decree, whether in terms of the decree itself or its actual execution, is 'the manifestation of the glorie of God'.[2] This decree is 'that by which God in himselfe, hath necessarily, and yet freely, from all eternitie determined all things'. This decree, 'inasmuch as it concerneth man, is called Predestination'.[3] Predestination is 'that by the which he hath ordained all men to a certaine and everlasting estate: that is, either to salvation or condemnation, for his owne glory'.[4]

God accomplishes predestination by 'the creation, and the Fall'.[5] Man was created 'in an excellent estate of innocency' which included free will.[6] Following Beza, Perkins says that our first parents were created 'perfect, but mutable: for so it pleased God to prepare a way to the execution of his decree'.[7] Perkins's chart graphically illustrates this, but here, as in Beza, is his rationale for this view:

For the will of God is the cause of causes: therefore we must take our stand

---

[1] *Workes*, ii, facing page 689. [2] Ibid. i. 15. [3] Ibid. 16. [4] Ibid.
[5] Ibid. [6] Ibid. 16–17. [7] Ibid. 18. Cf. *supra*, p. 31 n. 2.

in it, & out of or beyond it no reason must be sought for: yea indeed there is nothing beyond it. Moreover, every man (as Paul avereth) is unto God, as a lumpe of clay in the potters hand: and therefore God according to his supreme authoritie doth make vessels of wrath, he doth not find them made.[1]

Thus the decree is with regard to men not yet created, much less fallen.

Through the Fall man lost the fullness of God's image; what remains is the conscience. The conscience, in which the image of God resides, is 'part of the understanding in al reasonable creatures, determining of their particular actions, either with them or against them'.[2] The soul is framed so that it has two faculties, understanding and will. Understanding is the faculty whereby we use reason; it is 'the more principall part serving to rule and order the whole man'. It is the 'wagginer in the wagin'. The will is that whereby we choose or refuse a thing, and is joined by the affections. The burden of Perkins's argument is that 'conscience is not placed in the affections nor will, but in the understanding: because the actions thereof standes in the use of reason'. The understanding, however, has two parts: 'Theoricall' and 'practicall'. The former 'standes in the view and contemplation of truth and falsehood: and goes no further'. But the practical understanding, the essence of the conscience, searches whether a particular action is good or bad.[3] Because conscience is in the understanding, and assurance comes via a good conscience, Perkins will put the seat of faith in the understanding as well. It will be seen below, however, that this is ill placed by him.

Conscience, moreover, is 'a naturall' faculty, or a 'created qualitie, from whence knowledge and judgement proceede as effects'—as accusing or excusing. It is a power in the soul, 'the propertie whereof is to take the principles and conclusions of the minde and apply them, and by applying them either to accuse or excuse'.[4] Conscience is 'of a divine nature, and is a thing placed of God in the middest betweene him and man, as an arbitratour to give sentence & to pronounce either with man or against man unto God'.[5] It is here Perkins seems to follow Ursinus: this judgement comes 'in or by a kinde of reasoning or disputing, called a *practicall syllogisme*'.[6] In the making of this reasoning conscience 'hath two assistants: mind, and memorie'. The mind is the storehouse and keeper of 'all manner of rules and principles', comparable to a book

---

[1] *Workes*, ii. 694. Cf. *supra*, p. 30 n. 3.   [2] *Workes*, i. 510.   [3] Ibid.
[4] Ibid.   [5] Ibid. 511.   [6] Ibid. 529. Cf. *supra*, p. 40 n. 12.

of laws. The mind thus presents to the conscience the rule of divine law 'whereby it is to give judgment'. The memory brings to the mind 'the particular actions which a man hath done or not done, that conscience may determine of them'. It is here that the syllogism works.

Every murtherer is cursed, saith the minde:
Thou art a murtherer, saith conscience assisted by memorie:
Ergo, *Thou art cursed*, saith conscience, and giveth her sentence.[1]

Perkins also states that it is the function of conscience not to conceive a thing in itself but to reflect on what has been conceived, hence 'know what I know'.[2] This is the rationale behind what will be called reflex act in the experimental predestinarian tradition.

Inasmuch as the Word of God binds the conscience,[3] 'every man to whome the Gospell is revealed, is bound to beleeve his owne election, justification, sanctification in, and by Christ'.[4] Here Perkins's treatment of the conscience clashes head on with his rational doctrine of predestination. Since all men are not similarly predestined, obviously some are bound to believe what is not true.[5]

Indeed, predestination has two parts: 'Election, and Reprobation.'[6] Election is God's decree 'whereby on his owne free will, he hath ordained certaine men to salvation, to the praise of the glorie of his grace'.[7] Reprobation is 'that part of predestination, whereby God, according to the most free and just purpose of his will, hath determined to reject certaine men unto eternal destruction, and miserie, and that to the praise of his justice'.[8] To the elect a Saviour is given; to the reprobate no Saviour is given. The chosen are provided for by the office of a mediator, Jesus Christ.[9]

As our priest Christ performed 'al those things to God, wherby is obtained eternall life'.[10] Christ's priesthood consists of two parts: satisfaction and intercession. The former is 'whereby Christ is a full propitiation to his Father for the elect'.[11] The satisfaction consists in His passion and fulfilling the Law. In His death Christ was a 'ransome for the sinnes of the elect'. Moreover, the Father accounted Christ a transgressor since man's sin was imputed to Christ.[12] Christ fulfilled the Law by 'the holinesse of his humane nature' and by obedience to the works of the Law.[13] Christ's

---

[1] *Workes*, i. 529.   [2] Ibid. 511.   [3] Ibid. 512–13.   [4] Ibid. 517.
[5] His manner of handling this will be treated below.
[6] *Workes*, i. 24.   [7] Ibid.   [8] Ibid. 106.   [9] Ibid. 24.
[10] Ibid. 27.   [11] Ibid.   [12] Ibid. 28.   [13] Ibid. 29.

performance, in any case, was in behalf of the elect only: 'limited to the elect alone' by the Father's decree.[1] Moreover, the intercession of Christ at the Father's right hand is the application of the 'merit of his death' and the 'request by his holy spirit, in the hearts of the Elect, with sighs unspeakable'.[2] The end of the intercession is the perseverance of the elect.[3]

The 'outward meanes' of executing the decree of election is by God's covenant with His elect.[4] It is here that Perkins incorporates the contribution of the Heidelberg theologians into Beza's *ordo salutis*.

Gods covenant, is his contract with man, concerning the obtaining of life eternall, upon a certen condition. This covenant consisteth of two parts: Gods promise to man, Mans promise to God. Gods promise to man, is that, whereby he bindeth himselfe to man to be his God, if he performe the condition. Mans promise to God, is that, whereby he voweth his allegiance unto his Lord, and to performe the condition betweene them.[5]

There are 'two kindes' of this covenant: 'the covenant of workes, and the covenant of grace.' The former is made with the condition 'of perfect obedience, and is expressed in the morall law'. This Law demands perfect obedience which, if performed, issues in eternal life. But the transgression of this Law issues in 'everlasting death'. The Ten Commandments are 'an abridgement of the whole law, and the covenant of workes'.[6] At this point Perkins discusses the Ten Commandments, one by one.[7] The Law has three uses for the unregenerate: to make sin known; to effect and augment sin; and to pronounce eternal damnation for disobedience.[8]

The covenant of grace is 'that whereby God freely promising Christ, and his benefits, exacteth againe of man, that he would by faith receive Christ, and repent of his sinnes'.[9] The Gospel promises that for 'all such as repent and beleeve in Christ Jesus, there is prepared a full remission of all their sinnes, togither with salvation and life everlasting'.[10]

---

[1] *Workes*, ii. 693. This may be the first time in English theology the word 'limited' is used concerning Christ's death for the elect.

[2] Ibid. i. 29.   [3] Ibid.   [4] Ibid. 31 f.   [5] Ibid. 32.

[6] Ibid. Perkins, however, does not seem to be the first English divine to employ this motif. Cf. Dudley Fenner, *Sacra Theologia* (1586?), 88: 'Foedus duplex est. Operum foedus. Gratuitae promissionis foedus.'

[7] *Workes*, i. 32–70.   [8] Ibid. 70.   [9] Ibid. 71.

[10] Ibid. We do 'not so much offer, or promise any great matter to God, as in a manner only receive'.

Perkins describes the *ordo salutis* from the decree of election to the final consummation in terms of four 'degrees' of God's love: effectual calling, justification, sanctification, and glorification. Effectual calling, 'the first degree of the declaration' of God's love to the elect, is the severing of the sinner from the world into the family of God.[1] This is a spiritual union and is made 'by the spirit of God applying Christ unto us: and on our parts by faith receiving Christ Jesus offered unto us'. Because Christ is the head of the faithful, the latter are also crucified, buried, and raised up with Him.[2] However, the members of Christ's body are to be distinguished between how they appear before men and how they appear before God. Before men they are members of the Church; before God they *may* be reprobates.[3]

While the catholic Church is 'the company of the predestinate',[4] the Church is to be understood as having two parts: the Church Triumphant (in heaven) and the Church Militant (on earth). The former is made up of the departed saints.[5] The Church Militant, also called the visible Church, is 'a mixt company of men professing the faith assembled together by the preaching of the word'. Thus the visible Church includes 'true beleevers and hypocrites, Elect and Reprobate, good and bad'.[6] This is why men must be distinguished between how they appear before men and how they appear before God. On the other hand, they may appear unworthy before men but true believers before God—'dying members' of Christ, who fall into sin and must be excommunicated. These are not members in terms of 'externall communion with the Church' until they are repentant.[7] Those who appear worthy before men but not before God form the basis for Perkins's doctrine of temporary faith.

While temporary faith is the result of an ineffectual calling, as will be seen below, saving faith owes its origin to irresistible grace. But this is accomplished 'by certaine meanes'. The first is 'the saving hearing of the word of God' through preaching. Since the elect are born into the state of unbelief, they do not so much as 'dreame' of their salvation. The task of preaching then is to begin with the Law, 'shewing a man his sin, and the punishment thereof'.[8] For when God brings men to Christ, 'first, he prepareth their hearts, that they might be capable of faith'.[9] This preparation is by 'bruising them' or 'humbling them', and this humiliation is accomplished by giving them a 'sight' and 'sorrow' for their sins.[10] It is the function of the

---

[1] Ibid. 78.   [2] Ibid.   [3] Ibid. 79, 310ff.   [4] Ibid. ii. 348.   [5] Ibid. i. 308.
[6] Ibid. 310.   [7] Ibid. 79.   [8] Ibid.   [9] Ibid. 5.   [10] Ibid.

Law to produce such a sorrow. One may see that Perkins follows Beza and the Heidelberg theologians and not Calvin by propounding the need for the Law to precede the Gospel in bringing men to Christ.

However, the Law of itself cannot produce faith or repentance; such is the proper work of the Gospel.[1] The Law 'shewes us our sinnes, and that without remedy'.[2] It makes us 'dispaire of salvation in respect of our selves'. The Law, then, is our 'schoolemaster, not by plaine teaching, but by stripes and correction'. It is the Law that prepares; the Gospel 'stirres up faith'.[3] In any case, 'preparation is a worke of God' by which the heart is humbled.[4]

It seems to have been very well known that Perkins himself practised this method of putting the Law before the Gospel. Clarke relates an instance when, after one was duly touched by the horror of God's justice, he burst into tears, when 'Master Perkins finding that he had brought him low enough, even to Hell gates, he proceeded . . . to shew him the Lord Jesus . . . stretching forth his blessed hand of mercy . . . as made him break out into new showres of tears for joy'.[5]

Perkins appears to put preparation in the regeneration process. He does not say precisely when regeneration sets in, only that the work of conversion itself must be distinguished between 'beginnings of preparation' and 'beginnings of composition'.[6] The former 'go before' conversion, and are 'no graces of God' but fruits of the Law and of an accusing conscience. The beginnings of preparation may not make 'any chaunge at all'.[7] Such is 'the mollifying of the heart' which, by the use of 'foure principall hammers' (the knowledge of the Law, of sin, a sense of God's wrath, and 'an holy desparation'), brings a man to the place that he is adequately prepared to receive faith.[8]

Following the hearing of the word and the mollifying of the heart comes faith itself: 'a miraculous and supernaturall facultie of the heart, apprehending Christ Jesus applyed by the operation of the holy Ghost, and receiving him to it selfe'.[9] What Perkins never

---

[1] *Workes*, i. 454. [2] Ibid. ii. 290. [3] Ibid. [4] Ibid. 204.
[5] Clarke, *Marrow*, 416. [6] *Workes*, i. 628. [7] Ibid.
[8] Ibid. 79. Perkins incorporates Augustine's fivefold use of grace: preventing, preparing, working, co-operating, and the gift of perseverance. Perkins seems to believe that, while the beginnings of preparation are not 'graces', God's prevenient grace nevertheless underlies the whole process of regeneration, which includes 'preparing grace'. Ibid. ii. 725 f.
[9] Ibid. i. 79.

makes clear, however, is whether a 'prepared' heart is always given saving faith. But it would seem that it is not. For the reprobate may advance to a state that is virtually identical with the process of preparation outlined above. Perkins therefore holds out no guarantee that the four 'hammers' will be effectual every time. He seems rather to suggest that, if one *is* blessed with saving faith, this is how it happened; not that a 'sorrow' for sin inevitably issues in true conversion.

He theoretically holds at any rate that when God wills to regenerate a man, 'His worke cannot be resisted'.[1] What Perkins's theology does not provide is the immediate and conscious realization to the sinner that God's irresistible grace is in fact at work. Perkins does raise this question: When does faith first begin 'to breede in the heart?'[2] His answer is, 'in thirsting there is a measure of faith'.[3] He goes so far as to say 'the will to beleeve is faith'.[4] Indeed, 'the desire to beleeve, is faith in deed: and the desire to repent, repentance itself'.[5] On the other hand, he says that this desire is 'not faith in nature, but only in God's acceptation, God accepting the will for the deed'. This desire is the 'spring time of the ingrafted word' which will follow in 'leaves, blossomes, and fruite'.[6] Indeed, regeneration 'is like the sappe of the tree that lies hid within the barke; repentance is like the budde that speedily shewes it self, before either blossome, leafe, or fruite appeare'.[7]

The question, therefore, must be put to Perkins, What is faith 'in nature'? If it is not the desire, or the will; and if that which 'shewes it selfe' is repentance rather than regeneration, what is the 'nature' of saving faith? His answer to this question is that the 'essentiall propertie thereof' is 'to apprehend Christ with his benefits, and to assure the very conscience thereof'.[8] At first glance, this answer sounds much like Calvin. Perkins even says that 'there can be no justification' without 'some apprehension and assurance'.[9] But this statement flies in the face of his assertion that the will to believe is accepted of God. If faith must assure before it justifies, Perkins cannot hold out certain hope after all to the one who merely has the 'desire' or 'will' to believe.

This dilemma stems from Perkins's vacillation between Calvin and Beza, of which he does not seem to be aware: his efforts to define faith show him agonizing to retain Calvin's concept (faith as

[1] Ibid. 716.	[2] Ibid. ii. 295.	[3] Ibid. 296.
[4] Ibid. 756.	[5] Ibid. i. 629.	[6] Ibid.
[7] Ibid. 453.	[8] Ibid. 631.	[9] Ibid.

a persuasion, assurance, or apprehension) and that of Beza (applying or appropriating). Perkins's problem appears to be that he does not see that there is a substantial, qualitative difference between the two Genevan reformers. He wants simultaneously to define faith both ways, and is torn between holding out hope to the weak one who has but the desire to believe and maintaining the undoubted opinion of Calvin that faith assures. He puts forward this ambivalent statement: 'Whoever feeles in his heart an earnest desire, and a striving against his naturall doubtings, both can and must assure himselfe that he is indued with true faith.'[1] This assertion says one 'can' be assured, as though he is so assured; but that he 'must' be so assured implies he is not assured after all.

Behind this dilemma lies Perkins's valiant effort not merely to hold on to both Calvin and Beza at the same time but to make faith a persuasion simultaneously within the context of a doctrine of limited atonement. But he does not succeed. Perkins seems afraid to call a spade a spade; he insists that the 'seate of faith' is in the 'mind of man, not the will'. He thinks this is so because faith 'stands in a particular knowledge or perswasion, and there is no perswasion but in the minde'.[2] Perkins ought to have said that *assurance* is seated in the mind, not faith. But he will not even concede that faith is 'partly in the mind, and partly in the will' since a 'single grace' cannot 'be seated in divers parts or faculties of the soule'. Hence the nature of faith for Perkins must be 'a supernaturall gift of God in the minde, apprehending the saving promise'.[3] The 'nature' of faith stands in a 'certaine power or apprehending' Christ.[4] It is 'an undoubted and sure affiance' in Christ.[5] These definitions concur with Calvin's but are threatening to the weak believer who fears most of all he is not elected to start with.

Perkins knows this and has a solution ready. There are 'certaine degrees and measures of true faith'.[6] Perkins believes he can 'reduce to a minimum the conditions on which one can receive this assurance of salvation',[7] and keep faith as a kind of persuasion at the same time. And his claim that faith is not 'partly in the mind, and partly in the will' may be an accurate one—but not because he places the seat of faith in the mind; Perkins ought to say it is in the *will*. He should say faith is seated in the *will*, assurance is in the mind. For behind these intellectualist definitions of faith lies

---

[1] *Workes*, i. 630. This is a quotation from Ursinus.
[2] Ibid. 126.   [3] Ibid.   [4] Ibid. 362.   [5] Ibid. 393.
[6] Ibid. 631.   [7] Christopher Hill, *Puritanism and Revolution* (1969), 214.

Perkins's assumption that the *will* is always to be moved. This is why he defines faith in his catechism as 'a wonderful grace of God, by which a man doth apprehend & apply Christ, and all his benefits unto himselfe'.[1] Again, faith is 'apprehending and applying Christ'.[2] We must 'apply him and his benefits unto our selves'.[3]

Here is how he justifies this teaching on faith: 'This application is made by a supernatural act of the understanding, when we beleeve that Christ with his benefits is really ours.'[4] Perkins's phrase 'when we beleeve' that Christ is 'really ours' is the key to this dilemma: it clearly presupposes that the will has acted and that assurance comes by the reflex act. Perkins does not say this but he should have. The reason he can say faith is assuring is because he has the syllogistic tool in hand which will immediately deliver assurance after all. Perkins's followers will make clear what Perkins does not: faith is in the direct act, assurance is in the reflex act.

Perkins refuses to say that the act of faith itself must be a persuasion; but he cannot bring himself to lay to rest the doctrine of faith that the venerable Calvin espouses. He does not seem to realize that Beza's doctrine is new wine and does not preserve well in Calvin's wineskin. Perkins is forced to employ the practical syllogism; he really embraces a distinction between faith and assurance but he never admits this is what he does.

But the whole of his theology betrays where the roots of his doctrine lie. In the main he looks to Beza and the Heidelberg divines who connect 2 Peter 1: 10 to proving saving faith to ourselves via a good conscience. Justifying faith is that 'whereby a man is perswaded in his conscience'.[5] The will to believe in and of itself cannot deliver the immediate assurance but the conscience can do it, by reflecting upon itself. The sap behind the bark does not assure; but buds and blossoms do. The 'will to be regenerate' is the 'testimony of regeneration begun',[6] but it is the conscience which assures that regeneration in fact took place; for the conscience works *by* the practical syllogism.

Perkins says there are five degrees of faith.[7] These overlap with the preparation stage. The 'beginnings of preparation' in fact are so closely akin to the 'beginnings of composition' that it is impossible to say at what chronological point the former ends and the latter begins. This is the basic dilemma that haunts the experimental predestinarian tradition in so far as the issue of preparation is

---

[1] *Workes*, i. 5.   [2] Ibid. 362.   [3] Ibid. ii. 240.
[4] Ibid.   [5] Ibid. iii. 29.   [6] Ibid. i. 715.   [7] Ibid. i. 80.

concerned. Perkins at any rate says that the beginnings of composition are 'all those inward motions and inclinations of Gods spirit,
that follow after the work of the law'.[1] The 'lowest degree' of faith is
ὀλιγόπιστα, which is like 'a graine of mustard seede, or smoking
flax'.[2] Perkins employs Isaiah 42: 3 and infers a doctrine from the
text upon which Richard Sibbes will base his most popular sermons:
'Christ shall not quench the smoking flaxe, nor breake the brused
reed.'[3] The 'highest degree' of faith is πληροφορία, a 'full assurance,
which is not onely a certen and true, but also a full perswasion of the
heart'.[4] The five degrees of faith are: (1) the knowledge of the
Gospel, which may also be the 'general faith' from which one may
apostatize; (2) the hope of pardon, believing one's sins are 'pardonable'; (3) a hungering after Christ's grace; (4) flying from the terror
of the Law to the throne of grace; and (5) 'an especiall perswasion'
by the Holy Ghost 'whereby every faithfull man doth particularly
applie unto himselfe those promises which are made in the Gospel'.[5]
Full assurance, then, is the consequence of applying the promise;
but this assumes the primacy of the will.

While Perkins maintains that the 'leaste sparke of faith' is the
'serious desire to beleeve',[6] like Beza he propounds two works of
grace, the second of which validates the first. It is this very concept
which Arminius will seize upon. Perkins says that faith is weak when
the 'application' of the promise is 'very feeble'.[7] The second grace is
that which secures such an application. His voluntarism emerges
more clearly in the unfolding of this teaching. While the will to
believe is owing to God's prevenient grace, this role of the will is not
absent in the process of conversion in the way that 'our creation
was'.[8] Our will, then, is very much involved indeed, even if 'to wil to
beleeve, to will to repent and to obey, is the least grace and signe of
Gods favour'. For this reason, the renewed will is unable to bring
forth good works 'unlesse God further give a double grace'. Such is
'assisting grace' and 'exciting grace'.[9] Thus conversion comprises 'a
first grace', and 'a second grace'. But the first grace, despite
Perkins's assertion that the will to be regenerate is regeneration
begun, 'is not effectuall without the second'.[10] Yet the second grace
'is nothing else, but the continuance of the first grace given'.[11]
Perkins says these graces may be described in terms of 'preventing
grace' or the 'grace of regeneration' (the first grace), and 'the

---

[1] *Workes*, i. 628.   [2] Ibid. 81.   [3] Ibid. 628.   [4] Ibid. 81.
[5] Ibid. 80.   [6] Ibid. 81.   [7] Ibid.   [8] Ibid. 718.
[9] Ibid.   [10] Ibid. iii. *148.   [11] Ibid. ii. 15.

inspiration of good desires, and motions' (the second grace).[1] Perkins made his mistake when he called the first grace regeneration, as Arminius will show.

But at this point Perkins struggles further still with the place of man's will. He states that in the 'first conversion' the will is passive; it is the work of God. But in the 'second conversion' the will is active. Therefore the second grace

is *Active*, whereby man beeing converted by God, doth further turne & convert himselfe to God, in all his thoughts, words, & deeds. This conversion is not onely of grace, nor onely of will; but partly of grace, and partly of will: yet so as grace is the principall agent, & will but the instrument of grace. . . . thus there is a cooperation of mans will, with Gods grace.[2]

It is because only God can give the desire to believe that Perkins can infer that the will to believe is faith itself. At this point he is not suggesting man's will, much less man's initiative; it is rather the proof that God is at work. But, now that the desire is there, man must actively prove to himself that this will is indeed God's efficacious work; he must co-operate with grace and continue in faith and repentance. Thus the first grace 'is not effectuall, unlesse it be confirmed by the second grace following it'.[3] If one has only the first grace, then, he shows he is but a reprobate, who 'may go thus farre'; if one does not continue to the second, he will 'undoubtedly soone loose' the first after all, 'and finally fall away'.[4] Thus Perkins warns: 'The foresaid beginnings of grace are counterfeit unlesse they increase.'[5]

Perkins's theology of conversion discloses finally that it is man's will after all which must be moved before saving faith may be truly said to have emerged. Since man is passive in the first grace but active in the second; and the second must come forward or the first is rendered void, obviously it is the will at the bottom of the process after all which makes conversion effectual. While Perkins insists that only the elect can achieve this, Arminius will show that such a position is essentially no different from his. Moreover, William Ames will profit from Arminius's criticisms of Perkins's position.

Perkins claims to have Calvin's support for this teaching. This weak measure of faith—the desire to believe—is the same thing Calvin teaches about implicit faith, Perkins thinks.[6] There are, no

---

[1] Ibid. 204f. [2] Ibid. 205. [3] Ibid. 725.
[4] Ibid. 15. [5] Ibid. i. 632. [6] Ibid. 598-9.

doubt, similarities between Calvin's doctrine of implicit faith and Perkins's doctrine of the weak faith. But it will be recalled that Calvin says that implicit faith, which even the maturest Christian has, is nevertheless a full persuasion. The essential difference between Perkins and Calvin here is that Perkins makes a weak faith the *will* to believe; Calvin makes it a limited knowledge. Perkins thinks Calvin's doctrine of implicit faith ought to be grasped for two reasons: (1) it serves 'to rectifie the consciences of weake ones' who think faith must always be a 'full perswasion'; and (2) it rectifies 'sundrie Catechismes' that propound a faith 'at so high a reach, as few can attaine unto it'.[1]

Perkins's assessment of Calvin's doctrine of implicit faith further illustrates that he does not understand Calvin. Perkins does not understand that implicit faith for Calvin is based upon the freely given promise of Christ to all; implicit faith is still a full persuasion because the believer sees that Christ died for him if he can see nothing else. Perkins does not understand that it is not the idea of full persuasion itself that is out of reach but making full persuasion the essence of faith within the context of a system of limited atonement. This Perkins does not appear to see, and it seems to be the reason he misapprehends Calvin.

Full assurance does not come 'at the first calling', Perkins declares, and if any man thinks one is fully assured 'at the first, he deceiveth himselfe'.[2] What we must do, then, is to 'give all diligence' to make our 'election sure, and to gather manifold tokens thereof'.[3]

---

[1] *Workes*, i. 599.   [2] Ibid. 129.   [3] Ibid. 633.

5

WILLIAM PERKINS'S
DOCTRINE OF TEMPORARY FAITH

BEHIND Perkins's urging men to make their calling and election sure lies not only his belief that full assurance comes via the second work of grace but also his view that the predestined reprobate may excel in certain graces so that he too gives the appearances of being the true elect of God.[1] Thus we are back where we started, perplexed by another dilemma: how do we know we are not reprobate with but a temporary faith? Perkins clearly has his work cut out for him. But he thinks that the conscience which God has given man is sufficient to produce the conclusion that one is elected.

It will be recalled that *Whether a Man* begins with the doctrine of reprobation: 'Certaine propositions declaring how farre a man may goe in the profession of the Gospell, and yet be a wicked man and a Reprobate.'[2] In *A Golden Chaine* Perkins has this teaching crystallized in systematic form under the assumption of God's ineffectual calling of the reprobate, a concept he apparently borrows from Beza. Such a calling is *vis-à-vis* the effectual calling of the elect.[3] The reprobate can never be effectually called, justified, or glorified, because he was never elected. The reprobate is born into the world already doomed, no matter what he does in his lifetime. It does him no good to make his calling and election sure; his lot is unalterably fixed and decreed by God, whose right it is to take the lump of clay from which man is to be created and make him a vessel of dishonour.

This assumption, then, is where Perkins begins in *Whether a Man* and that which shares a position of equal prominence with that of the doctrine of election in *A Golden Chaine*. The horror of horrors for a disciple of Perkins is the thought that he could be a reprobate. This awesome projection is brought home and intensified by the knowledge that the reprobate may be given a 'taste' of God's

---

[1] It is curious that this matter of temporary faith has been overlooked by scholars. The writer knows of no theologian or historian of this period, including Perkins's interpreters, who has come to grips with this salient issue.

[2] *Workes*, i. 356.   [3] Ibid. 107 ff.

goodness which issues in a change of behaviour. If so, how do we
know that the 'taste' and change which we have experienced is not
what the reprobate may experience?

There are 'two sortes' of reprobates of 'riper age';[1] they that are
called, 'namely, by an uneffectuall calling', and those never called.
The ineffectual calling has three degrees in its execution: the calling
itself, the inevitable apostasy, and the final condemnation.[2] Those
reprobates who are never tapped for a temporary flourishing live
out their lives in 'ignorance' and 'hardnesse of heart', but are no less
condemned in the end than the reprobates who respond to God's
beckoning.[3] This calling is whereby the reprobates 'for a time, do
subject themselves to the calling of God, which calling is wrought by
the preaching of the word'.[4] The impact from preaching may be so
powerful that it makes a profound impact upon the reprobate;
indeed, he is 'esteemed' and 'taken for a Christian'.[5] Reprobates may
be 'often so like' Christians that 'none but Christ can discerne the
sheepe from the goates, true Christians from apparent Christians'.[6]
This is why Perkins urges his hearer diligently to 'trie and examine
himselfe, whether he is in the state of damnation or in the state of
grace: whether he yet be under the yoke of Satan, or is the adopted
child of God'.[7]

As Perkins propounds five degrees of saving faith, so he sets forth
five degrees of the ineffectual calling of the reprobate.[8] The first is
the enlightening of the mind 'whereby they are instructed of the holy
Ghost to the understanding and knowledge of the words'.[9] The
second degree is 'a certaine penitencie' whereby

the Reprobate, I. doth acknowledge this sinne. II. Is pricked with the feeling
of Gods wrath for sinne. III. Is grieved for the punishment of sinne. IV.
Doth confesse his sinne. V. Acknowledgth God to be just in punishing
sinne. VI. Desireth to be saved. VII. Promiseth repentance in his miserie, or
affliction . . .[10]

It is at this point that Perkins's voluntarism gets him into trouble,
not to mention bringing his hearer or reader into greater confusion.
While holding out hope to the weak believer whose 'desire' to
believe is faith, Perkins says above that the reprobate may actually

[1] *Workes*, i. 107. Reprobates 'are either infants, or men of riper age'.
[2] Ibid.   [3] Ibid. 109.   [4] Ibid. 107.
[5] Ibid. 361.   [6] Ibid. 362.   [7] Ibid. 361.
[8] Ibid. 107. In *Whether a Man* Perkins puts thirty-six propositions to show 'how
farre' the reprobate may advance. Ibid. 356 ff.
[9] Ibid. i. 107.   [10] Ibid.

desire to be saved. If we take comfort from his words 'the will to be regenerate' is the 'testimony of regeneration begun', we are brought back to nought when we learn that the reprobate too may have the desire to be saved. Indeed, if the work of preparation is to give 'sight' and 'sorrow' for our sin, we are no better off than the reprobate who 'hath oftentimes feare and terrour of conscience' when 'he considereth the wrath and vengeance of God, which is most terrible'.[1] Moreover, the reprobate 'may humble himselfe for some sinnes which he hath committed, and may declare this by fasting and teares'. The reprobate may confess his sins, 'even his particular sinnes', because he is tormented by them.[2] If we want to be saved, what more can we do when we are tormented by the sight of them? But there is more; the wicked in distress may pray, and 'God may heare their prayers, and grant them their request'.[3]

The third degree of the ineffectual calling is 'a temporarie faith'.[4] Here Perkins appears to follow Calvin, stating that the reprobate 'doth confusedly beleeve the promises of God'. It is at this juncture Perkins claims to posit the deciding difference between the elect's faith and that of the reprobate. He says that the reprobate believes 'some shall be saved' but not that 'he himself particularly shall be saved'. The reprobate is content with a general faith and 'doth never apply the promises of God to himselfe', nor does he even 'desire, or indeavour to apply the same'.[5] Perkins is highly confusing on this crucial point. If a desire to be saved is not a desire to apply the promise, one must ask of Perkins what such is.

Perkins's doctrine of assurance is in fact most ambiguous at the very place he intends to bring the greatest comfort. He has taken his doctrine of temporary faith too far; if the reprobate can do anything that the elect can do save one—apply the promise—Perkins should not have said the reprobate may desire to be saved. Or does Perkins simply mean that the elect alone have the rational powers to think syllogistically? Surely not, for all men have a conscience, the essential function of which is the practical syllogism. It must therefore be the syllogism at work if the reprobate too 'may be perswaded of the mercie & goodnes of God towards him for the

---

[1] Ibid. 357.   [2] Ibid.   [3] Ibid. 358.
[4] Ibid. While in this place Perkins attributes temporary faith to the 'third' degree of the ineffectual calling, he uses the same idea of temporary faith interchangeably with the reprobate's transitory flourishing as a whole. Perkins also calls this a 'common' faith as opposed to the 'faith of Gods elect'. Of the former there is (as Ursinus put it), 'historicall' faith, a temporary faith, and the 'faith of miracles'. Ibid. 125. Cf. Ibid. iii. *271.   [5] Ibid. i. 107.

present time in the which he feeleth it'.[1] It seems that what is the
basis of the reprobate's persuasion is but the conclusion of some
event—as knowledge or experience.

But Perkins is adamant in his insistence that the ability to apply
the promise lies solely within the grasp of the elect. The reprobate

> may seeme for a time to be planted in the Church, for he doth beleeve the
> promises of God made in Christ Jesus, yet so that he cannot apply them to
> himselfe. The reprobate *generally in a confused manner* believeth that Christ
> is a Saviour of some men: and he neither can nor desireth to come to the
> particular applying of Christ. The elect beleeveth that Christ is a Saviour of
> him particularly.[2]

The difference, however, between the 'confused manner' of the
reprobate's persuasion and what may be our doubtings and waver-
ings is the crucial question Perkins never solves. Regrettably, also,
Calvin is not much more helpful on this point.

In his catechism, having stated that faith is to apprehend *and*
apply Christ, Perkins claims that 'this applying is done by *assurance*,
when a man is verily perswaded by the holy spirit, of Gods favour
towards himselfe *particularly*, and the forgiveness of his *owne*
sinnes'.[3] Moreover, the essence of Perkins's doctrine of assurance is
in his dependence upon the practical syllogism.

> Although this particular expression, *I am elected*, is not expressely set
> downe in the Scriptures, yet is it inclusively comprehended in them, as the
> *Species* in his *Genus*, as the Logitians speake: so that it may by just
> consequent be gathered out of Gods word, if we reason thus: They which
> truly beleeve are elected, Joh. 6. 35. I truly beleeve; for he which beleeveth
> doth know himselfe to beleeve: therefore I am elected. The first proposition
> is taken from the Scriptures: the second, from the beleevers conscience, &
> from them both, the conclusion is easily derived.[4]

Thus 'the conclusion' for Perkins is the assurance. Furthermore,
since Christ told his disciples to rejoice that their names are written
in heaven, He 'signifies, that men may attaine to a certaine knowledge of their owne election'. Indeed, 2 Peter 1: 10 is given to us 'in
vaine' if the diligence therein commanded does not result in the
knowledge of our election 'without an extraordinary revelation'.[5] It

---

[1] *Workes*, i. 358.

[2] Ibid. Temporary faith issues in rejoicing in the Gospel, 'yet it doth not
thoroughly apply Christ with his benefits'. Ibid. 126.

[3] Ibid. 5.　　　　[4] Ibid. 106.　　　　[5] Ibid. 290.

follows that the 'application of the promises of the Gospel' is made 'in the forme of a practicall syllogisme, on this manner':

Whosoever beleeveth in Christ, is chosen to life everlasting. This proposition is set downe in the word of God . . . [then] comes the spirit of God and enlightens the eyes, and opens the heart, and gives them power both to will to beleeve, and to beleeve indeede: so as a man shall with freedome of spirit, make an assumption and say, *but I beleeve in Christ,* I renounce my selfe, all my joy and comfort is in him: flesh and blood cannot say this, it is the operation of the holy Ghost. And hence ariseth the blessed conclusion which is the testimonie of the spirit; *therefore I am the childe of God.*[1]

This certainty 'by little and little' is conceived 'in a forme of reasoning or practicall syllogisme':

Everyone that beleeves is the child of God:
But I doe beleeve:
Therefore I am the child of God.[2]

The fundamental idea which Perkins believes is that knowledge of our election is not by 'revelation' but through the practical syllogism.[3] It appears that the elect alone have the ability to reason this way.

However, Perkins uses the practical syllogism in two ways: (1) to prove the witness of the Spirit and (2) by the inference of sanctification. Apparently following Beza, Perkins posits that we cannot ascend up to the 'first causes' of election, therefore we must gather the knowledge of our election from 'the last effects thereof: and they are especially two: The testimonie of Gods spirit, and the workes of Sanctification'.[4] The testimony of the Spirit, however, is but 'a divine manner of reasoning framed in the minds of them that beleeve and repent, on this manner', which Perkins calls 'the practicall syllogisme of the holy Ghost' and 'the earnest of the spirit':

He that beleeves and repents, is Gods child.
    Thus saith the Gospell:
But I beleeve in Christ and repent: at the least I subject my will to the
    commaundment which bids me repent & beleeve: I detest my unbeleefe,
    & al my sinnes: and desire the Lord to increase my faith.
Therefore I am the child of God.[5]

---

[1] Ibid.   [2] Ibid. 541; 510–48, *passim.*
[3] Cf. ibid. ii. 21.   [4] Ibid. i. 114.
[5] Ibid. ii. 322.

Such reasoning, then, *is* the full persuasion; it is what Perkins means by 'applying' the promises 'by assurance'.

However, 'if the testimonie of Gods spirit be not so powerfull in the elect'—by which Perkins seems to mean the inability to reason well—'then they judge of their election, by that other effect of the holy Ghost: namely, Sanctification: like as we use to judge by heate that there is fire, when we cannot see the flame itselfe'.[1]

Perkins lists these 'effects' of sanctification: (1) feeling bitterness of heart when we have offended God by sin; (2) striving against the flesh; (3) desiring God's grace earnestly; (4) considering that God's grace is a most precious jewel; (5) loving the ministers of God's word; (6) calling upon God earnestly, and with tears; (7) desiring Christ's second coming; (8) avoiding all occasions of sin; and (9) persevering in these effects 'to the last gaspe of life'. Moreover, if these effects are but 'very feeble', we should not be dismayed; it means God is testing us. For the absence of these effects does not mean we are reprobate. God 'doeth oftentimes prefer those which did seeme to be most of all estranged from his favour'.[2]

The fourth degree of the ineffectual calling is 'a taste of heavenly gifts: as of Justification, and of Sanctification, and the vertues of the worlde to come'.[3] Such a tasting is 'verely a sense in the hearts of the Reprobates, whereby they doe perceive and feele the excellencie of Gods benefits'. But they do not digest what they tasted: it is one thing 'to taste of dainties', another thing 'to feede and to bee nourished thereby'.[4] This 'taste', Perkins says, issues in a heart-felt 'sweetnes of Gods mercies, and a rejoycing in consideration of the election, adoption, justification, and sanctification, of Gods children'. This taste is not the same as digesting, although those who taste 'truly resemble the reprobates'. Indeed, this taste by itself produces 'many fruits', even doing 'outwardly all things which true Christians doe'.[5]

As for the sanctification which issues from saving faith, it has two parts: mortification (abating the power of sin) and vivification (inherent holiness begun).[6] Issuing from sanctification is repentance: the will and endeavour to relinquish former sins and 'to become a new man'.[7] From repentance emerges 'new obedience', an 'infallible mark of the child of God'.[8] This denial is, in turn, the Christian warfare and the patient bearing of the cross.[9] Under the Christian

---

[1] *Workes*, i. 115. Cf. *supra*, p. 36 n. 8.   [2] *Workes*, i. 115.
[3] Ibid. 108.   [4] Ibid. 358.   [5] Ibid.   [6] Ibid. 84.
[7] Ibid. 86.   [8] Ibid. 292.   [9] Ibid. 86. Cf. *Inst.* III. vii, viii.

warfare we must bear the armour of God against the wiles of Satan, who attacks by three 'assaults': against our effectual calling, our faith, and our sanctification.[1] The patient bearing of the cross is persevering through God's appointed afflictions.[2] The profession of faith is 'calling upon God' in prayer.[3]

This, in brief, is Perkins's doctrine of sanctification. With the exception of desiring Christ's second coming, there is not any virtue described herein that Perkins does not also, at some point, impute to the reprobate by virtue of the ineffectual calling. Yet it is the effects of sanctification which Perkins posits as the ground of assurance if the testimony of the Spirit 'be not so powerfull'.

The fifth degree of the ineffectual calling illustrates that the reprobate can resemble true Christians in all of these things.[4] The 'taste' of God's heavenly gifts may issue in a zeal in the profession of religion. The reprobate may love God's ministers, even love God Himself, and, like the Christian who sometimes succumbs to Satan's temptations,[5] may, after sinning, 'amend & reforme his life', having 'great holiness outwardly'.[6] Perkins says that the true Christian has inward holiness while the reprobate's holiness is only outward. But if the reprobate can be utterly sincere, even like the fallen Galatians who 'would have plucked out their eies' for St. Paul,[7] how can we believe our sincerity is really inward holiness? But Perkins says that the reprobate's outward holiness is but for a time, although, while it lasts, there is 'amendment of life in many things'.[8] By the gift of prophecy the reprobate may be able to 'interpret and expound the Scriptures'[9] and may therefore be 'a preacher of the word'.[10] In any case, a reprobate may be in the visible Church, 'obey it in word and discipline, and so be taken for a true member of Christ'.[11]

Finally, the reprobate's ineffectual calling fails in the end. As the elect's glorification is predestined, so the flourishing reprobate is guaranteed an apostasy, sometimes executed by blaspheming the Holy Ghost, which is the unpardonable sin.[12] The destiny of all reprobates, called or uncalled, is eternal damnation. There is, however, a consolation for the reprobate who had some outward holiness: 'his paines in hell shall be lesse'.[13]

Perkins's doctrine of assurance, then, is administered by the practical syllogism, whether by the witness of the Spirit or the effects

---

[1] *Workes*, i. 87 ff. Cf. Beza's teaching, *supra*, p. 37 n. 2.
[2] *Workes*, i. 90 f.   [3] Ibid. 91 f.   [4] Ibid. 108.   [5] Ibid. 89 f.
[6] Ibid. 359.   [7] Ibid.   [8] Ibid. 108.   [9] Ibid. 274.
[10] Ibid. 359.   [11] Ibid. 360.   [12] Ibid. 108 f.   [13] Ibid. 358.

of sanctification. Perkins claims that the testimony of the Spirit is 'weake in most men'.[1] Full assurance comes 'not at the first, but in some continuance of time' after one is 'well practiced in repentance'.[2] Indeed, such a measure of faith is 'not incident to all beleevers, but to the Prophets, Apostles, martyrs; and such as have beene long exercised in the schoole of Christ'.[3]

Perkins's sole advice to the doubting Christian is embodied in 2 Peter 1: 10 , 'the charge of the holy Ghost upon every child of God' to 'get the assurance thereof sealed' by the 'saving graces of Gods spirit'.[4] He claims that 2 Peter 1: 10 means 'nothing else but to practise the vertues of the moral Law'.[5]

On the issue of faith and repentance in the *ordo salutis* Perkins claims that repentance follows faith 'as a fruite thereof'.[6] This is Calvin's order, but when Perkins makes a change of life the ground of assurance, he reverses the practical order Calvin intends. For Perkins says that the assurance of pardon of sin is upon the 'condition' of man's repentance: 'For then the pardon of sinne is simply and fully without condition, applied and revealed to the conscience.'[7]

Perkins does not apparently realize that this incorporation of the theology of Beza and the Heidelberg divines into his scheme requires a significant departure from Calvin, 'that worthie instrument of the Gospel'.[8] Perkins mentions Calvin eleven times, Luther twelve times, and Beza nine times. Ursinus, Olevianus, and Zanchius are mentioned once each. It is clearly Beza, combined with the thinking of these Heidelberg divines, who provides the foundation for Perkins's doctrine of faith.[9]

The central question to which Perkins devotes himself is the one he never satisfactorily answers: how a man 'maie discerne' he is in the state of grace. Beza's doctrine of limited atonement and Calvin's doctrine of temporary faith are the two main ingredients that flavour Perkins's thinking in this connection; but these ingredients

---

[1] *Workes*, i. 369.
[2] Ibid. 6. Cf. Ibid. 129, 367 ff.
[3] Ibid. ii. 241.   [4] Ibid. iii. *382.   [5] Ibid. ii. 24 f.
[6] Ibid. i. 454.   [7] Ibid. ii. 214.   [8] Ibid. iii. 210.
[9] Cf. L. J. Trinterud, 'The Origins of Puritanism', *CH* (1951), 37–57. Trinterud argues that 'Puritanism was indigenous, not exotic, to England'. By 'Puritanism' he mainly means a covenant theology. His argument stems largely from the fact there was a covenant theology in Tyndale. This is not doubted, but it seems that Trinterud claims too much in this statement, for it is clearly the Continental divines who give shape to Perkins's theology and it is largely Perkins to whom most English covenant divines look thereafter.

do not mix well, and can hardly be digested into a system that revolves around the premiss that sanctification is the ground of assurance. Perkins's kind of assurance is not an improvement over the reprobate's persuasion 'for the present time in the which he feeleth it'.[1]

Perkins's system ultimately requires a 'descending into our owne hearts',[2] the introspection Calvin warns against. The teaching of limited atonement is preponderantly the doctrine which forfeits faith as assurance in Perkins's thought. Since there is no way, apart from extraordinary revelation, that one can know he was one of those for whom Christ died, one must *do* certain things and infer his assurance. As Beza shows what are truly good works, so does Perkins.[3] As for the obvious problem that follows Perkins's assertion that every man is bound to believe his own election, Perkins admits a difficulty. He solves it by saying that every man is not bound to believe his election 'absolutely'. Instead, men are bound conditionally, 'according to the tenour of the covenant of grace', namely, 'to beleeve in Christ'.[4] Believing in Christ to Perkins means sooner or later to descend inside ourselves; the eventual result is not merely introspection, but a doctrine of faith that could easily breed legalism. The doing of good works, while not the ground of faith, is the ground of assurance. The apostle's admonition in 2 Peter 1: 10 is the Spirit's charge that, 'by keeping a continuall course in good works', we may have 'the most evident tokens of election'.[5]

Thomas Fuller says that Perkins reportedly died 'in the conflict of a troubled conscience'. This is 'no wonder', for God 'seemingly leaves his saints when they leave the world, plunging them on their death-beds in deep temptations, and casting their souls, down to hell, to rebound the higher to heaven'.[6]

Samuel Ward, who visited the dying Perkins, wrote in his diary: 'God knows his death is likely to be an irrecoverable loss and a great judgment to the university, seeing there is none to supply his place.'[7] On 25 October 1602 James Montagu (d. 1618) preached the funeral sermon, using Joshua 1: 2: 'Moses my servant is dead.'[8]

When the bells tolled Perkins's death Thomas Goodwin, who became a prominent Westminster divine, was two years old. Goodwin came up to Cambridge in 1613, and later wrote that the town

---

[1] *Workes*, i. 358.
[2] Ibid. 290.
[3] Ibid. iii. 30 ff. Cf. *supra*, p. 37 n. 3.
[4] *Workes*, iii. 32.
[5] Ibid.
[6] Fuller, *Holy State*, 82.
[7] Knappen, *Two Elizabethan Diaries*, 109.
[8] Breward, op. cit. 13.

was filled 'with the discourse of the power of Mr. Perkins's ministry'.[1] John Cotton, however, secretly rejoiced over Perkins's death. Perkins's sermons had deeply disturbed the eighteen-year-old Cotton, who was relieved to have Perkins out of the way.[2] Cotton was converted later by Richard Sibbes, who had been converted by Paul Baynes, Perkins's successor at St. Andrews. Cotton converted John Preston.

Perkins's legacy is the experimental predestinarian tradition. He did not intend to create such a phenomenon, but the time had come for a ministry such as his. 'Calvin, Beza, Perkins' were 'often cited as the trinity of the orthodox.'[3] It was Beza not Calvin, however, whose thought was predominant in Perkins and whose theology Perkins perpetuated. Perkins's legacy reached to the Westminster Assembly of Divines through whom his theology was given credal sanction. The study now turns to that legacy.

[1] *The Works of Thomas Goodwin* (1861), II. lviii.
[2] Larzer Ziff, *The Career of John Cotton* (Princeton, 1962), 22.
[3] Christopher Hill, *Puritanism and Revolution*, 213.

PART THREE

THE EXPERIMENTAL
PREDESTINARIAN TRADITION

6

SOME CONTEMPORARIES OF
WILLIAM PERKINS

BY 1609 the popular treatise *A Garden of Spirituall Flovvers* had reached its fifth edition.[1] This work is a manual to show the way to godliness, which, in turn, is depicted as the means by which assurance of election is obtained. The title-page states that these flowers were 'Planted by Ri. Ro. Will. Per. Ri. Green. M.M. and Geo. Web'.[2] Selected writings of these men were compressed into this volume in order (1) to help men see their misery, (2) to show how they are delivered from this misery, and (3) to instruct them to walk with God daily.[3] This treatise is an introduction to the kind of divinity that characterizes the experimental predestinarian tradition generally.[4]

The Church of England during the period covered by this study was predominantly predestinarian in soteriology,[5] a perspective which may be usefully termed *credal* predestinarianism.[6] While John Reynolds (d. 1607) was not successful in his bid at the Hampton Court Conference (1604) to have the Lambeth Articles officially appended to the Thirty-nine Articles,[7] predestinarian theology

---

[1] The earliest extant volume states 'The fift time imprinted'. Published by T. Pavier, 1609. This reached fourteen editions by 1643.

[2] M. M. Knappen, *Tudor Puritanism*, 392, identifies these as Richard Rogers, William Perkins, Richard Greenham, Miles Mosse, and George Webbe.

[3] *A Garden of Spiritual Flovvers* (1638), preface. These writings were gathered by Richard Rogers. Ibid. 20.

[4] See especially ibid. 191–244, for the emphasis on assurance of salvation by way of godliness.

[5] N. R. N. Tyacke, 'Arminianism in England, in Religion and Politics, 1604–1640' (D.Phil. thesis, Oxford, 1968), *passim*.

[6] This term is used to designate the position of the majority of the bishops during the period of this study who, though not generally known for their stress upon experimental divinity, were none the less predestinarian in their theology as a whole. Tyacke, op. cit., convincingly demonstrates that predestinarianism, which he unfortunately calls Calvinism, was preponderantly the position of most clergymen in the Church of England from 1604 to 1640.

[7] The Seventeenth of the Thirty-nine Articles states that 'predestination to life' is the 'everlasting purpose of God' whereby He has decreed to deliver from damnation 'those whom He hath chosen in Christ'. This statement is ambiguous; it does not say

nevertheless enjoyed greater royal favour under James I than under Elizabeth.[1] But the experimental predestinarian tradition should be distinguished from the credal predestinarianism on the one hand, and the cautious approach of popular preachers like Henry Smith (d. 1591)[2] and Bishop Lancelot Andrewes (d. 1626)[3] on the other. The experimental predestinarians were mainly pastors who not only believed but vigorously stressed that one's election *may* be known by experimental knowledge; indeed, it *must* be known lest one deceive himself and, in the end, be damned. This chapter will deal with the leading contemporaries of Perkins who take this position.

upon what basis the decree is made (whether upon God's predetermined choice of certain men or foreseen faith). However, the Lambeth Articles (1595) unambiguously state that some men are predestined to life, others reprobated to death, the cause not being foreseen faith 'but only the absolute and simple will of God'. The number of the predestined 'cannot be increased or diminished'. Philip Schaff, *The Creeds of the Evangelical Protestant Churches* (1877), 497, 523-4.

[1] Tyacke, op. cit. 31-5. 'Calvinist predestinarian teaching was . . . a crucial common assumption, shared by a majority of the hierarchy and virtually all its nonconformist opponents, during the Elizabethan and Jacobean periods'. Nicholas Tyacke, 'Puritanism, Arminianism, and Counter-Revolution', *The Origins of the English Civil War* (1973), 128. In 1615 James Ussher drew up the Irish Articles. They incorporate a rigid predestinarianism that agrees with the Lambeth Articles. The number of the elect can be neither 'increased' nor 'diminished'. Ussher is said to have been influenced by Perkins (Breward, op. cit. 102). Ussher's first three Articles, moreover, follow the order set forward in Zanchius's *Confession*: (1) of Scripture, (2) of God and the Trinity, and (3) of predestination. *The Whole Works of the Most Rev. James Ussher, D.D.* (1847), I. xl.

[2] 'Silver-tongued Smith' is generally called a 'puritan' because of his scruples concerning the subscription. *DNB* article. He is the only sixteenth-century English divine to rival Perkins in number of sermons published. The *STC* gives 127 listings (including repeated editions of sermons). The thrust of Smith's preaching is devotional, while his soteriology can hardly be called experimental predestinarian. He claims that while our election is certain with God, 'in respect of ourselves it is uncertain'. Therefore we 'must *strive* to make the same sure by good works'. He never says that election becomes certain in ourselves. *The Sermons of Mr. Henry Smith* (1866), ii. 96. See 'Questions gathered out of his own confession, by Henry Smith, which are yet unanswered'. Among a large number of 'yet unanswered' questions are these: 'Whether predestination, election, &c., are to be preached unto laymen? . . . what free-will remaineth unto us?' Ibid. 419. *STC* is *A Short-Title Catalogue of Books . . . 1475-1640*, ed. A. W. Pollard and G. R. Redgrave (1926).

[3] Andrewes has thirty-four listings in the *STC*. His position on predestination is highly modified. In his 'Judgment of the Lambeth Articles' Andrewes insists that predestination is too great a mystery to be disputed over, and that saving grace would be conferred upon all men were they not obstinate. Paul A. Welsby, *Lancelot Andrewes 1555-1626* (1958), 43f. Cf. *Two Answers to Cardinal Perron and other Miscellaneous Works of Lancelot Andrewes* (Oxford, 1854), 30: 'We think it not safe, for any man, peremptorily to presume himself predestinate.'

RICHARD ROGERS (1550?-1618)

Richard Rogers was born in Chelmsford in Essex. He matriculated as a sizar of Christ's College, Cambridge, in 1566. He graduated BA in 1570, and was ordained deacon and priest that year. He took his MA in 1574, after having migrated to Caius College. A year or two later he settled in Wethersfield, Essex, where he was lecturer until his death.

Besides his production of *A Garden of Spirituall Flovvers*, only one of Rogers's writings achieved repeated editions.[1] In the preface to *Seven Treatises* Stephen Egerton (d. 1621?) describes Rogers as 'another Greenham'. Rogers says that *Seven Treatises* is primarily set out 'to helpe and direct the weake Christian throughout from his first entrance into the knowledge of Christ Jesus'.[2] He notes that some have 'attained to the assurance of their salvation', while others take their assurance for granted and 'deceive themselves'. Rogers also recommends 'reading other treatises concerning the matter' and cites 'Maister Perkins workes, namely, his booke intituled the graine of mustard seede'.[3]

Rogers's writings do not reflect a systematic, theological mind; his concern is chiefly pastoral, with a special emphasis upon godly living. The same may be stated for all the figures in this chapter. Rogers says that God's calling and the granting of assurance are 'a double linck of that golden chaine' of Romans 8: 30, and that there is no other way 'to seeke out the certaintie of our election, but by the meanes which serve to our calling'. The means to the assurance of that calling is godly living: 'yea looke what affections he worketh in such as he will bring to the certaintie and assurance of salvation'.[4]

Rogers's use of 2 Peter 1: 10 is like that of Perkins,[5] but the passage he cites more often is Hebrews 3: 12, with the stress being placed upon the heart.[6] Since Rogers assumes at the outset that godliness is the means by which we make our calling and election sure, he labours to list 'helpes to increase godliness'.[7] Once our

---

[1] *Seven Treatises leading and guiding to true happiness* (six editions from 1603 to 1627). Hereinafter called *Seven Treatises*, this was published in an abridged form as *The practice of Christianity* (four editions between 1618 and 1638). Other writings of Rogers are: *A Commentary vpon the whole booke of Ivdges* (1615) (hereinafter called *Judges*); and *Certaine Sermons* (1612).

[2] *Seven Treatises*, 113.   [3] Ibid., preface.   [4] *Judges*, 656.

[5] Ibid. 140. Cf. *Certaine Sermons*, 140; *Seven Treatises*, 50, 137, 209, 270, 424.

[6] *Judges*, 97, 121. Cf. *Seven Treatises*, 102, 109, 136, 243, 298, 308, 322, 401.

[7] *Seven Treatises*, 211 ff.

hearts are cleansed, 'we should keepe them so with all diligence', that is, 'watch, trie, and purge them from all defilements, whereby they are wont to be tainted, and poysoned'.[1] For there are 'many times, yea hours in the day, wherein the heart may start aside from God, that is, from doing his will'.[2]

Rogers claims that there is a 'Double benefit' of Christ's death; 'not onely to save' us from eternal death but 'also to worke the death of sinne our most deadly enemie, and to mortifie it'.[3] His stress, then, is on the second benefit of Christ's death; the first, he apparently feels, needs no detailed exposition. But the second is emphasized since by it we have assurance of the first benefit. The title-page of *Certaine Sermons* summarizes Rogers's fundamental concern; it also keeps alive the notion of temporary faith:

First, to bring any bad person (that hath not committed the sinne that is unpardonable) to true conversion. Secondly, to stablish and settle all such as are converted, in faith and repentance. Thirdly, to leade them forward (that are so settled) in the Christian life, to bring foorth the fruite of both.

Rogers says that reprobates cannot be converted, but they can blaspheme the Spirit (Matthew 12: 31).[4] Indeed, they may experience affections like those of God's elect. Rogers lists four marks in those not elected but who seem none the less to be effectually called: (1) 'sorrow for their miserie'; (2) confession of their sins to God; (3) 'feare of His displeasure for the same'; and (4) 'desiring some kinde of amendment of life'. 'Even thus farre a man may goe in the profession of Christian religion' (Perkins's language), although 'not sealed up to salvation', Rogers concludes. He insists that he makes these statements not 'to discourage any: but partly to drive them from deceiving themselves' and also 'to make the true testimonies of eternall life to be more pretiously esteemed of those which have them'.[5]

Rogers's stress at any rate is upon the heart. He believes that the 'diligence' to be followed in making our calling and election sure is the keeping of a pure heart. One will be assured if he perseveres in this enterprise; it is 'experimentall knowledge' which 'wee gather by proofe' that assures us of our election.[6]

MILES MOSSE (*c.* 1558–1615)

Miles Mosse was admitted as a pensioner at Caius College, Cambridge, in 1575. He took the BA in 1578–9; the MA in 1582; the BD

---

[1] *Seven Treatises*, 140.   [2] Ibid. 308.   [3] Ibid. 208.
[4] *Certaine Sermons*, 140.   [5] *Seven Treatises*, 45.   [6] Ibid. 278f.

in 1589; and the DD in 1595. He was ordained priest at Lincoln in 1583, and was made vicar of St. Stephen, Norwich, in 1585. He was rector of Combes, Suffolk, from 1597 to his death in 1615.[1]

Mosse's theme is that the reprobate may have considerable knowledge but it is to be distinguished from the knowledge of saving faith. The reprobate, like the devils, can see, hear, and observe much about God.[2] Mosse cites Calvin; wicked men may have 'some speciall graces of God' and still not have saving faith.[3] While the wicked man may have 'some extraordinarie grace' and be 'fitted to particular workes, or speciall callings', he cannot be 'ingrafted into Christ by faith' or 'possesse the spirit of sanctification'.[4]

Saving faith is believing the Gospel 'with application, and so to apply and appropriate the benefits contained in it'.[5] This he calls 'a lively, or experimentall feeling'.[6] Indeed, 'to have this feeling knowledge of Christ, is an invincible argument that Christ dwelleth in us by his Spirit, and so is an assurance unto us of eternall life'.[7]

GEORGE WEBBE (d. 1637)

George Webbe matriculated as a sizar at Trinity College, Cambridge, in 1582–3. He took the BA in 1586–7; the MA in 1591. He was ordained deacon and priest in Lincoln on 29 June 1587. He was vicar of Leighton Bromswold, Huntingdonshire, from 1594 to 1607. He was rector of Preston Capes, Northamptonshire, from 1605 to his death.[8]

Webbe calls *A Posie of Spirituall Flowers* 'an Enchiridion to make you more and more in love with godlines'.[9] This treatise is more devotional than doctrinal, and is intended to say more about godliness than God. Webbe stresses in any case that coming to assurance of salvation is not 'an easie and a triviall thing'.[10]

Webbe's *Briefe Exposition* is virtually Perkins's catechism, although he curiously refers to 'mine owne paines in writing' it.[11] His definition of faith is typical of how he repeats Perkins verbatim:

---

[1] In 1614 Mosse published *Justifying and Saving Faith. Distingvished from the faith of the devils.*

[2] Ibid. 7–11, 81.　　　　[3] Ibid. 15.　　　　[4] Ibid. 17.

[5] Ibid. 44.　　　　[6] Ibid. 81.　　　　[7] Ibid. 82.

[8] Webbe published *A Posie of Spirituall Flowers* (1610); *The Practice of Quietnes* (seven editions from 1615 to 1638); and *Briefe Exposition of the Principles of the Christian Religion* (1612, 1617). Hereinafter called *Briefe Exposition*.

[9] *A Posie of Spirituall Flowers*, preface.　　　　[10] Ibid. 120.

[11] *Briefe Exposition*, preface.

'Faith is a wonderfull Grace of God, by which a man doth apprehend & apply Christ and all his benefits to himselfe.'[1] He goes on to repeat Perkins's teaching that there is a weak faith and a strong faith, and that the latter comes 'not at the first, but in some continuance of time, when hee hath beene well practiced in Repentance'.[2]

Webbe's more creative contribution is his basing godliness upon 'the practice of quietnesse'. By quietness he means a tranquil conscience.[3] Using circular reasoning he says that those who would have assurance 'must be quiet',[4] but that quietness does not come apart from godliness.[5]

JOHN DOD (*c.* 1555–1645) AND ROBERT CLEAVER (d. 1614)

John 'Decalogue' Dod and Robert Cleaver are often linked together owing to their joint publications. Many treatises indicate a joint authorship, making it difficult to determine which Dod penned[6] and which were written by Cleaver.[7]

---

[1] *Briefe Exposition*, unpag. (sect. V). Cf. *supra*, p. 63 n. 2.
[2] *Briefe Exposition* (sect. V). Cf. *supra*, p. 74 n. 2.
[3] *The Practice of Quietnes* (1615), 84.   [4] Ibid. 16.   [5] Ibid. 85.
[6] No historian to date has attempted to determine the exact authorship. Those which appear to be Dod's are: (1) *A Plaine and Familiar Exposition of the Tenne Commandements* (no less than twenty editions between 1603 and 1662), hereinafter called *Tenne Commandements* (1617). While many of the editions indicate a joint authorship, the 1617 edition says the author is Dod. It is possible that Cleaver joined with Dod in refining the work; in the 1603 edition R. C. says the treatise represents 'the labours of a faithfull Pastour'. (2) The first six of *Ten Sermons tending chiefly to the fitting of men for the worthy receiving of the Lords Supper* (1611, 1621). The title-page says, 'The six first, by I. Dod. The foure last, by R. Cleaver.' (3) *A Remedy against Privat contentions* (three editions: 1610, 1614, 1618), hereinafter called *A Remedy* (1610). (4) *A Plaine and Familiar Exposition on the Lords Prayer* (1635), hereinafter called *Lords Prayer*. (5) The second of *Two Sermons on the Third of the Lamentations . . . The one by I. D. the other by R. C.* (1610), hereinafter called *Lamentations*. The latter is Dod's according to a marginal note in Cleaver's *Three Sermons vpon Marke* (1611), 27. (6) The latter two of *Fovre Godlie and Frvitfvl Sermons: two preached at Draiton in Oxfordshire . . . two other sermons on the twelfth Psalme* (1610, 1611), hereinafter called *Fovre Godlie* (1611). Since Cleaver was located in Drayton, Dod probably preached the latter two. (7) The first two of *Three Godlie and Frvitfvll Sermons; The two first preached by Maister Iohn Dod; the last by Maister Robert Cleaver* (1610). However, in (8) *Seven Godlie and frvitfvll sermons. The six first preached by Master Iohn Dod: the last by Robert Cleaver* (1614) (hereinafter called *Seven Godlie*) the third sermon (on Ps. 14) is the same as the third in *Three Godlie*, which is attributed to Cleaver. Finally, the study will draw from *Old Mr Dod's Sayings* (1678).
[7] Those which seem to be Cleaver's are: (1) *A Sermon Preached by Master Cleaver: on Psalme 51, verse 1* (1610). (2) *Fovre Sermons, The two first, of Godly Feare: On Hebrewes 4. Verse 1.* (1613). (3) *A Declaration of the Christian Sabbath* (1625, 1630),

Robert Cleaver was born in Oxfordshire. He matriculated at St. Edmund Hall, Oxford, and received the BA in 1580-1. He was made rector of Drayton, Oxfordshire, in 1598. He died about 1614.

Cleaver stresses the moral Law. His conviction is that men are 'made able by grace to do that which is termed: keeping the law'.[1] He believes that Christians should maintain a 'constant watchfulnesse' and a 'holy feare of falling' since the heavenly rest to which they aspire 'is promised unto all that faithfully labour to attaine thereunto'.[2] He asks: 'If wee carelessely reject his holy lawes, may not his spirit justly forsake our soule?'[3]

Cleaver claims that 'the hearing of the promises is not sufficient for the procuring of our eternall happinesse', but there must also be an 'apprehending and applying of the same',[4] which is Perkins's phrase. We must 'labour for a working faith, and a diligent love, that so not onely we our selves, but others also that have the spirit of discerning, may know that we are the elect of God, by the fruits of godlinesse, appearing in us, and proceeding from us'.[5] Behind Cleaver's conviction about a 'holy feare of falling' is an interpretation of Hebrews 6: 4-6, which he understands as describing those who were not 'sincere in affection'.[6] Cleaver puts a heavy emphasis upon

hereinafter called *Christian Sabbath* (1630). (4) *Three Sermons vpon Marke, the ninth chapter, 22. 23 verses* (1611). (5) The first of *Two Sermons on the Third of the Lamentations* (see fifth listing under p. 84 n. 6). (7) The first two in *Fovre Godlie* (see sixth listing under p. 84 n. 6). (8) The last four in *Ten Sermons* (see second listing under p. 84 n. 6). The authorship of the third in *Three Godlie* and the same in *Seven Godlie* remains unsolved (see eighth listing on p. 84 n. 6). There is a considerable corpus of writings pertaining to the book of Proverbs that is probably Cleaver's. Cleaver is stated as the author of (9) *A Briefe Explanation of the Whole Booke of the Prouerbs of Salomon* (1615). But Dod apparently wrote the dedication, although both names are attributed to it. Cleaver was dead by 1614; the dedication states 'one of us undertook the explications of the Proverbs of Salomon, and the other to further the same by inspection, and assistance' and that the Lord interrupted things 'by visiting one of us, even him who was to doe the worke, and sustaine the burthen of the businesse'. Cleaver is stated as the author of (10) *A Plaine and Familiar Exposition of the First and Second Chapters of the Prouerbs of Salomon* (1614). A series of expositions on Proverbs (similarly entitled) survive, which are probably Cleaver's: (11) on the ninth and tenth chapters (1606, 1612); (12) the eleventh and twelfth chapters (three editions: 1607, 1608, 1612); (13) the thirteenth and fourteenth chapters (four editions from 1608 to 1631); the fifteenth, sixteenth, and seventeenth chapters (1609, 1611); (14) the eighteenth, nineteenth, and twentieth chapters (1610, 1611); and (15) *Bathsebaes Instructions to her Sonne Lemvuel* (1614), an exposition of the thirty-first chapter of Proverbs. The writings from Proverbs will be referred to as (e.g.) *Proverbs 1-2*.

[1] *Christian Sabbath*, 40.   [2] *Fovre Sermons* (Heb. 4: 1), 18.
[3] Ibid. 17.   [4] Ibid. 23.   [5] Ibid. 35.   [6] Ibid. 37.

sincerity. Hebrews 6 should thus induce us 'to goe forward in the wayes of godlinesse, working out our salvation in feare and trembling'.[1] We must 'labour to performe those duties, whereby wee may be assured of forgivenesse'.[2]

Like Richard Rogers, Cleaver stresses the heart. Where Christ 'doth helpe anie one in mercie, hee first helps his heart'.[3] Indeed, 'whosoever would have sound happiness, must have a sound heart'.[4] A 'sound hearted man' is known (1) by his actions, since he has 'innocent hands'; (2) by his affection, for he 'setteth not his heart on any earthly thing'; and (3) by his speeches, as he does not speak 'deceitfully'.[5] But there is more; an upright heart is known by its (4) 'universall obedience', having 'respect to every commaundement of God, to the first table as well as to the second, and to the second as well as to the first'; (5) 'a continuall increase in godlinesse'; and (6) a careful use of 'all the good meanes of attaining to goodnesse, and to eschew all the inducements that may allure unto evill'.[6] Cleaver's convictions are summed up: 'Strict obedience [is] to be laboured for.'[7]

Cleaver believes that the first step to repentance is that 'hearts must bee crushed and broken'.[8] For 'till the heart bee broken for sinne, there can be no plaine confession of sinne, and therefore no repentance'.[9] This prerequisite is a 'godly sorrow'.[10] The second step to repentance is 'a true, full, particular, and hearty confession' of sins.[11] The third step is requesting God for the pardon of our sins.[12] We must moreover 'strive to be perswaded' that our sin is 'pardonable, yea and that it shall be pardoned unto us', a point that was integral in Perkins's morphology of conversion.[13] This persuasion is helped along by a 'speedy judging of our selves', for 'the more speedily we judge our selves, the more mercifully the Lord will deale with us'.[14]

Cleaver does not assert here that we *know* that our sins have been pardoned; his *ordo salutis* seems to come short of this. The nearest he appears to come is that there is 'comfort to them that proceed in the waies of the Lord with a good conscience, whose workes doe testifie for them that they are upright and sincere'.[15] The 'promise of

---

[1] *Fovre Sermons* (Heb. 4: 1), 37.   [2] *A Sermon* (Ps. 51), 19.

[3] *Three Sermons vpon Marke*, 17.   [4] *Ten Sermons*, 183.

[5] Ibid. 184.   [6] Ibid. 187-9.   [7] Ibid. 197.

[8] *Fovre Godlie*, 2 f.   [9] Ibid. 3.

[10] Ibid. Godly sorrow is 'a soveraigne remedy'. *Lamentations*, 7.

[11] *Fovre Godlie*, 12.   [12] Ibid. 13.

[13] Ibid. 15. Cf. *supra*, p. 64 n. 5.   [14] *Fovre Godlie*, 31.   [15] Ibid. 44.

all Gods mercies is made to them that live a godly life'.[1] Moreover, 'they that are beleevers, and obedient, have Jesus Christ for their mediator, and redeemer, and how then can but they be saved?'[2]

John Dod was born in Shotlidge, Cheshire. He matriculated as a sizar from Jesus College, Cambridge, in 1572. He took the BA in 1575-6; the MA in 1579, and was a Fellow from 1578 to 1585. He was ordained a deacon in London in 1579 and a priest at Ely in 1580. He became rector of Hanwell, Oxfordshire, in 1585, but was suspended for nonconformity in 1604. In the years following he and Cleaver did most of their publishing. They write in 1606: 'We are now willing to make some worke for the Presse because we have no imployment in the Pulpit.'[3] In about 1624 he was presented with the rectory of Fawsley, Northamptonshire, where he remained to his death in 1645.

Dod was Richard Greenham's son-in-law.[4] Like Greenham, Dod was often sought for counsel by perplexed souls, and Clarke states that hundreds were converted under his ministry.[5] Fuller calls him 'a passive nonconformist' and 'a good decalogist'.[6]

Dod and Cleaver have in common an assumption that God's Law can be kept by the regenerate. Dod explains that there is a difference between keeping God's commandments and fulfilling them.[7] Only Christ fulfilled the Law; but 'every Christian man may so far forth keepe Gods law, as that hee shall be accepted and also *rewarded*'.[8] However, he insists this is 'not for the merit of the worke' but because of 'the mercy of him that accepts the worke'.[9] Dod claims that assurance of salvation comes 'if our conversation bee truely religious, and our profession beautified with the workes of pietie, mercie, and of upright and Christian dealing in the whole course of our lives'.[10]

Dod has a rationale for this approach to assurance, which he thinks coheres with his predestinarianism as a whole. Since he wants to maintain that 'God esteemes of every man and woman, according to their will and affection',[11] he explains that 'all good and holy desires come from God' (Philippians 2: 13).[12] The reason, then, that God has 'regard unto the deed' is 'because it is his owne worke: and

[1] *Proverbs 15-17*, 80.   [2] *Proverbs 18-20*, 69.
[3] *Proverbs 9-10*, preface.   [4] Knappen, *Tudor Puritanism*, 387.
[5] Samuel Clarke, *General Martyrologie* (1677), 176.
[6] Fuller, *Church History*, vi. 306.
[7] *Tenne Commandements*, 82 f.   [8] Ibid. 83.   [9] Ibid.
[10] *Lords Prayer*, 56.   [11] *A Remedy*, 30.   [12] Ibid. 31.

is not the will his worke as well as the deed?' (he again cites Philippians 2: 13).[1] Thus Dod says that 'so long as wee finde not this affection in some measure in our hearts, wee want an excellent argument of the certaintie of our salvation'.[2] It seems to follow then that if this affection is there, one should conclude that God's effectual work is behind it all; hence assurance may be inferred.

The Christian man therefore is rewarded with assurance if he 'keepes' the Law. Dod lists three instances that in turn indicate that the Law is being kept: (1) 'wee must aime at all' of the commandments, which is what Cleaver means by universal obedience. For 'if one lie in any sin, and break any Commandement wilfully' he is 'guilty of all'.[3] (2) 'This obedience must be done willingly, with a free & cheerfull heart', he says. And (3) the end of our actions 'must be good, to shew our loyalty to God, to approve our hearts to him, in obedience to his Commandements'. Thus Dod concludes: 'Hee that hath all these things, keepeth the law of God.'[4]

Dod makes a distinction between 'faith' and 'feeling'. He warns that it does not follow, 'Because you have no feeling, therefore you have no faith'. One may have 'the true comforter in his soule, and yet for a time be without sense of comfort'.[5] Dod's depicting a 'two-fold assurance' appears to be an elaboration of this distinction between 'faith' and 'feeling'; such he calls '1. A Sun-shine. 2. A Moon-shine Assurance'.[6] The first is 'full assurance'; the second 'is that of the Word'—called 'the faith of Adherence, when we want' full assurance. The 'Sun-shine' assurance, however, 'is given but to few, and that but seldom'.[7]

This distinction between 'Sun-shine' and 'Moon-shine' assurance is really the same as the distinction between the direct act and the reflex act of faith. Dod would not have known—nor would those who state that assurance is an act of reflection—that the light of the moon is but the reflection of the sun. In any case, this astronomical-theological analogy made by John Dod provides an interesting frame of reference for the experimental predestinarians' doctrine of faith generally.

Finally, Dod and Cleaver hold in common a belief that uprightness of heart is a ground of assurance. While Cleaver does not espouse a doctrine of temporary faith, Dod treats such minimally. Dod does say that 'hypocrites may go as farre as Christians in many

---

[1] *Ten Sermons*, 98.
[2] *Lords Prayer*, 101.
[3] *Tenne Commandements*, 83.
[4] Ibid.
[5] Ibid. 262.
[6] *Old Mr Dod's Sayings* (1678), xxii.
[7] Ibid.

things'.[1] While the true Christian 'digges deepe, and casts out the loose earth, that so his foundation may bee firme and sure', the hypocrite 'makes quicke work, all his building is above ground'.[2] Only true Christians 'so search their hearts, and lament their corruptions'. Moreover, hypocrites are 'never troubled' about 'the assurance of their election'.[3] Thus Dod's treatment of temporary faith is carried out in a fashion so that the deeply concerned soul need not be worried about his being non-elect. For if hypocrites are never troubled about the assurance of election, it would seem that one who *is* so troubled is elected.

WILLIAM BRADSHAW (1571–1618)

William Bradshaw was born at Market Bosworth, Leicestershire. He was admitted as a sizar at Emmanuel College, Cambridge, in 1588. He received the BA in 1592–3; the MA in 1596. He was made Fellow at Sydney Sussex College in 1599. Through Chaderton's influence he became lecturer at Chatham, Kent, in 1601, but was afterwards suspended. In subsequent years he lectured at Burton-on-Trent, Staffordshire, and Repton, Derbyshire.[4]

Bradshaw generally follows Perkins when he says there are 'certaine degrees of Gods speciall love' towards the elect: (1) God's free choosing of 'the number of them that were to be saved'; (2) the 'execution' of the decree to the elect 'while they were in the loynes of Adam, before they had any personall being'; and (3) God's ordained 'meanes' to attain salvation.[5] Concerning the 'third degree', the means are 'inward' and 'outward'. The inward means is sanctification. Those whom God 'hath decreed to save, he hath also decreed to sanctifie'.

Bradshaw posits sanctification as a means to the attaining of salvation. He seems to be the only figure in the experimental predestinarian tradition explicitly to say what many tend to imply. Bradshaw does not call this preparation before conversion; yet such

---

[1] *Seven Godlie*, 57.   [2] Ibid. 58.   [3] Ibid. 58–60.

[4] Bradshaw wrote *A Treatise of Ivstification* (1615) and *A Plaine and Pithy exposition of the second epistle to the Thessalonians* (1620), hereinafter called *Thessalonians*. Most of Bradshaw's writings are devoted to ecclesiological matters. His best-known is *English Puritanisme: containeing the maine opinions of the rigidest sort of those that are called Puritanes* (1608). This was translated into Latin by William Ames in 1610. It contains the rudiments of a congregational polity. Cf. G. F. Nuttall, *Visible Saints* (1957), 9 ff.

[5] *Thessalonians*, 135–8.

counsel to one seeking salvation may well suggest that his task primarily is to strive for sanctification. For Bradshaw claims that 'this Sanctification is the very first act, and entrance into our Salvation'. And 'once we begin to be sanctified, then are we within heaven-gate, we have one foote, as it were, over the threshold'.[1] Consequently 'whosoever feeles these motions in him (for they are not dead and senseles motions) may thereby assure himselfe, that he is one of Gods elect'.[2] The 'second inward meanes, is, Faith in the Truth'.[3] As to whether 'this be first or second in nature, I will not stand here to discusse'.[4]

The 'outward' means is 'nothing else but the Ministerie of the Gospell'.[5] Bradshaw also follows Perkins in his description of faith; saving faith 'apprehendeth and applyeth' Christ's righteousness.[6]

ARTHUR HILDERSAM (1563-1632)

Arthur Hildersam was born in Stetchworth, Cambridgeshire. He entered Christ's College, Cambridge; he graduated MA and was made a Fellow in 1583. In 1587 he became lecturer in Ashby de la Zouch, Leicestershire. He was in and out of Ashby for the next forty-five years; his nonconformity brought him before the High Commission not a few times. At one period he lectured at Burton-on-Trent, Staffordshire, and Repton, Derbyshire, in conjunction with William Bradshaw. He returned to Ashby on 3 August 1625, was suspended on 25 March 1630 for not using the surplice, but was restored on 2 August 1631. His last sermon was preached at Ashby on 27 December 1631.

Hildersam's writings indicate an unsettledness in his earlier years but which seems to develop into a more consistent theology as he grew older. This is evident by comparing the writings composed before 1625,[7] and those that came during or after that year, when Hildersam returned to Ashby.[8] The significance is that the earlier

---

[1] *Thessalonians*, 138.   [2] Ibid. 139.   [3] Ibid. 140.
[4] Ibid. He does discuss it briefly, however, and indicates that the order is unimportant.
[5] Ibid. 141.   [6] *A Treatise of Ivstification*, 87.
[7] These are: (1) *The Doctrine of Communicating Worthily in the Lords Svpper* (eight editions from 1609 to 1630), hereinafter called *Communicating Worthily* (1630); (2) *Lectvres upon the fovrth of John* (four editions from 1629 to 1656), hereinafter called *Fovrth of John* (1629). John Cotton wrote the preface to this work, which includes 108 sermons from 1608 to 1611.
[8] *CLII Lectures upon Psalme LI* (three editions from 1635 to 1662), hereinafter called *Psalme LI* (1635). These sermons were delivered from 1625 to 1631.

writings show him sometimes describing faith as assurance, while those after 1625 find him repudiating such a position.

The 'early' Hildersam. 'The faith of Gods elect is no vaine fancy nor uncertaine hope', Hildersam declares, 'but a certaine assurance.' This assurance is 'wrought in the heart by the Spirit of God'.[1] Justifying faith includes being 'certainely and undoubtedly perswaded, that Christ and all his merits doe belong unto him: hee may bee in this life certainely assured, that he shall be saved'.[2] Hildersam claims that the covenant of works and covenant of grace motif was given expressly for the purpose of furthering our assurance.

> Now God hath given us his word to assure us of this, and put us out of doubt in this matter. The Apostle makes this the reason, why God made a new Covenant with us, abolished the Covenant of workes, and gave us the Covenant of grace, and promised eternall life upon condition of Faith, and not of workes.[3]

Hildersam says, however, that one should 'prove by the Word, that Christ dyed for him'.[4] By this he does not mean that Christ died for all but that Christ's death was for the elect only.

It seems to be in connection with a doctrine of limited atonement that Hildersam discloses what he means when he says one may be assured. On 20 November 1610 he states that 'there is great certainty and assurance in true faith. It is more than opinion, than a conjecture, than to hope well: it is a certaine and undoubted perswasion of the heart'.[5] But two weeks later (4 December 1610) he states that one may be 'fully assured indeede' *if* he can prove that Christ died for him. This he thinks is to be done by looking for certain fruits of faith; 'a man that hath Faith, may (by the fruits of it) certainly know that hee hath it indeede'.[6] The certainty of faith consists in 'the uprightnesse of their hearts'.[7] Behind these assertions lies a thinking that agrees with Perkins; what the reprobate cannot do is 'to apply Christ to himselfe, and to relye upon him, to trust and put his affiance in him, for his owne salvation'.[8]

The 'later' Hildersam. After 1625 Hildersam's doctrine of faith is more consistent. He now claims that faith regarded as 'a full perswasion and certaine assurance' of salvation is to be shunned. 'I answer, That is a dangerous errour to define faith so. This assurance is indeed a sweet fruit, and effect of faith, but it is not faith it selfe;

---

[1] *Communicating Worthily*, 88.   [2] *Fovrth of John*, 300.   [3] Ibid. 305.
[4] Ibid.   [5] Ibid. 299.   [6] Ibid. 308.   [7] Ibid. 306.
[8] Ibid. 653. Cf. *supra*, p. 69 n. 5.

the essence and being of faith, consisteth not in this.'[1] The 'essence' of faith consists in 'an obedientiall affiance and trusting in Christ'.[2]

When an humbled sinner feeling his owne misery through sin, can beleeve that in Christ there is help and comfort enough to be found, and rest, and rely upon him only for mercy with a mind willing to obey him in all things, this man certainly hath true faith, though hee have no assurance.[3]

Those then who make faith 'a full perswasion, and stedfast assurance' are 'much deceived in defining faith thus; and that this is a dangerous mistake, and such as hath bred much needlesse feare and trouble of mind in many a good soule'.[4]

Faith consists in 'foure acts of the soule': two in the 'understanding' and two 'of the will'. These are: (1) the knowledge of the Gospel; (2) 'the assent, and credit that the mind giveth' to the Gospel; (3) 'the consent that the will giveth' to the Gospel; and (4) 'a resting and relying upon Christ'. The fourth act he calls 'the chiefest act of the soule in true faith, and that wherein the being and essence of it doth chiefly consist'.[5]

Hildersam warns his hearers not to imagine that 'Christ died for the world' and that He 'payed every mans score, satisfied Gods justice for every mans sin'.[6] For 'there be very few' that Christ 'hath in speciall undertaken for'. He urges, 'let thou and I labour to know that we are some of those few, of that small number'. Consequently he describes four 'signes and notes whereby we may know' Christ died for us and thus 'not be deceived'.[7] These signs describe those who have the Holy Spirit: (1) one does not obey his lusts; (2) there is a change in his affections; (3) a willingness to obey God 'in all his commandments'; and (4) a refusal to let the knowledge of Christ's death keep one from feeling troubled for his sins.[8]

Hildersam's fourth point is quite revealing. Hildersam will not allow us to look at Christ's death directly; only indirectly after we have mourned sufficiently for our sins:

If the *knowledge* of this that Christ died for *thee*, keepe thee from being troubled at all in thy mind for any of thy sinnes; nay if thou have not felt *more* hearts griefe and bitternesse in thy soule for thy sinnes, and *canst* more heartily sue to God for the pardon of them *since* thou didst believe in Christ, then ever thou didst before, certainly it was *never* the Spirit of grace, but thy owne foolish fancy that hath perswaded thee that Christ was pierced for thy sinnes, or that thou hast any thing to doe with the merits of his passion.[9]

---

[1] *Psalme LI*, 652f.   [2] Ibid. 653.   [3] Ibid.   [4] Ibid. 410.   [5] Ibid. 411-13.
[6] Ibid. 610.   [7] Ibid.   [8] Ibid. 611.   [9] Ibid.

What Hildersam apparently wants is that we sufficiently grieve for sin first, then enjoy the knowledge that Christ died for us. This illustrates the practical result of placing repentance before assurance in the *ordo salutis*; assurance, or joy of sins forgiven, is not to be sought directly in the death of Christ. Hildersam rather urges that we should 'labour to be assured upon good grounds'.[1] The 'good grounds' appear to be our own godliness, or, at least, sufficient mourning over sin. His apparent fear of Antinomianism prohibits even the joy of trusting Christ's death alone.

CONCLUSION

The figures of this chapter have in common the belief that assurance of saving faith is grounded in our godliness. Whether it be in terms of keeping the heart pure (Rogers), having an 'experimentall feeling' (Mosse), being 'more in love with godlines' (Webbe), being sincere (Cleaver), keeping the Law (Dod), beginning with sanctification (Bradshaw), or labouring to be assured on the 'good grounds' of our mourning for sin (Hildersam), these divines think that full assurance is not to be obtained easily. This is why John Dod suggests that most Christians must be content with 'Moon-shine' assurance.

[1] Ibid.

7

PAUL BAYNES AND RICHARD SIBBES

PAUL BAYNES (d. 1617)

UPON the death of William Perkins, Paul Baynes was chosen as lecturer at Great St. Andrews. Baynes, like some of Perkins's contemporaries, was well known to his own generation but relatively unknown to posterity. Baynes continued the Perkins tradition, not only by his theology but by perpetuating a kind of dynasty in the experimental predestinarian tradition. Baynes converted Richard Sibbes; Sibbes converted John Cotton; Cotton converted John Preston; Preston converted Thomas Shepard. William Ames compared Perkins and Baynes to Elijah and Elisha (2 Kings 2: 9): 'this M. Bains, upon whom also the spirit of that Elias, was by experience founded to be doubled.'[1] Richard Sibbes, Baynes's most famous convert,[2] when commending Baynes's commentary on Paul's letter to the Ephesians, affectionately spoke of him as 'our Paul'.[3] While nothing was published by Baynes himself, no fewer than ten writings emerged from the press under his name within a year of his death.

Baynes is to be seen as a pivotal figure in the experimental predestinarian tradition. He not only succeeded Perkins at St. Andrews but built upon the latter's soteriology, filling out his doctrine of faith while cautiously reassessing the doctrine of temporary faith. In Sibbes's words, Baynes 'succeeds him in opinion whom he succeeded in place'.[4] In receiving Perkins's mantle, moreover, Baynes may have inherited acute pastoral problems that Perkins's awesome teaching of temporary faith could have precipitated. This is at least one explanation for Baynes's carefully worked-out treatment of this haunting problem.

Baynes was born in London. He matriculated as a pensioner at Christ's College, Cambridge, in 1590-1. He received the BA in

[1] Preface to Paul Baynes, *The Diocesans Tryall* (1621).
[2] Samuel Clarke, *The Lives of two and twenty English Divines* (1660), 166.
[3] Preface to Paul Baynes, *A Commentarie vpon the first Chapter of the Epistle of Saint Pavl, written to the Ephesians* (1618).
[4] Ibid.

1593-4, the MA in 1597. He was a Fellow from 1600 to 1604. His lectureship at St. Andrews continued from 1602 to 1607, when he was silenced by Archbishop Bancroft, apparently for refusing subscription. Baynes lived out his days in extreme poverty and poor health, not having 'a place to rest his head in'.[1] Clarke calls him 'an excellent Casuist, and thereupon many doubting Christians repaired to him for satisfaction in cases of Conscience', but adds that he, somewhat like Perkins, 'went out of this world, with farre lesse comfort then many weaker Christians enjoy'.[2]

Baynes was one of the first Englishmen to answer Arminius, whose radical modification of the reformed doctrine of predestination was becoming well known in this country from 1610 to 1620.[3] In 1618 Sibbes published Baynes's commentary on Ephesians 1; the title-page says: 'Besides the Text fruitfully explained: some principal Controversies about Predestination are handled, and divers Arguments are examined.'[4] Baynes's most popular writings were his published letters,[5] followed by two commentaries,[6] several sermons,[7] a catechism,[8] and an ecclesiological treatise published by William Ames.[9]

---

[1] *Diocesans Tryall*, preface.

[2] Clarke, *Lives*, 30-1.

[3] William Ames was probably the first Englishman to counter Arminianism.

[4] Baynes mentions Arminius and 'Arminians' several times.

[5] These are: *Christian Letters of Mr. Paul Bayne* (four editions from 1620 to 1637); *Holy Soliloqvies* (three editions by 1620); *Comfort and Instrvction in Affliction* (1620); *Briefe Directions vnto a godly Life* (1618, 1637), hereinafter called *Briefe Directions* (1618); and *A Letter Written by Mr. Pavle Bayne, Minister of Gods word, lately deceased* (1617), hereinafter called *A Letter*.

[6] These deal with Ephesians and Colossians. Besides Sibbes's publication of Baynes's commentary on Eph. 1 (*supra*, p. 94 n. 3), Baynes's treatment of Eph. 1: 11 appeared in 1635 and 1645 under the title *The Judgement of Mr P. Bayn how farre God did will, or hath a hand in mans sinne*. Baynes's commentary on Eph. 6: 10 appeared as *The Spiritvall Armour* (1620). This study, however, will draw upon *An Entire Commentary vpon the Whole Epistle of the Apostle Paul to the Ephesians* (three editions from 1643 to 1658), hereinafter called *Ephesians* (1657). *A Commentarie vpon the first and second chapters of Saint Paul to the Colossians* appeared in 1634 and 1635, hereinafter called *Colossians* (1635).

[7] Most of these were not reissued: *A Caveat for Cold Christians* (1618), hereinafter called *A Caveat*; *A Covnterbane against Earthly Carefvlnes* (1618); *The Trial of a Christians Estate* (1618, 1637), hereinafter called *The Trial* (1618); *An Epitomie of Mans Misery and Deliverie* (1619); *Two Godly and Frvitfvll Treatises* (1619), hereinafter called *Two Godly*; and *The Mirrovr or Miracle of Gods Love vnto the world of his Elect* (1619), hereinafter called *The Mirrovr*.

[8] *A Helpe to trve Happinesse* (three editions from 1618 to 1635), hereinafter called *A Helpe* (1618).

[9] *The Diocesans Tryall* (three editions from 1621 to 1644).

While Baynes's defence of predestination is an enlargement of Perkins's supralapsarianism,[1] his treatment of temporary faith indicates a significant shift. Baynes poses a problem which epitomizes the experimental predestinarian concern:

Many of the faithfull are brought to that passe, that being perswaded that they are reprobates, are neere unto desparation; they have a sense of God his wrath, and are in great anguish of conscience: how shall they stay themselves in this estate?[2]

Baynes answers that 'they may be assured' that they 'have not sinned against the holy Ghost' because such 'desire to be partakers' of the truth. This anxiety about being reprobate is a 'delusion [that] commeth, even from Satan'.[3] For if one has the 'will and desire' to hate sin and delight in goodness, 'it is an infallible mark of Gods election & love towards him'.[4]

Behind his conviction that the 'will' to be godly is an infallible proof of election is Baynes's solution to the problem posed by the doctrine of temporary faith. He compares temporary faith to a dream-like state as opposed to being consciously awake. He discloses this idea when meeting an objection that many only 'think' they have 'true faith and holinesse' but do not have such in actual fact and are therefore deceived:

I answer; First, though a man dreame he eate, or be in this or that condition, and be deceived; yet a man who is this or that waking, doth know it, and is not deluded: So here, though the dreaming man, who is asleepe in sinne, may mocke himselfe; the man who is awake and walketh with God, is not mistaken.[5]

While 'many who have temporary graces, fall from them', such are not those who have an 'honest' heart; for the latter 'know' their grace abides.[6] It follows then, 'If we find that our hearts have that faith on Christ, by which they are purified, he who may know he hath that faith, which is the faith of the elect, he may know he is elected also; wherefore let us strive to make our election sure'.[7] As

---

[1] Baynes raises and rejects two opinions concerning predestination: that we are considered 'as fallen' and that election is based upon 'fore-sight of Faith'. What Baynes does not do is to refute Arminius's doctrine of faith. Moreover, he treats the doctrine of reprobation marginally.

[2] *Briefe Directions*, 24.   [3] Ibid. 24–5.

[4] Ibid. 58.   [5] *Ephesians*, 35–6.

[6] Ibid. 36.   [7] Ibid.

will be seen below, this solution coincides with Baynes's employing the idea of the reflex act.

While Perkins writes at length on 'how farre a reprobate may goe', Baynes instead speaks of 'how far an unbeleever may goe'.[1] The Christian must go 'further' than what may characterize an unbeliever, who can (1) be terrified by the spirit of bondage; (2) be penitent after committing a sin; (3) enjoy the exercises of religion; (4) have a taste of the life to come; and (5) have a reverence for God's ministers.[2] Going 'further' consists in this: 'we must willingly be reformed in what part of our life soever we can be justly challenged: & not blemish our profession in any thing.'[3] Baynes's substitution of 'unbeleever' for 'reprobate' tends to take away the horror of being eternally lost. But if one finds that the above progress is characteristic of himself, he need not take it as a sign he is but reprobate with temporary faith, but rather that he can go 'further' and become a believer. While Perkins's theology seeks to posit the same hope for the anxious soul, the term 'reprobate' with regard to an ineffectual calling gives the impression of being at a dead end. Baynes's shift—even if it is a semantic sleight of hand— showing how far an 'unbeleever' can go, suggests a dynamic rather than a static condition. Baynes shows more pastoral sensitivity with this ease of language.

If Perkins reduces to a minimum the conditions on which one may be assured, then, Baynes reduces the capacity for spirituality in the unbeliever. Baynes reserves the will to be godly, which he calls 'affectionate knowledge',[4] for the regenerate alone. While Perkins reduces to a minimum the conditions on which one may be assured but raises to a maximum the capabilities of the reprobate with temporary faith, Baynes retains Perkins's voluntarism while care- fully curtailing the spiritual potentialities of the 'unbeleever'.[5] Perkins fails to show us clearly how we can know we are not reprobate; Baynes succeeds by reserving 'affectionate knowledge' for the believer only. Baynes does not accomplish this by completely breaking out of Perkins's mould; he simply carries Perkins's voluntarism nearer to the place it should have had in Perkins's system. Baynes's contribution, then, is twofold: (1) he elevates the

---

[1] *Briefe Directions*, 30.   [2] Ibid. 30–1.
[3] Ibid. 33.   [4] *Ephesians*, 792.
[5] The nearest Baynes comes to ascribing a temporary faith to a 'reprobate' is *Ephesians*, 153: 'if there were no particular confidence in a Christians faith, the reprobate might have all that in his beleefe.'

role of the regenerate will, imputing to it an affection which cannot be rivalled by an unregenerate will; and (2) he restricts the will of the unbeliever to affections short of the desire for godliness. Behind this twofold secret is his point that the godly is fully conscious of his affections and is not in a dream-like state.

The Trial of a Christians Estate is devoted almost entirely to this matter of temporary faith. The 'spiritual gift of the temporizer doth meerely enlighten him to see Christ, but doth not move his will to go unto Christ'.[1] He equates this with 'the Papists faith'—a 'meere enlightning' without 'any confidence within the compasse of it'.[2] The 'temporizer' is never truly humbled but 'is superficial, insincere: in a word, such as doth not truly sanctifie him: by reason of which defect, it is not permanent'.[3] The temporizer's grasp is but 'an externall forme of knowledge', which produces a 'shew' by 'inferior works of the spirit'.[4] He nicknames these 'leap-Christians', in contrast to the true believer who 'is onely said to have an honest heart'.[5]

The 'leap-Christians' inevitably apostatize from this transitory state. Because 'the grace of the temporizer purgeth out the roote of no sinne',[6] the fall eventually follows. Baynes lists six 'symptomes' or 'signes of a declining soule', but does so by urging 'weake ones' not to imagine they should be dismayed or necessarily identify with these signs; for the apostasy of the temporizer is always 'willingly carried without remorse'.[7] These signs are: (1) the 'performance of duties in perfunctorie fashion'; (2) 'a preposterous appetite of unwholesome food'; (3) an 'indigestion of what we heare' as when 'meate is taken in, and passeth away not altered by the stomacke'; (4) an 'inordinate appetite' for 'worldly cares and pleasure'; (5) 'the dis-affecting of our brethren'; and (6) 'when there is felt no reluctation in regard of our daily weaknesses and lesser sinnes, but they digest with us'.[8] Baynes also acknowledges that there is a 'back-sliding' of God's chosen.[9] but this does not mean they will perish; 'once beloved, alwaies beloved'.[10] Baynes does not state the difference between the backslider's fall and that of the reprobate; he merely says that God may bring the former to 'untimely judgements', which afterwards fill him 'with his efficacie'.[11] This, however, should not let us imagine that our condition as backsliders is

---

[1] *The Trial*, 5.   [2] Ibid. Cf. *Two Godly*, 226f.   [3] *The Trial*, 6.
[4] Ibid. 8.   [5] Ibid. 9.   [6] Ibid.
[7] Ibid. 10.   [8] Ibid. 11 ff.   [9] Ibid. 16.
[10] Ibid. 17.   [11] Ibid.

that of the elect; we must rather 'stand constantly in our courses' to walk with God by 'resisting sloth'.[1]

Baynes is not only adamant that temporary faith is visibly distinct from 'justifying and saving Faith', but he makes the chasm so wide that one who possesses the latter need not be anxious about it.[2] Indeed, 'a true faith' may be discerned 'by the fruits, & namely by repentance'.[3] By repentance, 'I meane nothing else, but godly sorrow for sinne, wherein this soul humbleth it selfe before God, and cometh home to him'.[4] Baynes believes that a man knows whether or not he has repented; it is as simple as that.

As to the nature of faith itself, Baynes wants to make saving faith 'an assured perswasion'. But this is not a persuasion by a direct act; the persuasion itself is delayed since such is 'in regard of the sense and feeling of him who beleeveth'.[5] The persuasion then is not immediate or direct; it is rather 'a reflexed operation of [the] minde'.[6] Baynes stresses that there have been 'many true be[l]eeving soules, who long beleeve, before they come to see themselves to beleeve, and be able by a reflexed operation of minde to say, I know on whom I have beleeved'.[7] Faith itself, then, for a while, may be without assurance; it may purify hearts of men 'not yet assured'.[8]

Baynes's paramount conviction is that where godliness is, faith is. For 'godlinesse cannot be without true faith'.[9] Baynes believes that the Ten Commandments provide an outline 'of the duties of holynesse'.[10] He concludes not only that the Ten Commandments show the criteria for godly living but that the fruit of such 'is nothing else but for the person who is assured of Salvation'.[11] Godly living and faith, then, are inseparable. But the former confirms that the latter is there, since faith in and by itself is not easily 'felt'.

Although the love of God and Christ, the worke of the Spirit applying them, and faith apprehending them be the chiefe cause of our conversion, yet because they are not so easily felt of us, as they are sure and infallible grounds in themselves of Salvation; therefore it is necessary *to adde* some other effects or rather properties of true faith, that doe accompanie the love

---

[1] Ibid. 17–18.

[2] *Ephesians*, 248f. In this place Baynes shows the contrast between the temporary believer and the Christian in terms of the absence of godly affections in the former. Such a contrast, he says, is 'rich comfort to every beleever'.

[3] *A Helpe*, 223.   [4] *A Letter*, 4f.
[5] *A Helpe*, 189.   [6] Ibid. 191–2.
[7] Ibid.   [8] *Briefe Directions*, 61.
[9] Ibid. 47.   [10] Ibid. 130.
[11] Ibid. 181.

of God, and of Christ Jesus in us, and are the workes or fruits of the Holy
Ghost by the Gospell, which may more clearely testifie, that where these be,
there shall that be found also.[1]

There are 'degrees' of faith, moreover.[2] These degrees corre-
spond to Baynes's depiction of a Christian's growth, which he sees
as having three stages. The first is 'childhoode or infancie', a stage
during which one may not be able to lay hold of full assurance.[3]
Faith in this stage is in its 'weakest and least measure, when there is
as yet no assurance in the beleever, and yet inseparable fruits, &
infallible tokens of it'.[4] The second stage—'middle age'—is when we
are 'ever growing, though slowly'.[5] There is sometimes assurance in
middle age, but it is 'very weake'. The third stage is 'olde age, or the
experienced estate'.[6] Those in this stage are 'through long experience' much 'acquainted with the practice of a godly life'.[7] Such
godliness 'hath assurance accompanying it for the most part
usually, unlesse the beleever doe quench the Spirit in himselfe'.[8]
There may therefore be winter-time in the soul. Like Perkins, who
compares regeneration to sap within the bark, Baynes says that a
tree in the winter 'appeareth to be dead, yet is the sappe hidden in
the roote, which in due time will shew that the tree was never dead'.[9]

Baynes speaks of 'effectuall meanes' by which men come to
salvation: 'God hath not onely chosen some, but ordained effectuall
meanes, which shall most infallibly bring them to the end to which
they are chosen.'[10] Although Christ did not die for all,[11] one need
not despair if he makes a diligent use of the means 'which God hath
pointed, for our increase in Faith and Repentance'.[12]

Baynes has no doctrine of preparation for grace save in the
context of God's whole work. While these effectual means may be
'antecedent to our conversion'[13] Baynes never says that these means
are consciously used prior to faith. It is his belief that one who
actively employs the means does so because he has faith already.
The preparing is of God, who 'doth by his power often worke some
preparative change' in sinners 'before he doth by his power and
word worke the spirit of faith in them, and make them come to
him'.[14] God works 'conviction of sinne' in men to make them cry

---

[1] *Briefe Directions*, 34f. (my italics).   [2] Ibid. 44.   [3] Ibid. 93f.
[4] Ibid. 44f.   [5] Ibid. 92f.   [6] Ibid. 92.
[7] Ibid. 94.   [8] Ibid. 46.   [9] *Christian Letters*, unpaginated.
[10] *Ephesians*, 58.
[11] Ibid. 647. 'Christ did neither make intercession, nor dye for all.' *The Mirrovr*, 3.
[12] *A Helpe*, 292f.   [13] *Ephesians*, 59.   [14] Ibid. 174.

out, 'What shall wee doe to be saved?'[1] The 'sight of our misery' is owing to the Law.[2] However, 'these preparations are not absolutely necessary, for we see that God doth give to infants sanctifying grace, in whom none of these preparative operations can take place'.[3] But when the preparations do take place such may be called 'a spirit of bondage', which is that 'effect which the spirit worketh through the Law'.[4]

The Spirit of bondage is to be replaced by the 'spirit of promise', which seals us and assures our adoption into God's family.[5] Baynes shows what a seal is: (1) it 'maketh sometimes things sealed secret', thus the Spirit's graces 'make beleevers unknowne to the world, who have not received the same spirit with them'; (2) it distinguishes, thus believers are 'peculiar to God, are set apart'; (3) it makes things 'authenticall', thus believers are given full assurance of their salvation.[6] In spite of this analogy, this seal does not necessarily make itself known. Baynes thus states that 'true beleevers are not alwaies sure of their salvation in their sense and judgment'.[7] Hence he urges, 'Let us all strive to get our selves sealed to redemption'. However, it is 'the holy spirit, *and* the graces of the spirit' which 'are the seale assuring our redemption'.[8]

Baynes believes that the 'seal' or 'earnest' of the Spirit may be known 'in ordinary course'; hence the recipient of such may be 'infallibly assured'.[9] The knowledge of this seal of the Spirit is certain, but only by the possession of a good conscience.

This certainty is no other thing then the testimony of a renewed conscience, which doth witnesse through the spirit, that we are in a state of grace . . . I call it a testimony of the conscience . . . for the conscience doth but speake it as an eccho; that it testifieth to us both our present estate of Grace . . .[10]

This point coheres with what was seen above. Baynes believes that a man may be assured because he knows that he has repented. Such a man will not be deceived; he is not dreaming like the temporizer: 'they who have the testimony of a good conscience, may know that they obey God sincerely'.[11] This he also calls 'experimental knowledge'.[12]

Baynes places faith in the will and assurance in the understanding. The persuasion is in the understanding which reflects upon the

[1] Ibid.　　[2] *The Mirrovr*, 39.　　[3] *Ephesians*, 175.
[4] Ibid. 86.　　[5] Ibid. 142.　　[6] Ibid.
[7] Ibid. 143.　　[8] Ibid. (my italics).　　[9] Ibid.
[10] Ibid. 146.　　[11] Ibid. 148.　　[12] *Briefe Directions*, 277f.

act of the will. 'By assurance here is meant an assurance or confident perswasion, which is not onely, when the understanding determines that truth is spoken, but when the will doth confidently rest upon that good which is promised.'[1] By seeing the word is true, 'I have a confidence in my will, which maketh me rest' on what is said.[2] The act of faith consists in (1) the assent of the understanding and (2) the affiance of the will.[3] Baynes thus builds upon Perkins's soteriology but does not follow the latter in asserting that faith is to be seated only in the understanding; he is much more aware of the role of the will in this kind of theology.

Baynes's greater contribution, however, is that he reassesses the doctrine of temporary faith. He is sure that any serious inquirer need not be alarmed that he is reprobate. The godly knows he is not dreaming; one may, by a reflexed operation of the mind, know that he has repented and may thus apply the promise of salvation to himself. It will be recalled that Perkins believes the one thing the reprobate cannot do is to apply the promise to himself. Baynes concurs, taking this idea a step further: the ability to reflect upon oneself and thereby know humiliation for sin eludes the temporizer, who 'doth not reflect on himselfe, so as to be humbled'.[4] Baynes thus widened the chasm between the temporizer and the regenerate, a distinction that is virtually imperceptible in Perkins.

RICHARD SIBBES (1572–1635)

Of this blest man, let this just praise be given,
Heaven was in him, before he was in heaven.[5]

'The heavenly Doctor Sibbes' was born in Tostock, Suffolk. He was admitted at St. John's, Cambridge, in 1591. He received the BA in 1599; was made Fellow in 1601, and received the MA in 1602. His conversion under Paul Baynes, whom he called his 'father in the gospel',[6] came in 1602–3.[7] He was ordained deacon and priest in

---

[1] *A Helpe*, 187.   [2] Ibid. 188.
[3] *Ephesians*, 244. Cf. *Colossians*, 288.   [4] *The Trial*, 7.
[5] According to A. B. Grosart, 'Memoir of Richard Sibbes, D.D.', *The Complete Works of Richard Sibbes, D.D.* (Edinburgh, 1862), I. xx, Izaak Walton wrote these words with reference to Richard Sibbes in a copy of Sibbes's *The Returning Backslider*, now preserved in the Salisbury Cathedral library.
[6] Preface to Paul Baynes, *Ephesians*.
[7] Frank E. Farrell, 'Richard Sibbes: a Study in Early Seventeenth Century English Puritanism' (Ph.D. thesis, Edinburgh, 1955), 25. This thesis treats Sibbes's biography and theology. The latter is dealt with superficially, the doctrine of faith treated marginally.

Norwich in 1607-8, and was chosen one of the college preachers in 1609. He received the BD in 1610. In 1611 he was made lecturer at Holy Trinity Church, Cambridge, remaining in this position until 1615. During this period at Holy Trinity he converted John Cotton.[1]

In 1617 Sibbes was made preacher at Gray's Inn, London, and later complemented this lectureship by accepting the position of Master of Catherine Hall, Cambridge, in 1626. Soon after this appointment he received the degree of doctor of divinity. In 1627 he refused an offer of Archbishop James Ussher to be provost at Trinity College, Dublin. In 1633 Charles I presented Sibbes with the vicarage of Holy Trinity, Cambridge, where he had been lecturer once before. Sibbes appears to have held on to three positions (two in Cambridge, one in London) until his death on 5 July 1635.

Sibbes's pattern of conformity is quite like that of Perkins. Sibbes was a model churchman. It should be noted, moreover, that his prime years of preaching were carried out 'with Laud's eyes upon him'.[2] His sermons do not delve into ecclesiology at all. Because of Laud's power, men were forbidden to discuss issues like free will and predestination as early as 1628,[3] and this may account for Sibbes's small attention to the doctrine of predestination. However, Sibbes's pastoral concern leads one to suspect that he would almost prefer that men forget about the decrees of predestination. In any case, Sibbes appears to have bowed more and more to Laud's wishes. When in 1634 a vacant fellowship occurred in Catharine Hall, Laud recommended one whom Edmund Calamy (a Westminster divine) calls Laud's 'Bell-ringer at Lambeth' to the post. Calamy reports: 'The Doctor, who was not for provoking persons in Power, told the Fellows, that Lambeth House would be obey'd; that the Person was young, and might prove hopeful, &c.'[4]

Sibbes seems to have been more interested in publishing others' sermons than his own. As well as Baynes's commentary on Ephesians 1, Sibbes published sermons of John Preston,[5] Henry Scudder (d. 1659?),[6] Ezekiel Culverwell (d. 1631),[7] John Smith

---

[1] Larzer Ziff, *The Career of John Cotton*, 31.

[2] David Masson, *The Life of John Milton* (1881), i. 516.

[3] G. M. Trevelyan, *England under the Stuarts* (1965), 162.

[4] Edmund Calamy, *An Account of the Ministers, Lecturers, Masters . . .* (1713), ii. 605-6.

[5] He was joined in this effort by John Davenport (d. 1670); the sermons are listed *infra*, p. 118 n. 4.

[6] *Key of Heaven, the Lords Prayer Opened* (1620).

[7] *Time Well Spent* (1634); and *A Treatise of Faith* (c. 1622). The latter work went

(d. 1616),[1] John Ball (d. 1640),[2] and Richard Capel (d. 1656).[3] Apart from a collection of Sibbes's sermons that appeared anonymously under the title *The saints cordials* (1629),[4] only three volumes were published 'under his own sanction'.[5] But within five years of his death, no fewer than ninety-nine sermons appeared in print,[6] not counting the three volumes above or *The saints cordials*. Among those who wrote prefaces to his works were the future Arminian John Goodwin, John Dod, Ezekiel Culverwell, Thomas Manton, plus three future Westminster divines: Simeon Ashe, Philip Nye, and Thomas Goodwin.

The sermons of Sibbes, which Haller judges to be 'the most brilliant and popular of all the utterances of the Puritan church militant',[7] reflect the thinking of Perkins and Baynes.[8] Sibbes pays but perfunctory attention to the doctrine of temporary faith—and never uses the expression itself—and stresses instead the positive work of the Holy Spirit in the soul who is weary with sin—'the bruised reed'.[9] Sibbes was a preacher 'primarily devotional, not controversial';[10] indeed, the thrust of Sibbes's preaching is aimed at lifting up the weakest Christian and bringing him to a persuasion of his election in Christ.

into eight editions by 1648. Culverwell speaks of a 'two-fold' assurance: 'faith alone' (trusting the Word) and 'the certaintie of Sense', which comes from 'the conscionable indeavour to keepe Gods Commandments'. *A Treatise of Faith* (1630), 156-7.

[1] *An Exposition of the Creed* (1632). Smith says there are two kinds of assurance: 'absolute assurance, that whatsoever a man doth, or howsoever a man liveth, yet he shall be saved'; and 'conditional assurance', that 'which the Gospell teaches, that if we repent . . . then we may assure our selves that we shall be saved' (33).

[2] *A Treatise of Faith* (1631). This went into six editions by 1640. Ball may have influenced the Westminster divines. Cf. *infra*, p. 191 n. 4. Ball claims that the 'seat of faith' is in the 'heart'. By heart he means the 'will'. *A Treatise of Faith* (1631), 142.

[3] *Tentations: their Nature, Danger, Cure* (five editions, 1632 to 1637). Capel says much attention given to the doctrine of the unpardonable sin is the 'policy of Satan' (1633 edn., p. 279).

[4] This was reissued in 1637 and 1658, identifying the preacher of the sermons as Sibbes. However, one sermon ('The Poor Doubting Christian') is by Thomas Hooker. Cf. *infra*, p. 127 n. 11.

[5] Grosart, op. cit. xxiii. These are: *The Bruised Reed and Smoking Flax* (seven editions from 1630 to 1658); *The Souls Conflict with Itself* (five editions from 1633 to 1658); and *The Saints Safety in Evil Times* (three editions from 1633 to 1658).

[6] These came within at least sixty-three separate editions.

[7] Haller, *Rise of Puritanism*, 152.

[8] There are no less than 129 sermons. This study will draw from *The Complete Works of Richard Sibbes, D.D.* (seven vols., Edinburgh, 1862-4), hereinafter called *Works*.

[9] *Works*, i. 48 ff.

[10] G. F. Nuttall, *The Holy Spirit in Puritan Faith and Experience* (Oxford, 1947), 14.

A position that suggests an infralapsarian view of predestination may in part lie behind the enormous responsibility Sibbes imputes to men who hear the Gospel.[1] While God does not intend to save all—'we must let God do what he will'[2]—Sibbes preaches to men as though they held their destinies in their own hands. This approach has a significant effect upon his doctrine of faith. Whereas he believes men by nature are spiritually dead,[3] and that the Spirit alone can change this condition,[4] Sibbes urges men to 'labour to get into Christ' and by this 'grow more and more acquainted with the secret will of the Father to our salvation'.[5] He has no doubt that God's secret will can soon become known. To Sibbes, the issue is extraordinarily simple; we are commanded to believe in Christ: this 'binds'.

Reason not this, whether God hath elected or Christ hath died for thee. This is the secret will of God. But the commandment is, to believe in Christ. This binds. Therefore, yield to Christ when thou art called and bidden to cast upon him; then thou shalt find, to thy soul's comfort, the fruit of his death.[6]

Sibbes, like Baynes, considers it a delusion of the devil that men object, 'I be not one that Christ redeemed, and God elected'.[7] Sibbes's response is, 'Put this question out of question, by believing and obeying'. Indeed, 'Do thy duty' and 'be ruled by Him' and know then 'that thou art one of God's elect'.[8]

While Sibbes believes only the Holy Spirit can create life, and that 'we cannot prepare ourselves',[9] he encounters men as if the act of faith is in themselves. While the grace of faith comes by the Spirit, 'the act is ours, and comes immediately from us'.[10] Indeed, the work of conversion is 'as if we did it ourselves'.[11]

It is true, the grace is from the Spirit, but when the grace is received, the act is from ourselves, not only from ourselves, but immediately from ourselves. We cannot but confess it so. . . . we do not actually believe, but by an act of the Spirit; but yet the act of believing is our own.[12]

[1] God's secret purpose is the electing of some, 'and leaving others'. *Works*, v. 390. This suggests the 'others' were already fallen. Those whom God appointed to disobedience (1 Pet. 2: 8) were already blind and hostile to Him. Ibid. ii. 431. What will be 'hell in hell' is having to say, 'I have brought myself carelessly and securely to this cursed estate'. Ibid. iv. 92.

[2] Ibid. v. 511.   [3] Ibid. vii. 401 ff.   [4] Ibid. 408.
[5] Ibid. iv. 329.   [6] Ibid. v. 391.   [7] Ibid. 403.
[8] Ibid.   [9] Ibid. vi. 522.   [10] Ibid. iv. 449.
[11] Ibid. ii. 63.   [12] Ibid. iv. 449.

Moreover, 'all preparations are from God'. We cannot prepare ourselves or even 'deserve future things by our preparations; for preparations themselves are of God'. At the same time he thinks that God 'usually prepares those that he means to convert'.[1] This preparation Sibbes calls a 'bruising'. The reason there are lapses and apostasies is 'because men never smarted for sin at the first; they were not long enough under the lash of the law'.[2] This preparation, or bruising, is described as 'the first work of the Spirit' or 'the spirit of bondage'.[3] The tool used by the Spirit is the Law—'to drive them to an holy despair in themselves'.[4] The preaching of Christ 'is even to begin with the law to discover to people their estate by nature'.[5] 'Christ is not sweet till sin be bitter', Sibbes declares.[6]

While Sibbes is sensitive to the matter that some may linger in the bruised state needlessly long, he concludes that it is 'better to go bruised to heaven than sound to hell'.[7] If a man has 'stuck deep and long in sin, he must look for a greater measure and more certain time of his effectual calling'. Before such a one finds peace in mount Zion, God will speak to him from Sinai with thunder and lightning: this is a 'haling and pulling of such a man out of the fire with violence'.[8] It may be seen, however, that, while preparations are from God, Sibbes addresses the man under the Spirit of bondage as though he can pull himself out of the fire. Sibbes makes a distinction between 'humiliation' and 'humility', the former being the consequence of the Spirit of bondage, the latter being 'a grace itself'.[9] The Spirit of bondage issues in 'the principal, sanctifying, and saving work of the Spirit'—but in proportion to 'our humiliation and sorrow'. What we must do, then, is 'to take the rod betimes and beat ourselves'.[10]

Sibbes does not make it clear at what point one consciously graduates from the Spirit of bondage to the Spirit of adoption. This weakness in his theology is what keeps him from lucidly espousing a doctrine of full assurance. On the other hand, his solution to the problem of temporary faith may be regarded as filling out the attractive solution of Baynes. Sibbes solves the problem by avoiding it. He does not say whether the 'inferior work of the Spirit'—which he thinks is 'necessary before conversion'—*necessarily* issues in conversion.[11] He wants to hold simultaneously that the bruising is

---

[1] *Works*, vi. 522.　　[2] Ibid. i. 44.　　[3] Ibid. vii. 374f.
[4] Ibid. iv. 340.　　[5] Ibid. v. 506.　　[6] Ibid. vi. 171f.
[7] Ibid. i. 47.　　[8] Ibid. v. 376.　　[9] Ibid. 375.
[10] Ibid.　　[11] Ibid. i. 44.

prior to conversion but also that the bruised 'are secretly upheld by a spirit of faith'.[1] Indeed, 'Art thou bruised? Be of good comfort, He calleth thee.'[2]

The cause of 'relapses and apostasies', then, is insufficient bruising. Temporary faith is implied here. But Sibbes apparently does not want to inject anything into his preaching that will bring bruised souls to more sorrow. He therefore stresses the positive—that 'Christ will not "break the bruised reed"'.[3] Hence, rather than expound the possibility of relapse after one has advanced to the Spirit of bondage Sibbes holds simultaneously that the bruising is both a pre-conversion state and yet a 'spirit of faith, shewing itself in hidden sighs and groans unto God'.[4]

Sibbes in any case never speaks of 'temporary faith'—in any sermon or commentary. If Baynes builds upon Perkins's general structures but widens the chasm between the regenerate and the 'temporizer', Sibbes hardly lets one think there is a chasm at all. For the reprobate is 'not subdued to obedience, not to constant obedience'.[5] While castaways may have gifts, 'Christianity is a matter rather of grace than of gifts, of obedience than of parts'.[6]

As a consequence of this neglect of the doctrine of temporary faith, 'the heavenly Doctor Sibbes' has removed every hindrance that would inhibit the anxious soul who is willing to do anything he can to assure his election. Sibbes carries Baynes's compassionate care for souls a step further, but always building on the same foundation: that 'grace' affects the 'will'.

The main thing in religion is the will and affections, and when the will and affections are wrought on, the work is done in the matter of grace. And there is no other way to know whether the former work of the understanding and persuasion be effectual and to purpose or now, but this; to know whether the will choose and cleave to good things, and whether our affections joy and delight in them.[7]

It is not surprising then that Sibbes's theology of assurance is based upon a 'reflect act inbred in the soul'.[8] Indeed, 'there may be adherence without evidence; and there must be an act of reflection to cause faith of evidence'.[9] The act of reflection is the awareness of

---

[1] Ibid. i. 38.   [2] Ibid. 46.   [3] Ibid. 45.

[4] Sibbes does hold, however, that an inferior work of the Spirit operates in men never regenerate. It makes men 'civil'. Ibid. iv. 338. The Spirit may be given in some degree to reprobates, but the Spirit does not 'rule in them'. Ibid. i. 25. Cf. ibid. i. 163; vii. 8–9, 275, 497.

[5] Ibid. i. 25.   [6] Ibid. 242.   [7] Ibid. vii. 446.

[8] Ibid. ii. 47.   [9] Ibid. vii. 352.

holy affections. For the inferior work of the Spirit must progress; indeed, to the 'spirit of burning' (Isaiah 4: 4), 'to consume whatsoever opposed corruption like rust eats into the soul'.[1] This means that Christ governs the 'mind, will, and affections'.[2] For 'if the will be not inclined and wrought to go the best way, there is no work of grace at all'.[3]

Well, you see, therefore, that the grace wrought in the gospel it is not a mere persuasion . . . but a powerful work of the Spirit entertaining into the soul and changing it, and altering and turning the bent and inclination of the will heavenward . . .[4]

We must therefore 'labour' to make our calling and election sure, 'that is, in ourselves, and in our own apprehension'.[5] This certainty is increased by the avoiding of 'any sinful acts'. This care to keep 'our evidence clear' will allow 'that our consciences may witness' our calling and election.[6]

The act of reflection is really the second of a 'double act of faith', an idea Sibbes develops in the light of his observation that many a child of God waits 'long' before they have assurance.[7] Yet this is essentially Perkins's teaching of the two works of grace put in a slightly different way. The first act of faith is 'whereby the soul relies' upon God, Christ, and the promise. The second is 'the reflect act, whereby, knowing we do this, we have assurance'. Sibbes thinks 'man may perform the one act [the first] and not the other'.[8] The second merely proves that the first in fact took place. It is the first act which 'brings us into the state of grace' but this state is characterized by the want of assurance.[9] The first act Sibbes also describes as 'the direct act' which is followed by 'a reflect act, whereby I know I am in an estate of grace by the fruits of the Spirit'. But Sibbes is careful to maintain that it is 'by the first act that we are saved'.[10]

Sibbes therefore articulates the distinction between faith and assurance more clearly than any divine examined so far. This distinction is implicit in Perkins, although he speaks mostly of the lack of 'full' assurance. John Dod speaks of 'Moon-shine' assurance, the more common state of Christians. Sibbes's developed concept of the double act of faith issues simply in 'assurance', and that only by

[1] *Works*, i. 78.　　　　[2] Ibid.　　　　[3] Ibid. iv. 258.
[4] Ibid. 259.　　　　[5] Ibid. vii. 352.　　　　[6] Ibid. 353.
[7] Ibid. iii. 467.　　　　[8] Ibid.　　　　[9] Ibid. v. 393.
[10] Ibid. vii. 213.

reflection. Moreover, 'God gives the reflect act, which is assured hope, as a reward of exact walking'.[1] While we are saved by the direct act, assurance seems to be based on merit. We are saved by grace; we are assured by works. Other writers above have implied this; Sibbes says it. Assurance is 'a reward of exact walking'. It is this conviction that lies behind his assertion, 'faith is one thing, assurance another'.[2]

Sibbes builds upon Perkins's structures. Apart from a tendency towards infralapsarianism, Sibbes is squarely within Perkins's mould, the differences between them on temporary faith notwithstanding. It has been seen that Perkins's theology demands increased attention concerning man's will; his emphasis on 'applying' Christ is essentially voluntaristic. Sibbes says that 'true faith is an applying faith', and that the 'nature of faith' is to particularize, viz. to 'appropriate' Christ to oneself.[3] Sibbes's description of the 'seal' of the Spirit, moreover, is like that of Baynes.[4] While Baynes does not deal with the 'covenant of grace' and the 'covenant of works', Sibbes does so often, stressing the difference between the two.[5] His position is a replay of Perkins. While Perkins might not be happy with Sibbes's statement, 'Labour to be such as God may love us',[6] a strange comment for any predestinarian, such a remark reveals how far one can go towards an anthropocentric doctrine of faith when assurance is regarded as a reward for 'exact walking'.

---

[1] Ibid.   [2] Ibid. v. 448.   [3] Ibid. 391.
[4] Ibid. iii. 465ff. Cf. *supra*, p. 101 n. 6.
[5] e.g. see *Works*, i. 58f.; iv. 122; v. 342; vi. 4; vii. 352, 482, 198.
[6] Ibid. vi. 393.

8

JOHN COTTON (TO *c*.1632) AND JOHN PRESTON

JOHN COTTON (1584–1652)

THIS chapter will argue that John Cotton underwent a significant change of mind at some stage of his career prior to the Antinomian Controversy in America (1636–7). This shift of thought is transparent when his sermons preached in England are compared with those delivered in America.[1] It is fitting, moreover, that the 'early' Cotton and John Preston should be linked together, not merely because Cotton converted Preston but because 'it was grown almost a proverb, "That Mr. Cotton was Dr. Preston's seasoning vessel"'.[2]

With one exception,[3] the sermons which Cotton preached in England were published after he went to America, without his editing and probably without his permission.[4] Scholars have had no difficulty determining in which country the sermons were delivered,[5] yet the clear contrast which emerges from a comparison of the two sets of writings seems generally to have been overlooked.[6] This chapter will argue that Cotton's sermons in England present a consistent viewpoint on the nature of saving faith but one which Cotton repudiates in America. Incidentally, therefore, it will give support to Cotton Mather's statement that Cotton's sermons on the

---

[1] See Chapter 12.

[2] Cotton Mather, *Magnalia Christi Americana*, i. 260.

[3] *Gods Promise to His Plantation* (1630), Cotton's sermon at Southampton, delivered before those departing for Massachusetts Bay.

[4] For example, in the preface to *The way of life* (1641), William Morton writes: 'I could have wished (if it might have been) that it had passed under his owne censure.' Mather, op. cit. i. 280, says the sermons on 1 John were not published by Cotton. See *infra*, p. 111 n. 2.

[5] Larzer Ziff, *The Career of John Cotton* (Princeton, 1962), 261–8, and Everett H. Emerson, *John Cotton* (New York, 1965), 163–6, are in essential agreement as to the dates of Cotton's sermons. Cf. Julius H. Tuttle, 'Writings of John Cotton', *Biographical Essays: a Tribute to Wilberforce Eames* (Cambridge, Mass., 1924), 363–80.

[6] Emerson, op. cit. 50, notices a difference on the doctrine of preparation between *Christ the Fountaine of Life* and *Treatise of the Covenant of Grace*, but says: 'One can only fall back on the Reformed concept of the sermon as an explanation for this inconsistency.'

First Epistle of John,[1] 'preached in his youth, and not published by himself', contain 'some things therein which he would not have inserted',[2] a remark Mather probably made because he knew the theology for which his grandfather became controversial in America. In any case, the present writer will show the 'early' Cotton to be an experimental predestinarian but the 'later' Cotton to have espoused a position remarkably like that of John Calvin.

John Cotton was born in Derby in December 1584. He entered Trinity College, Cambridge, in 1597, when Perkins's influence was at its zenith. Cotton heard Perkins preach, 'but the motions and stirrings of his heart which then were, he suppressed'.[3] When he heard 'the Bell toll for Mr Perkins who then lay dying, he was secretly glad in his heart, that he should now be rid of him who had (as he said) laid siege to and beleaguer'd his heart'.[4] But later, under the preaching of Richard Sibbes, who 'shewed what Regeneration was not', Cotton 'saw his own condition fully discovered' and was converted. This experience 'begat in him a singular and constant love of Doctor Sibbes',[5] and Cotton kept a picture of Sibbes 'in that part of his house where he might oftenest look upon it'.[6]

Cotton received the BA in 1602, and, he later reflected, 'God kept me in the University'.[7] In 1603 he was made a Fellow at Emmanuel College, where he came under Laurence Chaderton's influence. He took the MA in 1606, was ordained at Lincoln in 1610, and became vicar of St. Botolph's, Boston, Lincolnshire, in 1612. He received the BD in 1613. Paul Baynes introduced him to 'a pious gentle woman' whom Cotton married.[8] Cotton's popularity increased while at St. Botolph's. His sermons were 'well attended by citizens from throughout the country side', one frequent attender being Mrs Anne Hutchinson.[9] John Preston, whom Cotton converted in Cambridge, often came to hear him, and frequently also sent students to do so.[10]

Cotton seems generally to have conformed to the establishment satisfactorily, although he refused to kneel to receive the eucharist.

---

[1] *Christ the Fountaine of Life* and *A Practicall Commentary . . . vpon The First Epistle Generall of John.*

[2] Mather, op. cit. i. 280.

[3] John Norton, *Abel being Dead yet speaketh; or, the Life & Death of . . . Mr. John Cotton* (1658), 12. Norton was Cotton's close friend and successor at the Boston church, New England.

[4] Ibid.   [5] Ibid. 13.   [6] Mather, op. cit. i. 255.
[7] Norton, op. cit. 11.   [8] Mather, op. cit. i. 258.   [9] Ziff, op. cit. 43.
[10] Ibid. 32–3.

In 1632 he learned he would be summoned by Laud to the Court of High Commission. He visited John Dod who advised him to leave the country. Cotton chose to go to America. He left on a June morning in 1633, sailing with his second wife (his first died of malaria) and daughter on the *Griffin*. With him was Thomas Hooker who had returned from Holland. Cotton's son, Seaborn, was born during the crossing, but his baptism was delayed, awaiting such a sacrament in a true church. The *Griffin* landed in the New Boston harbour on 4 September 1633.

Cotton's doctrine of faith in England[1] clearly mirrors the experimental predestinarian tradition, save for his aberration concerning the doctrine of predestination.[2] Concerning the latter, Cotton had worked out a scheme whereby election is totally by God's decree but reprobation is wholly in the hands of man. Cotton's position harmonizes with the highly activistic theology he espouses during this period. He wants to show that when men reject the Holy Ghost it is a real rejection,[3] and that the reprobate theoretically *could* be saved if they kept the covenant of works.[4] While Cotton never hints that the reprobate could keep such a covenant, he believes that their failure to do so vindicates God in damning them.[5] Twisse's concern is that Cotton's position is an implicit acquiescence in 'the sower leaven of Arminianisme'.[6]

While Twisse focuses upon the decrees of election and reprobation, Cotton's actual doctrine of faith is also closely akin to that of

---

[1] This is based on the following: *A Practical Commentary . . . vpon The First Epistle Generall of John* (1656, 1658), hereinafter called *1 John* (1656); *Gods Mercie mixed with his Ivstice* (1641), hereinafter called *Gods Mercie* (this was issued in 1658 as *The Saints Support & Life*); *Christ the Fountaine of Life* (sixteen sermons from 1 John 5: 12–16) (1656), hereinafter called *Christ the Fountaine*; *The way of life* (1655); and *A Treatise of Mr. Cottons, Clearing certaine Doubts concerning Predestination. Together with an Examination Thereof: written by William Twisse* (1646), hereinafter called *Predestination*.

[2] William Twisse (d. 1646), who became moderator of the Westminster Assembly of Divines, came upon Cotton's manuscript, which seems to have been passed around widely, and prepared a refutation which Cotton himself read prior to the latter's departure from England. Twisse reports in the preface that Cotton had been 'satisfied' by the rejoinder, implying Cotton changed his mind. Norton, op. cit. 31, states that Cotton did change, and, indeed, Cotton's predestinarianism after 1636 does not suggest the modified view which the treatise on predestination takes. Twisse says that he published the treatise in 1646 because he feared Cotton's position in the 1620s had become better known than his change of mind. Twisse's rebuttal is a defence of the supralapsarian view. The date of composition of *Predestination* was some time after the Synod of Dort, to which Cotton refers (39).

[3] *Predestination*, 93.   [4] Ibid. 62.
[5] Ibid. 172f.   [6] Ibid. 234.

Arminius. What the experimental predestinarians do not seem to be concerned with is that their doctrine of faith has very much in common with that of Arminius. It is possible that their excessive interest in the issue of the decrees of predestination has lured them away from noticing the parallel that exists between Arminius's doctrine of faith and their own.[1]

Indeed, Cotton states that conversion is comprised of 'a double act of God' (He stands and knocks) and 'a double act of ours' (our hearing His voice and opening the door—Revelation 3: 20).[2] Moreover, while Cotton affirms that the cause of spiritual life is 'Gods owne good pleasure' and 'the Spirit of God',[3] for he is sensitive to being charged with 'ungracious Pelagianisme',[4] he asserts that all men are given 'such means and helps of seeking after the Lord, and finding mercy from him, that they are sufficiently enabled by him to doe much more then they doe'.[5] These means, moreover, 'are in some measure sufficient' to bring men to repentance and salvation.[6] Such means, or 'helps', come 'either of the knowledge of God in Nature, or of grace in Christ'.[7]

Thus Cotton imputes to the unconverted a remarkable measure of ability to prepare themselves for faith; not that natural men can convert themselves, but they are enabled 'to doe much more then they doe', by which he seems to mean that they could do more than they think they can, or, at least, generally act upon. What 'helps' that may not come from 'grace in Christ', then, come from God's knowledge in 'Nature'. In any case, Cotton comes the nearest of any figure examined so far in positing preparation on man's part *before* regeneration. Indeed, we must 'prepare a way for Christ to come in to us'.[8] In addition to an analogy between John the Baptist and Christ, Cotton leans heavily on his interpretation of Isaiah 40: 3–4 to support his doctrine of preparation.[9] As every mountain must be brought low and crooked places made straight, so it is that 'if we smooth the way for Him, then He wil come into our hearts'.[10]

---

[1] That the experimental predestinarians would have reassessed their doctrine of faith had they realized the similarity between Arminius and themselves on this is not implied. In any case this is a fundamental point that interpreters of Calvinism and Arminianism seem to have overlooked: Arminius's radical modification of the reformed doctrine of predestination is paralleled by his deviation from Calvin on the nature of faith; but on the latter issue Arminius and the experimental predestinarians have much in common. See Chapter 10.

[2] *Gods Mercie*, 2.　　[3] *1 John*, 396–7.　　[4] *Predestination*, 207.
[5] Ibid.　　[6] Ibid. 207–8.　　[7] Ibid. 207.
[8] *Christ the Fountaine*, 40.　　[9] Ibid. 40f. Cf. *1 John*, 387f.
[10] *Christ the Fountaine*, 41.

Cotton's favourite phrase in connection with preparation is 'fit for Christ'.[1] When 'we are willing to be whatsoever he would have us to be', we are then 'made fit for Christ to come into us'. That we are not so fit is evidenced by our unwillingness to 'part with such and such Lusts'.[2]

Crooked things must be made straight; there in our hearts many turnings in and out, these must be made straight, it's when we look with a single eye, and are willing to be guided by a straight rule, and aim singly at Gods ends, such an heart is fit for Christ, when it's cleansed from all hypocrisie.[3]

Cotton imputes an enormous power to the Law to accomplish this fitness. The Law 'doth kill sin in us, and thereby kils us, it kills all our former jollities and comforts in this world'.[4] 'When a man is once blasted by the ministery of the Law, a spirit of bondage breathing in it, it doth so darken and dead all his comforts, as that a man is dead to sin, and dead to the world.'[5] A 'further power in the Law', while it does not regenerate, is that as 'a Schoolmaster to drive us to Christ' it 'discovers to us our sins'. Sometimes—'occasionally'—this power of the Law, or Spirit of bondage, is accompanied by the spirit of Adoption 'striking with it'. This Spirit of adoption 'makes us cry out, What shall we doe to be saved?'[6]

Cotton does not clarify the last assertion. But his saying that 'occasionally' the Spirit of adoption may strike with the work of the Spirit of bondage reveals his sensitivity about when regeneration actually does set in, a point Sibbes also fails to make clear. It seems, however, that Cotton's lack of elaboration on this point is in some sense compensated by his frequent emphasis on what he means by being 'fit' for Christ. When 'wee will not allow our selves in any passage of sinne, but yeeld up our selves, soules and bodies and spirits and all to bee guided by him', then Christ 'will come in and dwell with us'.[7] It is here that Cotton, wittingly or not, equates being prepared with repentance—and therefore preparation with assurance. He seems to be saying that if we are prepared, that is, 'fit', we are simultaneously assured that the Spirit of adoption has come to dwell with us. The crux of Cotton's doctrine of preparation, in any case, is the abandonment of known sin. While being prepared includes a diligence to heed God's word, Cotton quickly comes to

---

[1] *Christ the Fountaine*, 41. Cf. *1 John*, 388.   [2] *Christ the Fountaine*, 41.
[3] *1 John*, 388.   [4] *The way of life*, 232.
[5] Ibid. 233.   [6] Ibid.
[7] *Gods Mercie*, 22.

the point: 'What ever known sins you have heretofore lived in, abandon them, and then God will poure out the riches of his mercy upon you . . . when you heare a sin reproved, turn from it, and then He will poure out His spirit upon you.'[1] This assertion, moreover, can hardly be regarded as anything but placing repentance before faith in the *ordo salutis*.

What Cotton does, then, is to demand repentance in a man before he can be 'fit'; and he must be 'fit' before Christ will come to dwell with him.

If there be nothing in a mans heart, but hee is willing to bee guided in it, by the straight rule of Gods word, and hee aimes directly at the glory of God, and the comming of his Kingdom, and the doing of His will, then is all a mans crooked wayes laid aside, and the heart lyes so levell, *then Christ will suddenly come* into His Temple . . .[2]

Indeed, since sanctification 'stands chiefly in two things: In the mortification of corruption, and quickening our spirits to holy duties, and faith doth both these',[3] the description of the heart 'fit' for Christ is essentially no different from what Cotton calls sanctification. While he affirms that faith mortifies and quickens, he simultaneously implies that sanctification is a prerequisite to faith.

Cotton's essential position is that when we do our part, God will do His part. Cotton comes quite close to saying that preparation for faith is entirely man's work—unless the knowledge of God in 'Nature' can be taken to mean that such is God's work. In any case, the Spirit of bondage prepares for the Spirit of adoption, and the former seems to be man's co-operation with the work of the Law which makes him, in turn, 'fit for Christ'. Cotton writes to Archbishop Ussher that there is no promise of grace to pardon sin 'before the heart be changed from stonyness to brokenness'. Indeed, 'faith in the promises' *before* this change has taken place 'is no better than the temporary faith, which is found in the stony soil' (Luke 8: 13).[4] Cotton is convinced that 'the Spirit will not lodge in an uncleane heart'.[5] He speaks in circles: 'Faith prepares my heart to receive this sealing spirit', and 'faith purifies our hearts'; but this purification is 'by applying all the Commandements of God to our soules, so as that we dare commit no iniquity, and so are cleane and marvellous innocent, ashamed, and dare not meddle with any sin'.[6]

---

[1] *The way of life*, 103.   [2] *Christ the Fountaine*, 43.
[3] *The way of life*, 351.
[4] *The Whole Works of the Most Rev. James Ussher, D.D.* (Dublin, 1864), xv. 331.
[5] *The way of life*, 326.   [6] Ibid.

From this circular argument one can but infer that man determines, if not controls, the Spirit's entrance by his willingness or unwillingness to abandon sin; the willingness must come before the Spirit does. It seems that it is not the Spirit who makes one willing, but the willingness which allows the Spirit to enter. Indeed, faith 'makes roome for the Spirit'.[1]

What Cotton does not clarify, moreover, is whether or not the operation of the Spirit of bondage can be aborted along the way. Such would pave the way for a doctrine of temporary faith. His reference to 'temporary faith' to Archbishop Ussher is not found elsewhere in his sermons preached before 1632.[2] Cotton therefore is to be seen in line with the experimental predestinarian tradition to protect the role of the will to obey God from being impugned with anything other than the sure sign that Christ *has* come to dwell in us.

The knowledge that we have this will to keep God's commandments is 'actio reflexa'.[3] For 'as I know that Fire burns from the light and heat, so then I know it by experience', the 'Effects'; and such effects 'cannot delude us'. Having been oppressed by the consciousness of sin, one 'knows that hee knows Christ' by 'the purifying of his conscience . . . purifying it from the lusts of sin'. Thus 'we know that we know him, if we keep his Commandements'.[4]

But such knowledge is hardly different from the knowledge of being prepared by a 'fit' heart; hence assurance of being prepared is simultaneously assurance of being elected. Cotton asks, speaking of this knowledge that we keep God's commandments, 'how shall we make it [our calling and election] sure, if we know not that we know it?'[5] The 'actio reflexa' is essentially reflecting upon our obedience— whether it be our fitness (preparation) or our keeping the commandments (regeneration). His counsel concerning preparation for Christ is really no different from his counsel concerning how we know we have Christ. The only difference, moreover, between assurance of preparation and assurance of regeneration is that Cotton does not explicitly say that sanctification precedes faith; only that if sanctification is there, 'then thy faith is a regenerating faith'.[6] It is obvious,

---

[1] *The way of life*, 326.

[2] Like Sibbes, Cotton refers to the common work of the Spirit. *1 John*, 26. He makes a passing remark that there may be zeal (as in Herod—Mark 6: 20), humiliation (as in Ahab—1 Kings 21: 29), and fear (as in Felix—Acts 24: 25). But these 'rest only upon the outwards of a man' and do not reach 'the Heart, and Will, which are the Castle wherein Christ abides'. *1 John*, 279.

[3] Ibid. 54.   [4] Ibid. 59.   [5] Ibid.

[6] Ibid. 345. Cf. *Christ the Fountaine*, 109 ff., where Cotton elaborates that the

obvious, however, that preparation for faith requires repentance, or sanctification—whatever name Cotton may wish to call being 'fit'.

Cotton later takes a radically different line. But his change of mind seems to have come after the era in which he was 'Dr. Preston's seasoning vessel'.

JOHN PRESTON (1587–1628)

John Preston was born in Upper Heyford, Northamptonshire, in 1587. In 1604 he matriculated as a sizar at King's College, Cambridge, but migrated to Queens' in 1606. At some point he became enamoured with Aristotle, his 'tutelary saint'.[1] He received the BA in 1607 and was chosen Fellow in 1609. In 1610 he was made prebendary of Lincoln Cathedral.

In 1611 Preston heard a sermon by John Cotton which challenged Preston's 'low opinion of the ministry & preaching' and which resulted in his conversion.[2] In 1620 he took the BD, and became dean and catechist of Queens'. Preston is the first in the experimental predestinarian tradition to gain royal favour; his close relationship with the Duke of Buckingham appears to have been responsible for his becoming Chaplain-in-ordinary to Prince Charles.[3] In 1624 he was awarded the DD by royal mandate. In 1622 Preston had been assigned to two posts. On 21 May he became the preacher at Lincoln's Inn, London, a congregation with a strong representation of Parliament men.[4] On 2 October he became Laurence Chaderton's successor as Master of Emmanuel College.[5] In 1624 he was made lecturer at Trinity Church, Cambridge, the pulpit made popular a few years before by Richard Sibbes. Thus, 'flying from pulpit to pulpit in London and Cambridge and taking his due turns preaching at court, Preston burned out the last two or

'effects' of sanctification prove our life in Christ (1 John 5: 12). These effects prove there is life: 'For we may as well argue from having of life that we have the Son, as from the having of the Son that we have life; they are reciprocall.' *1 John*, 396.

[1] Thomas Ball, *The Life of the Renowned Doctor Preston* (1885). 9. Preston 'continued longer in Aquinas, whose summes he would sometimes read as the Barber cut his haire, and when any fell upon the place he read, he would not lay down his booke but blow it off' (19). Ball's work first appeared in part in Samuel Clarke, *Martyrologie*.

[2] Ball, *Life*, 16.

[3] Irvonwy Morgan, *Prince Charles's Puritan Chaplain* (1957), 74ff. This is the only recent biography of Preston. It scarcely touches on his theology, nor does it list Preston's bibliography.

[4] Ibid. 111f.   [5] Ibid. 115.

three years of his life'.[1] He was buried at Fawley, Northampton-shire; 'Old Mr. Dod, the minister of that place, preached, and a world of Godly people came together, July 20. 1628'.[2]

By prior arrangement with Preston,[3] Richard Sibbes and John Davenport began publishing his London sermons,[4] while Thomas Ball and Thomas Goodwin produced those Preston preached in Cambridge.[5] Not a few volumes, however, emerged under Preston's name without an endorsement of these men,[6] to their dismay,[7] and an edition of Preston's abridged works appeared later.[8] Within ten years of his death, at least twenty-five separate volumes (over 100 sermons) were published under his name.

If Cotton influenced Preston, Grosart's comment should be added, that Preston and Sibbes loved each other 'with a love that was something wonderful'.[9] When Sibbes and Davenport call the *Breast-Plate* 'the summe' of Preston's labours,[10] they reveal perhaps as much about their own theological affinities as Preston's; but there is no doubt that Preston's works as a whole show him clearly to have embraced the thinking of that already seen in the more fully developed experimental predestinarian tradition.[11]

---

[1] Haller, *Rise of Puritanism*, 74.   [2] Ball, *Life*, 175.

[3] Sibbes and Davenport, preface, *The Saints Qvalification*, state that they were to publish the London sermons, and 'those friends of the Authors that resided in Cambridge' were designated by Preston to publish the sermons he preached there.

[4] These are: (1) *The Nevv Covenant, or The Saints Portion* (nine editions from 1630 to 1639), hereinafter called *New Covenant* (1630). (2) *The Saints Daily Exercise* (twelve editions from 1629 to 1636). (3) *The Breast-Plate of Faith and Love* (nine editions from 1630 to 1651; in three parts, each with new pagination), hereinafter called *Breast-Plate* (1630). (4) *The Saints Qvalification* (four editions between 1633 and 1637), hereinafter called *Qvalification* (1633). (5) *The New Creatvre: or a Treatise of Sanctification* (1633), hereinafter called *New Creature*. (6) *The Cvppe of Blessing* (1633).

[5] These are: (1) *Sermons preached before his Maiestie* (five editions from 1630 to 1637). (2) *The Golden Scepter held forth to the Humble* (two editions, both in 1638), hereinafter called *Golden Scepter*. (3) *The Churches Marriage* (1638). (4) *The Churches Carriage* (1638?). (5) *The Doctrine of the Saints Infirmities* (four editions from c.1630 to 1638), hereinafter called *Infirmities* (1638). (6) *Life Eternall, or A Treatise of the knowledge of the Divine Essence and Attributes* (five editions by 1634).

[6] It does not seem useful to list all of these (totalling no less than thirteen separate sets, although smaller than those cited above), with these exceptions: *Remaines of that Reverend and Learned Divine, John Preston* (1637), hereinafter called *Remaines*; *The Law ovt Lavved* (1633); and *The Deformed Forme of a Formall Profession* (1632).

[7] Preface, *Qvalification*. However, no theological variance appears in these un-authorized editions.

[8] *An Abridgement of Dr Preston's Works* (1648).

[9] Grosart, 'Memoir of Richard Sibbes', l.   [10] Preface, *Breast-Plate*.

[11] Preston has a sermon entitled 'Exact Walking'. Sibbes says that assurance is the

Moreover, Preston's use of the covenant of works and covenant of grace is more prominent than in any divine examined above. In addition, his interpretation of this motif discloses a subtle embellishment when compared to Perkins's treatment of it. Preston says:

> You must know that there is a double Covenant, there is a Covenant of Works, and a Covenant of Grace: The Covenant of Workes runs in these terms, Doe this, and thou shalt live, and I will bee thy God. This is the Covenant that was made with Adam, and the Covenant that is expressed by Moses in the Morall Law . . . the Covenant of Grace . . . runs in these termes, Thou shalt beleeve . . . and thou shalt likewise receive the gift of righteousnesse . . . and thou shalt grow up in love, and obedience towards mee, then I will be thy God, and thou shalt be my people.[1]

While Perkins says that in the covenant of grace 'we do not so much offer, or promise any great matter to God, as in a manner only receive',[2] Preston makes the condition of faith considerably more than mere receiving. Preston assumes (1) that the covenant of grace is designed primarily to invoke our love and obedience and (2) that God will be ours *when* that obedience is manifested.

In Preston's thought federal theology has made full circle, now becoming in effect a covenant of works after all. Indeed, although he says that the covenant of grace shows us that Christ's righteousness has satisfied the Law, Preston's main point is that the covenant of grace brings about a change and alteration in man's 'disposition'. The heart is softened, and man will come and serve the Lord 'with alacrity and cheerfulnesse'.[3] This cheerfulness is with particular reference to the Law of God, for man now 'lookes upon all the Law of God, as a wholsome and profitable rule of direction'.[4] The covenant of grace, however, is 'not of the letter, but of the Spirit' and is 'done by vertue of the Spirit'.[5] But while it is the Spirit who changes our disposition, Preston none the less has made the covenant of grace in effect a covenant of works because he requires that such a change consciously take place before one can have the assuring benefit of it.

The upshot is that we must concentrate on our attitude towards the Law rather than our receiving the righteousness of Christ. Preston urges that we must 'labour' to 'grow to assurance of the

reward for 'exact walking' (*supra*, p. 109 n. 1). Preston takes the same line in this sermon. *Sermons preached before his Maiestie* (1630), 73 ff. Cf. Preston's sermon, 'The New Life', ibid. 27 ff., based on 1 John 5: 12, as seen in Cotton. *Supra*, p. 116 n. 6.

[1] *New Covenant*, 317–18.   [2] *Supra*, p. 58 n. 10.   [3] *New Covenant*, 321.
[4] Ibid. 322.   [5] Ibid. 325.

forgiveness of our sinnes'.[1] This assurance is in the end derived entirely from the reflective knowledge of our 'sincerity' to keep the Law; God is 'willing to accept the sincerity of his obedience, though there be not a perfection of obedience'.[2] Indeed, the promise to Abraham, Preston claims, was not grounded in the 'particular act' of faith, 'but that habit, that grace of faith, that beleeving disposition'.[3]

Preston seems to realize, however, that his theology could encourage men to look directly toward the Law. He urges that 'the way is not to consider presently the Commandement, for a man to thinke with himself, this I ought to doe'.[4] Instead we must 'labour to grow in faith, in the beliefe of those promises of the Gospell'.[5] But this valiant attempt to get men to focus on the Gospel directly is soon transcended by his assertion that the condition of the covenant of grace is repentance: 'The Condition that is required of us, as part of the Covenant, is the doing of this, the action, the performance of these things, it is to repent, to serve the Lord in newnesse of life.'[6] While Preston hastens to mention that the ability to manifest this newness of life is within the context of God's initiative,[7] he says none the less: 'But the doing of this, the bringing forth the fruite of these inward abilities, of these inward habits and graces, that are planted in us by the power of Christ, that thing is required in us.'[8]

This circular reasoning is seen again when Preston comes to the matter of assurance of being in the covenant of grace. His answer to his raised question, 'How a man should know whether he be within the Covenant, or no?', is simply, 'to take Jesus Christ' as 'Lord and Saviour'.[9] But Preston does not leave it at that; he asks: 'But how shall a man know whether this faith be right or no?' He replies by disclosing how true faith passes the pragmatic test: 'if it be a right faith, it will worke, there will be life and motion in it.'[10] 'Thou maist know' that 'thou art within the Covenant' like Abraham 'because thy faith workes'.[11]

But there is still 'another way to know' one is in the covenant of grace: 'If thou have received the Spirit.' Again, circular reasoning emerges; Preston tells how 'to know whether you have the Spirit'.[12] It is at this point he develops the familiar Spirit of bondage *vis-à-vis* the Spirit of adoption. The former he calls the 'Antecedent' which

---

[1] *New Covenant*, 333.   [2] Ibid. 345.   [3] Ibid. 358.
[4] Ibid. 333.   [5] Ibid. 350.   [6] Ibid. 389.
[7] Ibid.   [8] Ibid. 390.   [9] Ibid.
[10] Ibid.   [11] Ibid. 392.   [12] Ibid. 393.

'of necessity must goe before' the Spirit of adoption. For 'no man can come to Christ, except the Law be a S[c]hoolemaster to bring him to Christ'.[1] Thus Preston not only stresses the role of the Law in preparation but states that, when the Spirit of bondage is joined with the Law, 'that makes it effectuall'.[2] Preston in this way fills out Cotton by implying that the Spirit of bondage cannot be aborted, a point Cotton does not make clear. Preston says the Spirit of bondage makes the Law effectual by melting the heart.[3] But elsewhere he states that it is not the Law but 'the Gospell that softneth the heart first'.[4] But in the latter place Preston is no less adamant that for 'a perfect worke of the Gospell the knowlege of the Law must precede'.[5]

The fact is that Preston's doctrine of faith is so intertwined with the Law that it is impossible to tell whether he thinks the Spirit of bondage is actually what softens the heart or if it is the Gospel that does it. He is consistent, however, in stressing that 'without Humiliation no man shall obtaine mercy',[6] and states that humiliation is 'passive, and active'.[7] This seems to be another way of stating Perkins's doctrine of two works of grace. The former makes the way for the second, while 'no promise is made' to the former, which he calls 'this passive Legal Humiliation'.[8] Preston further states that the Spirit of bondage is the same as 'active' humiliation,[9] which he also calls 'a fruit of Sanctification'.[10] And it is the 'active' humiliation 'unto which the promise is made'.[11]

It will be recalled, moreover, that a doctrine of temporary faith is latent in Cotton's use of the Spirit of bondage but that he does not deduce such from this frame of reference. Preston is clearer on this point, for he says that the Spirit of bondage is effectual since it is 'active' humiliation—a fruit of sanctification—to which the promise is made. Moreover, Preston tacitly leaves the door ajar concerning a doctrine of temporary faith. He claims that 'passive' humiliation 'may bee found in an unregenerate man'. Such a man has 'a sensible-nesse of sinne' and is 'fearefull of his estate'.[12] This passive humiliation, then, is short of 'active' humiliation, or sanctification.[13] Preston is somewhat reminiscent of Perkins when he says a 'Temporary

---

[1] Ibid. 394.   [2] Ibid. 395.   [3] Ibid.
[4] *Golden Scepter*, 254.   [5] Ibid.
[6] Ibid. 66. That humiliation must go before justification is 'a rule in Divinitie'. *Qvalification*, 6.
[7] *Golden Scepter*, 77.   [8] Ibid. 77-8.   [9] Ibid. 80.
[10] Ibid. 78.   [11] Ibid.   [12] Ibid. 78.
[13] *New Creature*, 47.

Beleever' may go 'thus far'; but unlike Perkins, Preston reserves sanctification for the regenerate. He wants to show 'how farre' the unregenerate 'fall short of them that be truely sanctified'.[1] While Perkins shows how far the reprobate may go but not how far they fall short, Preston shows how far the unregenerate may go, 'and yet how farre they fall short'.[2]

The difference between the temporary believer and the regenerate is summed up by Preston:

This rule will not faile, they [the unregenerate] are not generall in their obedience, there is not a generall change: Now the effect cannot goe beyond the cause, but it is true of the regenerate. They are New Creatures every way, and therefore there is a generall observation of the Law of God . . . I say, they have a respect to all the Commandements.[3]

Moreover, these unregenerate men have light 'shut up within the compasse of one faculty' only[4]—the mind, which is capable of a 'generall faith', which is 'an act of the understanding, assenting to something'.[5] For while a 'generall' faith is in the understanding only, saving faith must affect the will: 'there is an act also of the will required, which is to take and receive Christ: for this taking is an act of the will'. There must be 'a consent as well as an assent'.[6]

It may now more clearly be observed why Preston says the covenant of grace is designed to change our disposition; when our disposition is changed, 'then' God will be our God. But Preston has in effect made the covenant of grace a covenant of works since grace is not promised without 'active' humiliation on our part, namely, sanctification. It is not surprising, moreover, that Preston uses Cotton's term: 'you must labour to make your hearts fit to be humble',[7] even urging that we must 'labour to get some sense of holinesse'.[8] Since 'there is a time when God offers grace to a man' so that 'to refuse it' means 'eternall' misery, we must hasten to make our election sure by 'growing rich in good workes'.[9] If the heart is 'changed and sanctified', that is enough; 'then conclude, thou art in Christ'.[10] Inasmuch as holiness is an effect of election, we should 'set sanctification as high in our esteeme as Justification'.[11]

Preston recognizes 'infirmities' in Christians, which arise 'by reason of some impediment'.[12] Thus no Christian is perfect in holi-

---

[1] *New Creature*, 153f.   [2] Ibid. 163.   [3] Ibid. 159.
[4] Ibid.   [5] *Breast-Plate*, i. 47.   [6] Ibid.
[7] *Remaines*, 210.   [8] Ibid. 216.   [9] *New Covenant*, 603–4.
[10] *New Creature*, 58.   [11] Ibid. 36.   [12] *Infirmities*, 33.

ness. In the absence of this perfection Preston stresses 'sincerity'[1] and the 'desire' for holiness. Indeed, 'inwardly to desire holinesse for itselfe is an infallible sign' of true repentance—[2]which, as will be recalled, is the condition of the covenant of grace. But the 'lesse sincerity, and the lesse mourning for sin, and the lesse Humiliation, the lesse assurance'. Thus 'the more thou canst' be 'humbled', the more 'thou addest to thy assurance'.[3] This assertion is another indication that being prepared is simultaneously being assured.

Assurance itself Preston thinks to be the second of 'two acts of faith': (1) the 'direct act'—taking Christ—and (2) the 'reflect act' by which 'we know we have taken Christ'.[4] These two acts are 'very different' from each other; we can have the direct act of faith without the reflect act—the 'act of assurance'. The direct act moreover 'admits of no degrees' but there are degrees of the second act, which 'is grounded upon our owne experience'.[5]

Assurance is therefore increased in proportion to our sincerity, humility, and sanctification. In addition, one may check his spiritual pulse by how much he detests sin. If one wishes to know 'if hee be in the state of grace or no, if he lyes in the least knowne sinne that is, he is but counterfeit'.[6] Preston differentiates the real from the counterfeit in terms of having the 'power' of godliness over against a 'forme' of godliness. 'Those therefore that are able to stand against some lusts' but 'not against all', Preston declares, 'have not this power in them'.[7] Therefore 'if thou wouldest know whether thou have faith or no, looke backe, reflect upon thine owne heart, consider what actions have passed thorow there'.[8]

The experimental predestinarian tradition has reached in John Preston a stage that makes the doctrine of predestination itself virtually pointless; it has become a mere theory.[9] The decrees of predestination undoubtedly lay behind the motivation for being in the covenant, but the practical effect in the *ordo salutis* is one which seems divorced from the doctrine of election and effectual calling.

[1] *Qvalification*, 159. Cf. *New Covenant*, 1.
[2] *Remaines*, 25.
[3] *Qvalification*, 31.
[4] *Breast-Plate*, i. 63.
[5] Ibid. 63–4.
[6] *The Law ovt Lavved*, unpaginated.
[7] *The Deformed Forme*, 18.
[8] *Breast-Plate*, ii. 91.
[9] Preston's doctrine of predestination makes no contribution to this study. Cf. *Remaines*, 170; *New Covenant*, 507; *New Creature*, 150.

While Perkins makes sanctification the alternative ground of assurance if full assurance is lacking, Preston shows how far this option can be carried, especially when sanctification, or repentance, or a godly disposition is regarded as that to which the promise of grace is made. The result is that preparation for faith becomes *repentance*, which, in turn, assures. The consequence is an interest in godliness more than God.[1]

[1] I am indebted to Dr J. I. Packer for this expression.

9

THOMAS HOOKER

(1586-1647)

IN the theology of Thomas Hooker there is to be found a fully developed teaching of preparation for faith prior to regeneration. While many of the writers examined above espouse a strong doctrine of preparation for faith but generally manage to say that such preparation is in the context of the whole process of regeneration, Hooker clearly teaches that preparation may be prior to regeneration in the *ordo salutis*, and, in some sense, is in man's hands. This is most easily illustrated by the title of Hooker's treatise *The Vnbeleevers Preparing for Christ*. Miller calls Hooker 'the most exquisite diagnostician of the phases of regeneration, and above all the most explicit exponent of the doctrine of preparation'.[1] Pettit rightly notes that Hooker 'applied himself to the needs of the unregenerate with extraordinary vigor';[2] but whether Hooker 'developed a doctrine of assurance' that represents 'a considerable departure from what had come before'[3] is to be questioned. For Hooker's appeal to the practical syllogism to prove saving faith is merely a continuation of experimental predestinarian thinking.

Giles Firman (d. 1692) relates an interesting incident:

When Mr. Hooker preached those Sermons about the Souls preparation for Christ, and Humiliation, my Father-in-law, Mr. Nath. Ward, told him; Mr. Hooker, you make as good Christians before men are in Christ, as ever they are after; and wished, would I were but as good a Christian now, as you make men while they are but preparing for Christ.[4]

Thomas Hooker was born at Markfield in Tilton, Leicestershire. In 1604 he matriculated at Queens' College, Cambridge, but transferred to Chaderton's Emmanuel College. He received the BA in 1608, the MA in 1611, and was a Fellow from 1609 to 1618. In 1618 he was made rector of St. George's in Esher, Surrey.

[1] Perry Miller, '"Preparation for Salvation" in Seventeenth-Century New England', *Journal of the History of Ideas* (1943), 253.
[2] Pettit, *The Heart Prepared*, 101.
[3] Norman Pettit, 'Hooker's Doctrine of Assurance: A Critical Phase in New England Spiritual Thought', *New England Quarterly* (1974), 519.
[4] Giles Firman, *The Real Christian* (1670), 19.

There were two events in Hooker's life that seem to have affected him profoundly, laying the foundations for his well-known 'preparationist' ministry. The first was the nature of his own conversion. Rather than experiencing a sudden and unexpected conversion, Hooker underwent a long, agonizing process, crying out, 'While I suffer thy terrors, O Lord, I am distracted!'[1] The man who reportedly was of 'singular help' was the future Westminster divine Simeon Ashe (d. 1662), then a sizar at Emmanuel. After his conversion, Hooker had an inclination to pursue 'the application of redemption' in 'experimental divinity'.[2]

The second event deeply to affect Hooker was the role he played in the extraordinary conversion of Mrs Joan Drake (d. 1625), wife of Francis Drake. This story itself is illustrative of the very dilemma this study seeks to investigate.[3] In addition to having a series of maladies including 'migraine, perpetual heartburn, and insomnia', Mrs Drake became 'melancholy, distempered, and erratic' and confided that she was not happily married. Mr Drake was solicitous for her well-being but was unable to ameliorate her emotional state. Mrs Drake had become convinced that her maladies were owing to her having committed the unpardonable sin and that she was among the number of the reprobate, incapable of changing her appointed state.[4]

Over the next few years (*c*.1620-5) several eminent divines were called in to help Mrs Drake. The first was John Dod, 'the fittest man known' to help her.[5] When Dod arrived 'she suddenly flung upstairs' and 'shut her selfe in'. She came out only after Mr Drake threatened 'to beat down the door'.[6] But Dod's prayers and counsel—which lasted a month—did not avail. He returned several times in the ensuing months, but Mrs Drake remained convinced 'shee was a damned Reprobate, must needs goe unto Hell to live for ever', that it was 'in vaine, and too late for her to use any meanes'.[7]

---

[1] Mather, *Magnalia*, i. 333.

[2] George H. Williams, 'The Life of Thomas Hooker in England and Holland, 1586-1633', *Thomas Hooker* (Cambridge, Mass., 1975), 3.

[3] See George H. Williams, 'Called by Thy Name, Leave us Not: The Case of Mrs. Joan Drake', *Harvard Library Bulletin* (1968), 111-28; 278-300. The original account of Mrs Drake's conversion is found in the anonymous *Trodden Down Strength, by the God of Strength, or, Mrs. Drake Revived* (1647). This was republished as *The Firebrand taken out of the Fire*. Williams suggests that Hooker, who had married Mrs Drake's woman-in-waiting, promoted the publication of the 1647 treatise. Op. cit. 114.

[4] Williams, 'Called by Thy Name', 117.   [5] *Trodden Down Strength*, 18 f.

[6] Ibid. 19 f.   [7] Ibid. 23.

She wished Mr Dod 'to let her alone', for 'the Decree of her rejection and damnation' was 'past irrevocable';[1] moreover, Dod, who tried to show her that her case did not fit Hebrews 6: 4-6, was but 'an unwelcome Intruder'.[2] In the months that followed the future Archbishop of Armagh, James Ussher, John Forbes (d. 1634), a certain Dr Gibson, John Rogers of Dedham (d. 1636), a Mr (Ezekiel?) Culverwell, and Robert Bruce (d. 1631) at one time or other tried in vain to cure Mrs Drake.[3]

John Dod recommended Thomas Hooker, 'being newly come from the University' and who had 'a new answering methode'.[4] Hooker seems to have held his post in Esher but moved into the Drake manor house to be near Mrs Drake.[5] He 'was very assiduously industrious in watching her disposition, and various inclinations of her changes and tentations'.[6] She gradually improved. She became willing to 'the use of meanes: having prayer, catechizing, expounding and reading of the word, and singing of Psalms'.[7] She even 'much rejoyced to see' old Mr Dod.[8] Dod visited her some ten days before her death, and while he prayed with her, she exclaimed: 'I am assured the like was never heard or read before: which uncouth language (in shew a rapture of another world) a few words whereof the Relator can shew or expresse'.[9] During the last ten days of her life Hooker, Dod, and John Preston were often with her. John Preston preached the funeral sermon after her death on 18 April 1625.[10]

In the meantime Hooker had married Mrs Drake's woman-in-waiting. In late 1625 he became lecturer at St. Mary's in Chelmsford, and it was mainly at Chelmsford that Hooker's published sermons on preparation for faith were preached. With the exception of the immensely popular *Poor Doubting Christian Drawne vnto Christ* (1629)[11] and *The Sovles Preparation for Christ* (1632),[12] Hooker's sermons were published after he left for America on the *Griffin* in 1633.[13]

---

[1] Ibid. 24.　　　　　　　　　　　[2] Ibid. 32.
[3] Ibid. 68–108.　　　　　　　　　[4] Ibid. 120.
[5] Williams, 'Called by Thy Name', 124.　[6] *Trodden Down Strength*, 126f.
[7] Ibid. 127.　　　　　　　　　　　[8] Ibid. 128.
[9] Ibid. 139.　　　　　　[10] Williams, 'Life of Thomas Hooker', 5.
[11] Originally included in a collection of Sibbes's sermons, *The saints cordials* (1629), this sermon went into no less than sixteen editions by 1700, and several more by 1904. This study will draw from its reprint (carefully reconstructed from various editions) in *Thomas Hooker*, 152–86.　　　　　　　　[12] See *infra*, n. 13.
[13] It is crucial to grasp that Hooker's sermons on preparation are carefully woven into a cycle—'a long series of sermons known to have been repeated at least three

Williams judges that Mrs Drake's 'protracted conversion' remained for Hooker 'the underlying model for his theology of preparation for grace within the structures of predestinarian Puritanism'.[1] In *Poor Doubting Christian* one may overhear 'many of the arguments which he must have first presented to poor doubting Joan Drake in Esher'. One can almost hear 'her recurrent argument repeated by him and placed in the mouth of some generalized doubting Christian: "I am not elected, and God will not do me good, seeing I am not elected, and therefore it is vain for me to use means"'.[2] It is safe to say that the whole of Hooker's soteriological preaching may be summed up in one word: preparationism.

There is yet one more influence to be taken into account, namely

times in his life as a minister'. Sargent Bush, Jr., 'Establishing the Hooker Canon', *Thomas Hooker*, 379. The chronological order of composition (not necessarily coinciding with dates of publication) can be generally determined, not only by a familiarity with Hooker's thought as a whole but also by noting his occasional manner of referring to what sermon or subject immediately preceded and (sometimes) what sermon will follow. The order below, moreover, is not merely what seems to be the chronological order of composition but also Hooker's very *ordo salutis*—from the role imputed to unbelievers to contrition, humiliation, ingrafting, effectual calling, possession of Christ and being exalted with Him. Hooker follows a doctrinal plan and it is equally important to note that he preaches to his hearers as though they themselves are no further along (or behind) spiritually than the immediate subject (e.g. 'contrition') he is discussing. He therefore does not return to the original phase (the unbeliever's preparation) once he has moved on, and so does not seem to take into account that new people could begin hearing him and would not necessarily be aware of his original premiss. This point must not be forgotten, since it is only in the first work below that Hooker explicitly imputes an enormous responsibility to the natural man before regeneration. The apparent order is: (1) *The Vnbeleevers Preparing for Christ* (1638). (2) *The Sovles Preparation for Christ. Or, A Treatise of Contrition* (ten editions from 1632 to 1658), hereinafter called *Sovles Preparation* (1632). (3) *The Sovles Hvmiliation* (four editions from 1637 to 1640), hereinafter called *Hvmiliation*. (4) There is a corpus of editions that point to the same phase, following 'humiliation' but preceding 'effectual calling': *The Sovles Ingrafting into Christ* (1637); *The Soules Implantation* (1637), hereinafter called *Implantation*; and *The Soules Implantation into the Natural Olive* (1640). (5) *The Sovles Vocation or Effectval Calling to Christ* (1637, 1638), hereinafter called *Effectval Calling* (1638). (6) *The Sovles Possession of Christ* (1638), hereinafter called *Possession*. (7) *The Sovles Exaltation* (1638), hereinafter called *Exaltation*. This cycle is supplemented by the following, all preached in England and dealing with preparation: *Fovre Learned and Godly Treatises* (1638), hereinafter called *Fovre Learned*; *The Saints Guide* (1645); *The Christians Tvvo Chiefe Lessons* (1640), hereinafter called *Chiefe Lessons*; *The Covenant of Grace Opened* (1649); *The Faithful Covenanter* (1644); *The Pattern of Perfection* (1640); *The Sinners Salvation* (1638); *Spirituall Thirst* (1638); *The Stay of the Faithfull* (1638); and *The Properties of An honest Heart* (1638).

[1] Williams, 'Life of Thomas Hooker', 5. Cf. Williams, 'Called by Thy Name', 290 ff. Mather, op. cit. i. 334, also suggests this.

[2] Williams, 'Life of Thomas Hooker', 16. Cf. *Poor Doubting Christian*, 165.

that of his friend John Rogers of Dedham. Hooker's first published writing was his Epistle to the Reader in the second edition (1627) of Rogers's *The Doctrine of Faith*.[1] Hooker praises the way in which Rogers makes 'a saving contrition to go before faith'.[2] Another point Hooker emphasizes—one to be repeated often in his own treatises—is that vocation (effectual calling) is 'a saving work' but not 'a sanctifying work'.

Therefore every saving work is not a sanctifying work. Though therefore we must have faith before we can be in Christ, and the soul must be contrite before it can have faith, this saving work may be and yet this no work of sanctification.[3]

Hooker's discussion, as seen often above, is another way of stating Perkins's two works of grace. There is a 'sorrow of preparation', the other a 'sorrow of sanctification, and yet both [are] saving'. Moreover, a hatred and detestation of sin in a contrite person 'cannot be in a reprobate'. The difference between the sorrow of preparation and the sorrow of sanctification is that the former is wrought 'upon' us, the latter 'by us through the Spirit given to us and dwelling in us when we have received Christ'.[4]

As to the 'coming in of faith' itself, Hooker suggests the reader turn to page 175 in Rogers's treatise, which reads:

It is hard to say at what instant Faith is wrought, whether not till a man apprehends Christ and the promise, or even in his earnest desires, hungring and thirsting, for even these are pronounced blessed. Some having got hold, hold it faster than some by much, yet none but with doubtings sometimes; yet some are much privileged this way, especially that came hardliest by it.[5]

Hooker may have been especially impressed by Rogers's point that some are 'much privileged' who 'came hardliest by it', for in *The Sinners Salvation* Hooker says that 'faith is a hard thing to attaine;[6] indeed, 'to beleeve is the hardest thing that a man is put to doe under heaven'.[7] It is 'an easie matter to give the literal answer' to the question, 'What must I do to be saved?', namely, to believe on Christ; but to bring the soul to salvation indeed is 'very hard'.[8] It is like saying, 'How should I get up into the aire like a bird?'[9] For this

---

[1] Williams, 'Life of Thomas Hooker', 6. This treatise went into eight editions by 1640. Hooker's preface is in *Thomas Hooker*, 140–6, and will be used below. The study will also draw from Rogers's *The Doctrine of Faith* (1633). Rogers was vicar of Dedham, Essex, from 1605 to 1635.

[2] *Thomas Hooker*, 144.   [3] Ibid. 145.   [4] Ibid.
[5] John Rogers, *The Doctrine of Faith*, 175.   [6] *The Sinners Salvation*, 57.
[7] Ibid. 59.   [8] Ibid. 13.   [9] Ibid. 14.

reason Hooker thinks 'faith cannot be sudden'[1] because 'Christ will not enter by violence, where-ever hee dwells'.[2] However, Hooker does note that God 'may doe as he please' in saving men, but the long process 'is the course of God generally'.[3]

It is noteworthy that in Rogers's treatise the thorny problem of temporary faith is dealt with at the beginning. As though paying tribute to that in Perkins he accepts and that which needs correcting, Rogers says:

True Faith goeth further then this [which Perkins says but fails to clarify], for the beleever particularly applieth Christ to himselfe [Perkins's main point in his definition of faith] truly, and so lives by Him a true sanctified life, which this Temporary Faith fals short of [but which differs from Perkins's depictions of temporary faith].[4]

Hooker's doctrine of temporary faith is essentially like that of Rogers. Moreover, considering the quantity of Hooker's treatises (over 4,000 pages), his treatment of temporary faith is minimal— some forty pages. In treating this subject he points out the critical difference to be found in saving faith, the sign being a hatred of sin. True faith is to be contrasted with that in (1) the 'Civill man', (2) the 'Formalist', and (3) the 'Temporary Professour'.[5] Civil righteousness is 'the practice of some outward duties of the second Table, joyned with either a slight performance, or else negligent omission of the duties of the first Table',[6] by which he means the first five of the Ten Commandments. The 'grounds of civill righteousnesse' are (1) restraining grace—'a common worke of the spirit, whereby the corruption of mans nature is bridled'; and (2) 'Prevailing corruption', when one sin 'getteth the victory of another by reason of their opposite nature'.[7] In any case, 'the heart is not changed, or renewed, either in minde, will or affections'.[8]

'Formall righteousnesse' Hooker calls 'the practice of the outward duties of the first Table, joyned with a neglect of the duties of the second Table, and that by giving way to some grosse corruption'—for example, stealing, murder, adultery.[9] Judas, as well as Ananias and Sapphira (Acts 5: 1–11), is in this category.[10]

'Temporary Righteousnesse' is a common work of the Spirit 'whereby a man being enlightned to see the privileges that are in

---

[1] *The Sinners Salvation*, 70.   [2] Ibid. 48.
[3] Ibid. 71.   [4] Rogers, *The Doctrine of Faith*, 10.
[5] *Chiefe Lessons*, 213.   [6] Ibid.
[7] Ibid. 214. Cf. *Sovles Preparation*, 142.   [8] *Chiefe Lessons*, 214.
[9] Ibid. 224.   [10] Ibid. 231.

Christ for a time rejoyceth in them, yeeldeth some obedience to them; yet afterward he utterly falls away'.[1] Such a righteousness is compared to 'the morning dew, that vanisheth away with the Sunne'.[2]

The fact is that Hooker does not deeply concern himself with the matter of temporary faith.[3] Like Sibbes, he apparently prefers to ignore it. The whole of Hooker's theology may be summed up in these words:

Before the soule of a man can partake of the benefits of Christ, two things are required: First, that the soule bee prepared for Christ. Secondly, that the soule bee implanted into Christ.[4]

This preparation is 'the fitting of a sinner for his being in Christ'.[5] The theology of Hooker and that of the 'early' Cotton is closely akin.

You must come to this truth: for there is no justification nor acceptation within this; nay, there is no faith can be infused into the soule, before the heart bee thus fitted and prepared: no preparation, no perfection. Never humbled, never exalted.[6]

Moreover, this work of preparation is not to be confused with regeneration: 'the heart in this worke [of preparation] is not yet conceived to be in Christ, but only to be fitted and prepared for Christ'.[7]

The most significant development in Hooker's theology, however, is the power and freedom he imputes to the natural man. Hooker has carefully worked out a rationale which lies behind his remarkable assertions concerning this. While this scheme is also similar to Cotton's,[8] Hooker's is more sophisticated. Hooker makes a bold exhortation to men in their natural state: 'labour to get out of this naturall corruption'. This process is to be initiated by a speedy and constant perseverance 'in the meanes' God has appointed.[9] Hooker is fully aware moreover of the far-reaching implications in what he is saying.

But you will say, a naturall man cannot receive any good, why should hee

---

[1] Ibid. 233.   [2] Ibid.

[3] Hooker raises the question whether 'sound sorrow' can be in a reprobate; the answer is no. *Sovles Preparation*, 165 ff.

[4] *Vnbeleevers Preparing*, 1.   [5] *Implantation*, 26.

[6] *Sovles Preparation*, 165. Cf. *supra*, p. 114 n. 3.

[7] *Sovles Preparation*, 165.

[8] Cf. Cotton and man's 'Natural' knowledge of God. *Supra*, p. 113 n. 7.

[9] *Vnbeleevers Preparing*, 104.

then be counselled to receive the things of God, as grace and salvation; this is a cavill of Bellarmin and thus I answer it, we have no spirituall abilities in our selves to performe any spirituall duty, but yet wee have ability to performe some morall actions.[1]

While this last phrase is not in conflict with anything Perkins, Beza, or even Calvin, would hold, Hooker very subtly takes the doctrine of common grace a step—indeed, a huge step—further. A man has 'rest[r]aining and preventing grace whereby he is able to waite upon God in the meanes, so that he may be enabled to receive grace'.[2]

What Hooker has done, then, is to impute to the natural man an ability to attend to the *means* of grace by virtue of common grace. While Hooker never says the natural man is able to procure saving grace directly, he says that man can, nevertheless, by common grace, raise himself, as it were, to the plateau of *means*. From then on it is God's work; but man initiates the process of preparation by getting himself under the means: if man will but reach for the means, he may be 'enabled' to receive grace. Therefore,

As long as the parts and members of your bodies and the faculties of your soules continue, as long as your understandings and memories indure, why cannot you bestow your bodies to come to Church as well as to goe to the Alehouse? why cannot you bestow your eyes as well in reading, as in carding and dicing? God hath given you liberty to use these meanes, that so you might receive grace . . .[3]

Furthermore, 'God doth not punish a man because he cannot get faith, but because he will not use the meanes whereby he might get faith'.[4] For 'these things you may doe and those things you have power to doe'. Therefore 'you should use the meanes which God hath ordained for the working of grace in your soules', for 'hereby you may be converted'. Thus 'you must come, that so grace may be wrought in your hearts, and that you may be converted'.[5]

Lest one think at this point that Hooker is simply saying the natural man can 'come to Church' in these lines, there are to be noted 'three things which are in the power of natural men to performe'. The first is, that 'every naturall man' should be 'throughly convinced of the misery hee is in'.[6] Hooker urges: 'suffer your selves to be throughly informed and convinced of your own miserie and weaknesse'.[7] He intreats the natural man to take the course of the

---

[1] *Vnbeleevers Preparing*, 120 (not 220, as numbered).
[2] Ibid.   [3] Ibid. 120–1.   [4] Ibid. 121.
[5] Ibid.   [6] Ibid.   [7] Ibid. 122.

Apostle, and say, 'in me dwelleth no good thing' (Romans 7: 18).[1]
The natural man, then, has the 'power' to 'suffer' himself to say:
'I confesse I am a naturall and carnall man, and therefore in my
flesh there is no good at all.'[2]

No writer examined above makes a statement like this. In Hooker
the preparationist doctrine reaches full tide in the experimental
predestinarian tradition. While Perkins's language never comes
close to that seen in Hooker, the latter none the less has not violated
Perkins's doctrine of faith. Hooker merely takes Perkins's voluntarism to its logical conclusion. On the other hand, Arminius, examined
below, does not make such comments as Hooker makes in this
connection.

But there is more; the second thing the natural man can do is to
evolve to the stage whereby he says: 'Lord, what a stout heart have
I, what a many gracious promises and godly councells have I had.'
But realizing he has not given way 'to any of them' the natural man
says, 'therefore there is no good in mee'. The third thing the natural
man can do is depicted by Hooker in the imperative: 'when you
have done this, then *convince your owne hearts* that there is an All-
sufficiencie in the promise unto your soules'.[3]

We now turn to more of the details of Hooker's intricate doctrine
of preparation. It will be recalled that Hooker differentiates between
the 'saving' work and the 'sanctifying' work, although both are
'saving'. The former is a 'sorrow of preparation' (wrought 'upon'
us), the latter a 'sorrow of sanctification' (wrought 'by' us through
the Spirit).[4] It should be kept in mind that, while the sorrow of
preparation is wrought 'upon' us (by which Hooker apparently
means it is passive), we may first raise ourselves to the use of the
means before this sorrow of preparation begins. His word is 'suffer';
we must suffer or allow God to begin the sorrow of preparation.
While this sorrow of preparation is wrought 'upon' us, we actually
may take the initiative, albeit in our natural state, that we might
'receive grace'. We can make the first move, then, and God begins to
work 'upon' us. Yet the three things that Hooker claims we have the
'power to doe'—convince ourselves of (1) our misery, (2) our
unthankfulness, and (3) that God has promised to change us—so
coincide with the very 'sorrow' he also claims is God's work 'upon'
us, that there is little descriptive difference between what is in our
hands and what is God's work. Concerning the latter, after all is

---

[1] Ibid.　　　　　　　　[2] Ibid.　　　　　　　　[3] Ibid. (my italics).
[4] *Supra*, p. 129 n. 4. Cf. *Sovles Preparation*, 146.

said and done, Hooker has his doctrine of election to fall back on; he no doubt thinks that only the elect in the end will take his advice.

At any rate Hooker divides the work of preparation into (1) contrition and (2) humiliation.[1] While preparation is said to be God's work—'He pulls a sinner from sinne to himselfe'[2]—we know already it is in our power to attend to the means in order to let God pull us from sin. Moreover, Hooker defines contrition as 'when a sinner by the sight of sinne, and vilenesse of it, and the punishment due to the same, is made sensible of sinne, and is made to hate it, and hath his heart separated from the same'.[3] Hooker does not say exactly, chronologically, when the work of *God* begins in the morphology of preparation, i.e. when our 'power to doe' becomes His work 'upon' us.

The heart of the problem in any doctrine of preparation is to distinguish when regeneration sets in. But Hooker has a more serious dilemma which he never directly faces. His 'new answering methode' must lie either in his teaching that preparation itself is 'saving', or the surprising power he imputes to the natural man. He believes preparation is saving once 'sound sorrow' emerges. For 'by sound sorrow the soule is truly prepared and fitted for the Lord Jesus Christ'.[4]

Perkins's 'beginnings of preparation' and 'beginnings of composition' are basically what Hooker means by 'sorrow of preparation' and 'sorrow of sanctification'. The first is a sensibleness of sin, the latter a hatred for sin.[5] But it is the sanctifying work which 'justifies a poore sinner',[6] thus Hooker is found in the curious position of holding that the 'saving' work is not justifying; only the 'sanctifying' work is. Preparation is saving but not justifying since preparation is prior to faith (which justifies).

Hooker's method is comforting to the soul who wants assurance as soon as possible that, however long the process, there is no danger the process can be aborted along the way. As long as one feels sorrow for sin, seeing that he is 'miserable', his sorrow is sound. The consoling thought is that contrition is guaranteed to lead to a hatred of sin which 'cannot be in a reprobate'. Hooker has nipped in the bud the nasty problem of temporary faith. Let the natural man attend to the means straight away: he has the power to discover sin, and this discovery leads to the hatred of it. Once

---

[1] *Sovles Preparation*, 1 f. Cf. *Hvmiliation*, 131. [2] *Sovles Preparation*, 1 f.
[3] Ibid. 2. [4] Ibid. 160.
[5] Ibid. 248 f. [6] Ibid. 169.

contrition has set in, faith will follow. Thus Hooker not only believes in perseverance of faith but perseverance of preparation as well; both are 'saving'.[1] Pettit misses this crucial point when he says 'there can be no certainty of success' in Hooker's preparatory process.[2] The prospect of uncertainty is linked to temporary faith, the very root of Mrs Drake's horror.

What Hooker has done, then, is to take Calvin's doctrine of perseverance and push it backwards, as it were, to the preparatory process. For Hooker the doctrine is not only once saved, always saved, but once *prepared*, always saved. Preparation is saving, even if not justifying. But since justification is inevitable, the discussion is in a sense merely semantic. For Hooker believes 'if the heart be prepared, Christ comes immediately into his temple'.[3]

The irony of Hooker's teaching is that, though the process is expected to be long and hard, there is a very real sense in which Christ's coming into His temple is but a step away. The moment one takes seriously the means and discovers sin, instantaneous assurance is theoretically to be had. One need not worry therefore where he actually is in this preparatory pilgrimage; he may know the outcome from the start, and that is good enough: his destination is faith. His immediate concern is to feel the misery of sin; then the road to faith is easy. By making preparation 'saving', there is also but a semantic difference between Perkins's weak faith (which he implies is the 'beginnings of preparation') and Hooker's 'sorrow of preparation'. Hooker calls it 'saving' but oddly avoids calling it faith. He reserves the latter for a conscious hatred of sin. But pastorally Hooker's doctrine is vastly different from Perkins's. Perkins's awful doctrine of temporary faith looms large if the 'second grace' does not follow. Hooker's solution is far better. He takes the role of the will with utmost seriousness, eliminates the threat of temporary faith at the outset, and holds that contrition cannot be in a reprobate. He is so convinced of this theology that he raises the question—which he none the less brands as 'idle'—whether the prepared man could be lost if he dies 'before he come to have faith'.

I say it is an idle question, because it is impossible that he which is thus prepared [i.e. by a 'sound sorrow'] for Christ and grace, but he shall have them before he die . . . When the heart is fitted and prepared, the Lord Jesus comes immediately into it: the temple is the soule, & the way is the preparation for Christ . . .[4]

[1] *Supra*, p. 129 n. 4.   [2] Pettit, *The Heart Prepared*, 96.
[3] *Hvmiliation*, 170.   [4] *Sovles Preparation*, 165–6.

Humiliation is a necessary part of preparation because the 'nature of faith' is that it 'goes out of it selfe, and fetcheth a Principle of life, grace, and power from another'.[1] Humiliation immediately follows 'the Soule being cut off from sin', and 'pares it, and makes it for the ingrafting into Christ'. Humiliation is

when the soule upon search made despaires of all helpe from it selfe: he doth not despaire of Gods mercie, but of all help from himselfe and submits himselfe wholy to God, the soule strikes sale and fals under the power of Jesus Christ and is content to be at His disposing.[2]

Again, this is still but a preparatory state. The sinner is 'conceived not yet to be in Christ'.[3] We know, however, it is a saving work. Indeed, the sanctifying work is now supposed to have taken place. But Hooker believes there is a gap to be dealt with which lies chronologically between the hatred of sin and the soul turning heavenward: it is humiliation, wherein one learns fully to despair of himself. One can now see why Hooker intends this preparatory process for faith to be a long one.

I speak still of one that is not yet ingrafted into Christ: rebell against his sinne he will; but kill it, and subdue it, that he cannot: and hence it is, that the Lord lets in upon the Soule a great many infirmities, and a swarme of weaknesses that are present with the Soule: and so he seeth an utter inabilitie in himselfe to help himself against him . . .[4]

Thus the Lord 'tires a poore soule with his own distempers'.[5]

Not unlike Preston, then, who makes faith a disposition of the heart, Hooker's conviction is that faith will not emerge until the soul is humiliated; humiliation is preceded by contrition; contrition is preceded by man's willingness to attend to the means of grace.[6] In any case, the 'gate', or 'entrance of life, is Humiliation of heart'.[7] Hooker concludes: 'Now, if the heart bee once prepared and humbled, looke then immediately for Christ.'[8]

The next stage in Hooker's *ordo salutis* is 'the ingrafting into the Lord Jesus, the heart being thus prepared, it is implanted into the true vine, the Lord Christ'. This implanting is 'the worke of the Spirit, whereby the humbled sinner stands possessed of Christ, and

---

[1] *Hvmiliation*, 7, 130.   [2] Ibid.   [3] Ibid. 11.
[4] Ibid. 14.   [5] Ibid. 52.
[6] Hooker's doctrine of the covenant is an assumption in the whole of his doctrine of faith. His treatment of it, however, adds no contribution to this study. Cf. ibid. 128 ff.; *The Patterne of Perfection*, 208 ff.; *Effectval Calling*, 40 ff.; *The Faithful Covenanter*, 11 ff.
[7] *Hvmiliation*, 210.   [8] Ibid. 213.

is made partaker of the Spirituall good things in Him'.[1] There is, however, a chronological gap between humiliation and implantation: effectual calling. This Hooker calls *closing* with Christ.[2] It is the act of faith itself. In the meantime, 'Christ cannot bee hindred from coming into a Soule truly humbled, hee commeth speedily'.[3] Indeed, when 'all hinderances are taken out of the way that should stop Him', He 'must of necessity come'. After all, Hooker reasons, 'it must either lie on His part or on our part'; and if we have done our part 'there is nothing can hinder the Lord from comming'. If He does not come, 'it is either because wee love our selves, or cleave to our sinnes'.[4] But these impediments having been extinguished, Hooker lays down this imperative: 'immediately expect our Saviour, for Hee will come'.[5]

It is obvious that the doctrine of assurance emerges at this juncture. Hooker insists that if there is no wilful sin 'then Christ is come' already.[6] But lack of assurance, or feeling, does not mean He has not come. Hooker anticipates that the knowledge that He has come will not be accompanied by assurance: 'Christ is come, but thou perceivest it not', he predicts. But there is an explanation for this too: 'When Jacob awaked out of his sleepe, Surely (said hee) the Lord is in this place, and I perceived it not: And so the Lord is in thy soule, and thou perceivest it not: And so the Lord is in thy soule, and thou perceivest Him not.'[7] Our problem then, Hooker says is that 'wee judge Him by sense, and some extraordinary sweetnesse'.[8] We should simply understand that when the soul is truly humbled, 'Hee takes possession of it as His owne'.[9] We must look to the 'promise'[10] that tells us Christ has come, and not look for 'revelations and dreames'.[11] Hooker's doctrine at this point concurs with that of Baynes; we simply know whether or not we have repented. It is not surprising then that, after the laborious process of preparation, Hooker in the end appeals to 'a reflecting act, when a man lookes over his understanding, and labours to discerne the worke thereof'. We know that we know Him, 'if wee keepe his Commandements'.[12]

---

[1] *Ingrafting*, 3. The expression 'possessed of Christ' is also expounded in the treatise *Possession*. As contrition and humiliation are tied together—the former leads to the latter—so are the concepts of 'implanting' and 'possession'. On the heels of this, moreover, is 'exaltation', or union with Christ, which is the theme in *Exaltation*. A further exposition of these phases, however, does not seem useful.

[2] *Effectval Calling*, 33.   [3] *Ingrafting*, 7.   [4] Ibid. 14.
[5] Ibid. 15.   [6] Ibid. 16.   [7] Ibid.
[8] Ibid. 17.   [9] Ibid. 26.   [10] *Effectval Calling*, 61 f.
[11] Ibid. 63.   [12] Ibid. 87.

It is for this reason we are given 2 Peter 1: 10.[1] Still, however, 'a mans spirituall estate is not alwaies discernible to himselfe'.[2] The only way to know our adoption is by our regeneration; the only way to know our regeneration is by 'an alteration and change' in us.[3] Hooker resorts to this circular reasoning, and, in the end, to the question whether or not we have been sufficiently prepared.

In Hooker's theology, then, there is to be seen how far voluntarism can advance without violating Perkins's structures. While Hooker's claim that his doctrine of preparation is mostly 'passive' is to be seriously questioned, he does admit that faith is completed by the act of the will. Since vocation consists in God's call and our response, Hooker says the latter is in the will. Indeed, the 'root of faith' and the 'full growth of faith' is 'in the will'.[4]

It seems then that Hooker's doctrine of faith is voluntaristic from start to finish. All his pleadings about an 'effectual' calling of God are rendered meaningless by his appeal—indeed, his urgent and impassioned counsel—directly to man's will.

Hooker says that 'to beleeve is the hardest thing that a man is put to doe under heaven'. Moreover, 'once a man beleeves, the hardest is done, the worst is past'.[5] He would have been equally true to his thought had he said once a man is prepared, the worst is past.

---

[1] *Chiefe Lessons*, 204.   [2] Ibid. 208.   [3] Ibid. 295-6.
[4] *Effectval Calling*, 284.   [5] *The Sinners Salvation*, 59.

PART FOUR

THE CONTRIBUTION OF HOLLAND

10

JACOBUS ARMINIUS

(c.1559-1609)

Truly, Perkins, you have handled these matters more negligently than
befitted the dignity of the subject and your own erudition.[1]

JACOB HAEMENSZ, better known later as Jacobus Arminius, was
born in Oudewater, Holland. In 1575 he went to Marburg where he
studied for about a year. In 1576 he enrolled as a theology student at
the University of Leiden. In 1581 he came to Geneva to study under
Theodore Beza. Arminius seems to have become enamoured with
the thought of Peter Ramus, but his enthusiasm for Ramus brought
him to clash with Beza. Arminius was forced to leave Geneva, but
returned in 1584 and 'conducted himself in a milder manner'.[2] He
eventually earned Beza's restrained commendation as having 'an
apt intellect both as respects the apprehension and discrimination of
things'.[3]

In 1587 Arminius went to Amsterdam and took a pastorate. By
1591 he seems to have been brought into theological controversy by
being asked to defend Beza's doctrine of predestination in the light
of a pamphlet circulating against it. The upshot was that Arminius
became a convert to the very opinions which he had been requested
to refute.[4] He began questioning the general belief that the man in
Romans 7: 14-21 was regenerate.[5] In 1593 he took a position on
Romans 9 that shows him moving clearly in the direction for which
he is best known. When William Perkins's 1598 treatise on predestination emerged in Holland Arminius 'bought the book eagerly,
for he was an admirer of Perkins'.[6] In about 1602 Arminius
prepared an answer to Perkins, but did not publish it when he heard
of Perkins's death the same year.[7]

In 1603 Arminius was appointed professor of theology at Leiden

---

[1] J. Arminius, 'Examination of Perkins' Pamphlet', *The Works of Arminius* (3
vols., 1825, 1828, 1875), iii. 470.
[2] Carl Bangs, *Arminius* (Nashville, 1971), 71-3.   [3] Ibid. 74.
[4] Ibid. 138. Bangs surmises, however, that Arminius was never convinced of Beza's
position in the first place, but gives no conclusive evidence for this.   [5] Ibid. 40.
[6] Ibid. 209.   [7] Arminius's answer was published posthumously (1612).

and was made doctor of theology. He remained at Leiden to his
death in 1609, but those six years were characterized by intense
controversy, almost entirely over predestination.

The purpose of this chapter is to set Arminius's doctrine of faith
in the context of this study. While interest in Arminius's doctrine of
predestination has made it well known, less is known about his
doctrine of faith itself, especially the fact that this doctrine of faith is
remarkably like many in those who opposed him.[1] It is curious that
reformed theologians in the seventeenth century became exercised
over the abstractions of predestination, but did not see that their
doctrine of faith was hardly different from Arminius's. Indeed,
many objected to Arminius's claim that he too believed faith is the
gift of God, but refused to take him seriously since he changed the
structures of predestination. It is interesting indeed that the experimental predestinarians have not been questioned for virtually the
same kind of voluntarism that made Arminius suspect because of
his modification of predestination.[2] This chapter will argue that
Arminius's doctrine of faith is in effect no different from that in the
figures seen in the experimental predestinarian tradition.

Arminius's doctrine of predestination can be summarized briefly.
His contention, simply, is that God predestines 'believers'. His
doctrine is set forth in four decrees: (1) God appointed Jesus Christ
to be our Mediator and Redeemer; (2) God decreed 'to receive into
favour *those who repent and believe*' and 'leave in sin' all unbelievers;
(3) God decreed 'to administer *in a sufficient and efficacious manner*
all means which were necessary for repentance and faith'; and (4)
God 'decreed to save' those who 'He knew from all eternity' would
believe and persevere and to damn those 'He likewise knew' who
'*would not believe and persevere*'.[3]

Arminius is consistent in his thesis that 'election of grace is only
of believers',[4] for predestination 'is the decree of the good pleasure
of God in Christ, by which He determined within Himself from all
eternity to justify believers'.[5] If one believes, he is elected; if he does
not believe, he is not elected.[6]

---

[1] F. E. Stoeffler, *The Rise of Evangelical Pietism* (Leiden, 1971), 136, appears to be
the only scholar who has perceived a similarity. He observes that Ames's theology of
regeneration 'differed little from what the Remonstrants said, though Amesius fought
them vigorously'.

[2] *Works of Arminius*, ii. 51 f. In about 1608 Arminius was assailed by his opponents
for holding a number of heresies, one of which that he taught that faith is not God's
gift. Arminius denied this and insisted that he did indeed believe that faith is the gift
of God.   [3] Ibid. i. 589 f.   [4] Ibid. iii. 583.   [5] Ibid. ii. 392.   [6] Ibid. 67.

As to the charge that Arminius does not make faith the gift of God, he produces an illustration to show he does after all believe that faith is God's gift: 'A rich man bestows, on a poor and famishing beggar, alms by which he may be able to maintain himself and his family. Does it cease to be a pure gift, because the beggar extends his hand to receive it?'[1]

The crux of the matter, however, is that Arminius holds that grace can be resisted. For 'grace is so attempered and commingled with the nature of man, as not to destroy within him the liberty of his will'.[2] For the 'representations of grace which the Scriptures contain, are such as describe it capable of "being resisted" . . . and received in vain'. Indeed, it 'is possible for man to avoid yielding his assent to it; and to refuse all co-operation with it'. Arminius makes abundantly clear what he is rejecting: 'that grace is a certain irresistible force and operation'.[3]

The difference between Arminius and the reformed position is not to be underestimated, nor is the contrast semantic. Arminius has radically modified the reformed doctrine of predestination; on the order of the decrees the two schools are poles apart. Arminius ties election (though based on foreseen faith) to man's will to believe; the experimental predestinarians make the will to believe the proof one is elect. The similarity between the two schools of thought lies in the nature of saving faith; although not intended, the two ways of thinking overlap here. They meet each other coming from opposite directions.

The best vantage-point for observing the similarity of the two schools is by contrasting Arminius's doctrine of perseverance with the experimental predestinarians' doctrine of temporary faith. However much the latter avoided this teaching in their sermons, it was always around, and they could readily raise it when they needed it to explain an apostasy.

Arminius suggests that grace may be lost. His argument is subtle. He can affirm dogmatically that it is impossible for believers to decline from salvation. But what he means is that it is 'impossible for believers, as long as they remain *believers*, to decline from salvation'.[4] For 'if believers fall away from the faith and become unbelievers, it is impossible for them to do otherwise than decline from salvation,—that is, providing they still continue unbelievers'.[5] Whether or not a believer may in fact cease to believe Arminius

---

[1] Ibid. 52.   [2] Ibid. i. 564f.   [3] Ibid. 565.
[4] Ibid. 677f.   [5] Ibid. 678.

wants to put in suspension, and calls for 'a diligent enquiry from the Scriptures' whether some 'through negligence' desert the commencement of grace and render it ineffectual.[1] But he candidly thinks 'there are passages of Scripture which seem to me to wear this aspect'.[2]

The experimental predestinarians' ready solution to this and other similar scriptures is the temporary faith of the non-elect. Not only does a rejection of the Gospel prove one's reprobation but the falling away from the profession of faith as well. Arminius agrees; unbelievers are foreordained to condemnation by God's decree. Indeed, there is substantial agreement between the two schools that those who reject the Gospel or apostatize are reprobates. The difference is the theological rationale that lies behind those who accept and those who resist, and those who persevere and those who fall away. The experimental predestinarians explain that believers persevere because they were elected; Arminius says God elects believers whom He foresees will persevere. The experimental predestinarians draw upon their neat doctrine of temporary faith to explain apostasies.

Arminius knows this. This matter is crucial in his debate with Perkins. It will be recalled that Perkins holds to two works of grace; that the second (perseverance) authenticates the first. But the failure of the second to come forth means that the first was counterfeit (hence temporary faith). Arminius seizes upon this position of Perkins (and Beza). His arguments demonstrate that his own doctrine is effectively no different from Perkins's, and that Perkins, to be consistent, should admit this. For since Perkins holds that the 'first grace' is 'the gratuitous favour of God, embracing His own in Christ to life eternal'[3] but that the second grace must be achieved to validate the first, what happens if the first is not extended to the second? Arminius points out that this means that the believer really does 'fall from that very grace wherewith God embraces him unto life eternal'.[4] Thus Arminius demonstrates that his own position that a believer may fall is the consistent one. Indeed, if Perkins holds that the recipient of the first grace must obtain the second (perseverance) or the first is rendered invalid, there is no practical difference whatever in the two positions. If the believer does not persevere (whether Arminius or Perkins says it), such a person proves to be non-elect.

---

[1] *Works of Arminius*, i. 602.   [2] Ibid. 603.
[3] Ibid. iii. 459.   [4] Ibid. 460.

Moreover, Arminius reminds Perkins of Perkins's statement that if a believer grievously falls after receiving the first grace but does not repent, such a person will not obtain remission of sins.[1] 'Hence I conclude that they can lose that grace of the remission of sins', Arminius replies.[2] The example of David's restoration after his adultery and murder 'proves nothing', Arminius continues; there is no proof that David could not have been lost had he not repented; we simply know that David did repent.[3]

Arminius differs from the experimental predestinarians, then, on the theoretical position behind the practical events but not on the undoubted fact that men do sometimes fall. They differ merely in their explanation of that apostasy. Both parties agree that election, faith, and perseverance must be linked in the chain of salvation: the failure to persevere means a cessation of faith; the cessation of faith means reprobation. The experimental predestinarians have their doctrine of temporary faith to fall back upon. But Arminius has a doctrine of temporary faith too, equal in fact to any held in the experimental predestinarian tradition. He does not call it this, nor does he need to. He is merely arguing that Perkins should see the inconsistency of his own position. Arminius summarizes Perkins's doctrine of faith generally and then chides him:

In the beginning of faith in Christ and conversion to God the believer becomes a living member of Christ; and, if persevering in the faith of Christ, and keeping a conscience void of offence, remains a living member. But if it [should] happen that this member grows slothful, is not careful over itself, gives place to sin, by little and little it becomes half-dead; and so at length, proceeding still further, dies altogether, and ceases to be a member. These points are what should have been refuted by you; which you are so far from confuting that you rather confirm them by your distinctions. Truly, Perkins, you have handled these matters more negligently then befitted the dignity of the subject you have and your own erudition.[4]

Had Perkins lived to answer Arminius, he would have faced grave difficulties. It seems Perkins could (1) have repeated what he had already stated (setting forth his theory but lacking convincing proof that his doctrine of faith is different in effect), (2) admitted Arminius was right but stuck to the same predestinarian views,[5] (3) become an Arminian altogether, or (4) taken up Calvin's position.

Calvin's doctrine by this time had passed behind a cloud, although reformed predestinarianism was being called Calvinism. What

---

[1] Ibid. 462–3.   [2] Ibid. 463.   [3] Ibid.   [4] Ibid. 470.
[5] This is what Ames virtually does. See Chapter 11.

Arminius is refuting and Perkins defends is really Bezan theology.[1] Arminius does not directly attack Calvin's doctrine of faith. Whether he perceives a substantial difference between Calvin and Beza remains unknown.

Arminius in any case reverses Calvin's order regarding faith and repentance, which had been done effectively by the experimental predestinarians. God decreed 'to receive into favour those who repent and believe'.[2] He states that faith is obedience and there are three parts in this obedience.

The First is Repentance, for it is the calling of sinners to righteousness. The second is Faith in Christ, and in God through Christ; for vocation is made through the Gospel, which is the word of faith. The Third is the Observance of God's commands, in which consists holiness of life, to which believers are called, and without which no man shall see God.[3]

The debate between Perkins and Arminius is a case of two forms of voluntarism in opposition to each other. It will be recalled that Perkins maintains that the will co-operates with grace once the first grace has been bestowed.[4] Hence the failure to obtain the second grace is actually owing to man's will, although Perkins would say the man who fails to persevere was reprobate from the start. Arminius fully sees the structures of Perkins's system and realizes that, however much he is being accused of heresy, he is consistent, even within the prevailing structures of the reformed doctrine of faith. Arminius, moreover, appears to have recognized the voluntarism that was implicit in reformed theology since Beza.

Indeed, Arminius cites the Heidelberg Catechism: 'Salvation through Christ is not given to all them who had perished in Adam, but to those only who are ingrafted into Christ by true faith, *and who embrace his benefits*.'[5] Arminius replies: 'From this sentence I infer, that God has not absolutely predestinated any men to salvation; but that he has in his decree considered (or looked upon) them as believers.'[6] A believer for Arminius is one who does not resist grace. He also reminds Perkins that Perkins calls the recipients

---

[1] Bangs, op. cit. 68, seems to agree: 'Beza's doctrine of predestination is the fountain-head of what is often called "high Calvinism". It was the insistence on the details of his system as essential to Reformed orthodoxy which had a great deal to do with the precipitation of the Arminian controversy.'

[2] *Works of Arminius*, i. 589.

[3] Ibid. ii. 398. 'Repentance is *prior* to faith in Christ; but it is *posterior* to that faith by which we believe that God is willing to receive into his favour the penitent sinner.' Ibid. 723.   [4] Cf. *supra*, p. 65 n. 2.

[5] *Works of Arminius*, i. 558f.   [6] Ibid. 559.

of the first grace 'believers'. 'In the distinction of believers, those whom you name first in no way deserve to be called "believers": for hearing and understanding the word does not constitute a believer, unless there is added thereto approval of the same.'[1] By 'approval' Arminius means an act of the will. Arminius is not rejecting the basic structures of Perkins's doctrine of faith. In fact he adopts them, equally as seriously as Perkins himself does. What Perkins calls the first and second grace (the latter being brought to fruition by the co-operation of the will) Arminius calls the twofold work of the Spirit: 'the one sufficient, the other efficacious'. The former is seen when the man to whom it is applied '*can* will, and believe, and be converted'; the latter (virtually no different from Perkins's 'second grace') is that by which he 'on whom it is employed *wills*, believes, and *is* converted'.[2] Thus Arminius maintains that a believer is one who has added his 'approval', and that, if Perkins were consistent, he too would reserve the title 'believer' for the one who experiences the second grace. This is precisely what Ames will incorporate into his theology. Perkins's mistake, Arminius thinks, is calling the recipient of the first grace a believer inasmuch as the matter is really in suspension until the second grace has been obtained.

On the nature of saving faith, then, the views of Arminius and Perkins are reciprocal. Both are voluntaristic; Arminius realizes it. William Ames will fill out Perkins, probably profiting from Arminius's correction of Perkins. However, to the experimental predestinarians, the order of the decrees seems too precious to be given up, and the heat of the battle is over these decrees. Arminius's struggle to get men to see that he is in effect holding to the same doctrine of faith as that of the 'orthodox' seems not to have counted. His sin was bringing the decrees in line with his voluntaristic view of faith.

Arminius asks whether the term 'instrument' is the correct term to use regarding the nature of justifying faith. He is charged by his opponents with saying faith is not the instrument of justification.[3] He says that, while he does not deny that faith in some sense may be called an instrument, faith 'not as it is *an instrument*, but as it is *an act*, is imputed for righteousness, although such imputation be made on account of Him whom it apprehends'.[4] This is true because faith

---

[1] Ibid. iii. 459.

[2] Ibid. (my italics). Efficacious grace is that 'by which they not only can believe and be converted if they choose, but also *will* will, will believe, and will be converted'. Ibid. 316.   [3] Ibid. ii. 49.   [4] Ibid. 50f.

is 'the requirement of God, and the act of the believer when he answers the requirement'.[1] Thus 'the acceptance or apprehension itself is *an act*, and indeed one of obedience yielded to the gospel'.[2]

It may also be observed that Arminius's doctrine of faith easily coheres with the covenant theology of the experimental pre-destinarians. Arminius's calling faith an act correlates with the condition of the covenant of grace as seen by them. The opponents of Arminius seem not to have realized that his making faith an act was merely giving the correct term to the nature of faith that had become an assumption in reformed thinking. Arminius sees that retaining the term 'instrument', which seems to be but a remnant of Calvin's theology, is without sound reason. Arminius, then, is merely adjusting his doctrine of justification to his doctrine of faith. While we are justified 'solely by the obedience of Christ', and 'since God imputes the righteousness of Christ to none except believers I conclude' that 'to a man who believes Faith is imputed for righteousness'.[3]

The similarity between Arminius and the experimental pre-destinarians on the nature of saving faith is further broadened by looking at Arminius's doctrine of assurance. He thinks one may be 'certain and perswaded' of his salvation 'if his heart condemn him not'. Such a certainty is 'wrought in the mind' by the Spirit 'and by the fruits of faith,—as from his own conscience, and the testimony of God's Spirit witnessing together with his conscience'.[4] Thus the practical syllogism that is crucial to Perkins's doctrine of assurance is Arminius's ultimate appeal as well. For the certainty of salvation 'is dependent upon this decree,—"They who believe, shall be saved:" I believe, therefore I shall be saved'.[5] While Arminius does not employ the term reflex act to explain this assurance in the mind, this is what he means. His actual terms are 'mediate' (the capability of faith itself to apprehend) and 'immediate' (the apprehension itself), the latter 'being derived' from the former.[6] It is the same idea as the direct act (the will) and the reflex act (the mind) which has been seen often above. Arminius's doctrine of assurance, then, is also essentially no different from that seen in the experimental pre-destinarian tradition. Assurance comes from the 'fruits of faith,—as from his own conscience', a phrase that could have been uttered by any divine examined above in the Beza–Perkins tradition. The reason is because of the voluntarism that is implicit from Beza

---

[1] *Works of Arminius*, ii. 49 f.   [2] Ibid. 50.   [3] Ibid. i. 636
[4] Ibid. 603.   [5] Ibid. 555.   [6] Ibid. ii. 51.

onwards. Arminius takes this more seriously than any divine examined above.

Arminius has little to say about preparation for grace. This is possibly because the need for such a pastoral concept is considerably lessened by Arminius's taking the decrees out of eternity, as it were, and placing them in the here and now. He might well be called an existential predestinarian. He has succeeded in relaxing the tension whether or not one's lot is unchangeably fixed. His theology clearly brings the possibility of salvation within reach of anyone.[1] While the experimental predestinarians try to do this too, their need for positing a doctrine of preparation is undergirded, if not caused, by their making the number of the elect equal to the number for whom Christ died.

Arminius and Calvin have in common the belief that Christ died for all. They also agree that the death of Christ is of no value until we believe.[2] But the similarity ends there in so far as the doctrine of faith is concerned. Arminius insists that Christ prays 'also for the non-elect'.[3] When Christ said, 'I pray not for the world, but for those whom Thou hast given Me', Christ simply meant that He prayed for those 'who believed and those who were about to believe'.[4] Thus Arminius brings Christ's intercessory prayers in line with his doctrine of the atonement; the experimental predestinarians limit the scope both of Christ's death and His intercession, but to them neither can be enjoyed save by an active obedience to God's commands. Only Calvin holds that election may be enjoyed by looking directly at Christ. His view of the relation of Christ's intercession to His death seems never to have been considered; such a position would have been in opposition to the position of Arminius on the one hand and that of the experimental predestinarians on the other.

In the year following Arminius's death the Remonstrants kept their master's views alive. The Remonstrance of 1610 is a summary of Arminius's basic position. In summary, the Five Articles are: (1) God has decreed Jesus Christ as the Redeemer of men and decreed to save all who believe on Him; (2) Christ died for all but only believers enjoy forgiveness of sins; (3) man must be regenerated by

---

[1] Like the experimental predestinarians, Arminius believes God has predestined the means to the end. Ibid. ii. 394. He speaks vaguely about 'preparation for regeneration' that comes from the 'motion of the regenerating Spirit'. Ibid. 17. In any case, Arminius is more cautious than Thomas Hooker, if not also Cotton and Preston.

[2] Ibid. 325–32, 9–10.   [3] Ibid. iii. 326.   [4] Ibid. 326 f.

the Spirit; (4) grace is 'not irresistible'; and (5) perseverance is granted 'through the assistance of the grace of the Holy Spirit', but whether one can fall away from 'life in Christ' is left open.[1]

On 29 May 1619 the international Synod of Dordrecht (Dort) brought to an end a series of 163 sessions (beginning 13 November 1618), resulting in the condemnation of the Five Articles of the Remonstrants. Besides upholding the Heidelberg Catechism, the Synod issued Five Canons to counter the Five Articles of the Remonstrants. In summary the Canons of Dort are: (1) that God's eternal decree of predestination is the cause of election and reprobation, and that this decree is not based upon foreseen faith; (2) that Christ died for the elect only; (3) and (4) that men by nature are unable to seek God apart from the Spirit and that grace is irresistible; and (5) the elect will surely persevere in faith to the end.[2]

Three things are to be noted concerning the Canons of Dort: they (1) embrace the practical syllogism; (2) assume a voluntaristic view of faith; and (3) reverse the order Calvin intended regarding faith and repentance in the *ordo salutis*. Article 12 of the First Head of Doctrine states that men may have assurance of election 'not by inquisitely prying into the secret and deep things of God, but by observing in themselves' the 'infallible fruits of election'.[3] Moreover, those who lack this 'assured confidence' must not 'rank themselves among the reprobate' if they 'seriously desire' to please God, for God is merciful and 'will not quench the smoking flax, nor break the bruised reed'.[4]

The Synod of Dort represents a substantial departure from Calvin's doctrine of faith. Moreover, Perkins's idea of the least measure of faith, the will to believe, is given credal sanction at Dort. But there is more; Arminius has stolen from reformed theology Calvin's conviction that Christ died for all men.

[1] The full text of the Five Articles of the Remonstrants (also the Canons of Dort) are given in Peter Y. DeJong (ed.), *Crisis in the Reformed Churches: Essays in commencement of the great Synod of Dort, 1618-1619* (Grand Rapids, 1968), 207ff.

[2] Ibid. 229-62. These five statements became known as the Five Points of Calvinism. See *supra*, p. 1 n. 4.

[3] Ibid. 233.   [4] Ibid. 234-5.

11

WILLIAM AMES
(1576-1633)

I gladly call to minde, when being yong, I heard, worthy Master Perkins, so Preach in a great Assembly of students, that he instructed them soundly in the Truth, stirred them up effectually to seeke after Godliness . . .[1]

WHILE Perkins's most famous pupil undoubtedly retained a deep admiration for his mentor throughout his days, William Ames not only filled out Perkins's theology but, in doing so, was forced to break with his master at significant points. There is to be seen in Ames's soteriology an elaborate system that revolves almost entirely around the role of the human will. Ames possessed the greatest intellect in the experimental predestinarian tradition since Perkins. *The Marrow of Sacred Divinity* (1643)[2] was the first systematic theology to emerge within this tradition since *A Golden Chaine*.

Ames appears to realize that if sanctification is to be the ground of assurance, then (1) faith is an act of the will and (2) temporary faith has no convenient place in such a theological scheme. While the divines who followed Perkins moved gradually towards an explicit voluntarism and away from temporary faith, William Ames gave this trend his weighty sanction. Calvin's doctrine of faith, for all practical purposes, was now dead and buried. Ames espoused a voluntaristic doctrine of faith within a tradition that had already been shaking off Calvin's influence anyway.

There is no way to know certainly how Ames came to this position. It may have been simply his own perception that Perkins missed the point when placing the seat of faith in the understanding —that Perkins ought to have placed it in the will, since it is actually the will around which his system implicitly turns. If Perkins did not see this, he should have, as Ames virtually says.

However, the possible influence of Arminius and the Remon-

---

[1] W. Ames, *Conscience with the power and Cases thereof* (1639), To the reader. Hereinafter called *Conscience*, this was translated from *De Conscientia, et Eius Iure, vel Casibus* (1622 and 1630).

[2] Hereinafter called *Marrow*, the 1643 edition (used below) is the translation from *Medulla Theologiae* (1623, 1627).

strants upon Ames is to be noted. It seems likely that Ames read Arminius's *Examination of Perkins' Pamphlet on the Order and Mode of Predestination* (1612). In 1613, when Ames is found debating with the Remonstrant Nicholaas Grevinchovius—a quarrel 'momentous to both'[1]—Ames does not disagree with his opponent that faith is an act of the will. Grevinchovius says:

For since this very faith, or acknowledgment, and trust is an act of the will, it is necessary that the cause of that act be judged to be the will, faith thus being the effect of the will, on which it depends in just the same way as any event [has a cause].[2]

Ames concurs that 'the first outcome of efficacious grace is effectually to flow into the will'.[3] But this 'co-operation of the will is the effect of that efficacy', he insists.[4] While Ames wants to make efficacious grace the cause of the will's choosing the good, there is concurrence that it is the will none the less which immediately produces faith. Thus Ames seems to have come to a voluntaristic position at least ten years before the *Marrow* was written. If he is attracted to the option that faith is a persuasion in the understanding by virtue of efficacious grace, he gives no indication of it. When he acknowledges that faith 'commonly' is taken to signify 'an act of the understanding', this is quite probably an allusion to Perkins:

But because the will is wont to be moved thereupon, and to stretch forth it selfe to embrace the good so allowed, therefore Faith doth aptly enough set forth this act of the will . . . For it is a receiving . . . an act of election, an act of the whole man, which things doe in no wise agree to an act of the understanding.[5]

While logic perfects the intellect, theology perfects the will.[6] Theology is 'the doctrine of living to God'.[7] A contemporary of Ames, Gisbertus Voetius (1588–1676),[8] observed that while some theologians make faith to reside in the understanding (he cites Perkins and others), and some say faith resides in the intellect *and* the will, he only knew Ames to 'attribute it to the will alone'.[9]

[1] Keith L. Sprunger, *The Learned Doctor William Ames* (1972), 47. This is the definitive biography of Ames. It treats his doctrine of faith marginally. A very useful volume is *William Ames* (Harvard, 1965), which includes Matthew Nethenus's 1668 biography of Ames, an 1894 treatment by J. M. Stap (Holland), and a 1940 thesis by Karl Reuter (Germany). These treat the nature of faith marginally, however.
[2] W. Ames, *De Arminii Sententia* (1613), 28.   [3] Ibid. 31.   [4] Ibid.
[5] *Marrow*, 8–9.   [6] Ames, *Technometria* (1631), 34.   [7] *Marrow*, 1.
[8] Voetius was a Dutch theologian who studied at Leiden during the Arminian controversy. He defended the Calvinist party and was a delegate to the Synod of Dort. He became a professor at Utrecht in 1634 and was widely known in Europe as a defender of scholastic Calvinism.
[9] Voetius, *Selectarum Disputationum* (Utrecht, 1648–69), v. 289.

William Ames was born in Ipswich. In about 1593, when
Perkins's fame was reaching its peak, Ames went up to Cambridge,
matriculating as a pensioner at Christ's College, where he came
under Perkins's immediate influence. Ames's conversion, however,
seems to have taken place after Perkins had vacated his Fellowship
in 1595 but while he was still lecturing at St. Andrews. It pleased
God 'that the yong Ames should be called out of his naturall estate
of sin & misery, as Lazarus out of his grave, by the loud voice of
[Perkins's] powerful ministry'.[1] Ames received the BA in 1597-8,
and the MA in 1601, and was elected Fellow the same year. He
remained at Christ's another nine years.

It seems that Ames frequently objected to wearing the surplice.
But it was a sermon preached in the university church in 1609 which
ultimately proved too much for the authorities. The vice-chancellor
suspended Ames from all ecclesiastical and academic duties. Ames
tried to settle at Colchester as pastor of a congregation there, but
was forbidden to preach by the bishop of London, George Abbott.
'What a man Ames would make if he were a son of the Church', his
critics said.[2] Ames sought exile in the Netherlands. Before leaving,
his friend Paul Baynes warned him, 'Beware of a strong head and a
cold heart'.[3]

In Holland Ames soon took up debates with the Remonstrants,
most notably with Grevinchovius, the minister of a church in
Rotterdam. From about 1611 to 1619 Ames found employment at
The Hague as chaplain to Sir Horace Vere. In 1618 he was employed
by the Dutch Calvinist party to watch the proceedings of the Synod
of Dort, giving his opinions and advice when required. Ames
reportedly exercised enormous power behind the scenes, and was an
adviser to the president of the Synod. He seems to have distinguished himself at the proceedings, this being acknowledged by
George Abbott, now archbishop of Canterbury, who none the less
refused Ames a post in England, since he was not an 'obedient son
of his mother, the Church of England, but a rebel'.[4]

In 1622 Ames accepted the theological chair at Franeker and was
later made rector of the university. During the years 1622-32 he
attracted students from all over Europe. His most famous pupil was
Johannes Cocceius (d. 1669), with him from 1626 to 1629.[5] In 1632

[1] Quoted in Sprunger, op. cit. 11.   [2] Nethenus, in *William Ames*, 4.
[3] Mather, *Magnalia*, i. 245.   [4] Nethenus, in *William Ames*, 13.
[5] Cocceius embellished Ames's covenant theology and is sometimes thought of as
the father of federal theology.

serious illness (asthma) forced Ames to go to Rotterdam where he filled the post of pastor to the English Church. During this time he met with Thomas Hooker, who had fled to Holland in 1629. Hooker claimed that a man absorbed in Ames's thought would be 'a good divine, though he had not more books in the world'. Ames was impressed with Hooker as well, and said he 'never met with Mr. Hooker's equal, either for preaching or for disputing'.[1] Hooker wrote the lengthy preface to Ames's *A Fresh Svit against Human Ceremonies in Gods Worship* (1633) just before his own departure for America via England. Ames died in November 1633.

Ames's theological interests were vast. His ecclesiological writings, considering their later impact, justly make him 'the father of New England church polity'.[2] He is regarded as a popularizer of Peter Ramus's logic,[3] while the *Marrow* became the main textbook at Harvard and (later) Yale for many years.[4] He continued Perkins's essential casuistical divinity, systematically treating nearly every 'case of conscience' imaginable. Both his ecclesiology and soteriology became orthodoxy, as it were, at Massachusetts Bay. In any case, Ames's voluntarism appears to be the key to all he believes.[5]

Ames retains the structures of Perkins's supralapsarianism,[6] but sees the incompatibility of making good works the ground of assurance while simultaneously espousing an explicit doctrine of temporary faith. The evidence for this is not only the near total eclipse of temporary faith in Ames's writings,[7] but its conspicuous absence in the *Marrow*. Ostensibly the systematic *Marrow* is largely

---

[1] Mather, op. cit. i. 339–40.

[2] Perry Miller, 'The Marrow of Puritan Divinity', *Publications of the Colonial Society of Massachusetts* (Boston, 1937), 256.

[3] K. L. Sprunger, 'Ames, Ramus, and the Method of Puritan Theology', *Harvard Theological Review* (1966), 133 ff.

[4] Samuel Eliot Morison, *Harvard College in the Seventeenth Century* (Cambridge, Mass., 1936), i. 267; Edwin Oviatt, *The Beginnings of Yale (1701–1726)* (New Haven, 1916), 196–200.

[5] In addition to those cited above, the writings of Ames on which this study will draw are *The Svbstance of Christian Religion: Or, a plain and easie Draught of the Christian Catechisme, in LII Lectures* (1659), hereinafter called *Svbstance*; and *An Analyticall Exposition of Both the Epistles of the Apostle Peter, Illustrated by Doctrines out of Every Text* (1641), hereinafter called *Peter*.

[6] Ames wrote the preface to William Twisse's *Vindiciae Gratiae* (1632), a defence of supralapsarianism.

[7] In *Peter*, 14, he says those who have a temporary faith 'are wont to fall in the midst of afflictions', and, that in the unregenerate there may be 'a sudden motion of the minde' but this is 'not a rooted affection'. Ibid. 41. He seems forced to explain the apparent apostasy in 2 Pet. 2: 20–2: 'They had that faith which we use to call temporary faith, but they were never soundly rooted in faith.' Ibid. 229.

patterned after Perkins's *A Golden Chaine*—from God's decrees, to the Fall, the giving of a Mediator, and the *ordo salutis* (from predestination to glorification); but the doctrine of reprobation includes not a word about an ineffectual calling.[1] Indeed, while Perkins's *magnum opus* proceeds from the discussion on glorification to his elaborate doctrine of reprobation (with particular reference to the ineffectual calling of the reprobate), Ames's discussion on glorification (Chapter 30) is followed not by the doctrine of reprobation but by 'Of the Church mystically considered' (Chapter 31). While Ames's treatment of reprobation itself is as lucid (and harsh) as that of Perkins, there can be no doubt that Ames deliberately skirts the problem of temporary faith. Moreover, in the *Marrow* he does not refer to an effectual calling; it is merely 'calling'.[2] By this he means an effectual calling. But by simply referring to 'calling' he has implied there is no other kind of calling but an effectual calling. He is not only moving away from Perkins by departing from Perkins's system at the crucial point of temporary faith but has used a term that cannot be easily set in opposition to the very concept he does not wish to dignify. Any careful reader of Perkins is bound to notice what Ames has done. Ames evidently desires a system, however much he respects Perkins, that will be logically consistent throughout. He is not prepared to abandon his predestinarianism, but he is determined to have nothing to do with a system that suggests the reprobate may have sanctification.

There are two situations mentioned in the *Marrow*, however, in which the doctrine of temporary faith may be implied. Under the heading of 'calling' Ames states (in one line) that there may be an enlightening 'sometime, and in a certaine manner granted to those not elected'.[3] The second instance is his saying that a 'generall assent, which the Papists make to be Faith, is not Faith' since it may be 'without any life'.[4] But in any case, there is not the remotest hint

[1] *Marrow*, 121f. 'Reprobation is the predestinating of some certaine men, that the glory of Gods Justice might be manifested in them . . . [it] cannot properly be called election: because it is not out of love, *neither doth it bring the bestowing of any good*, but the privation of it' (my italics). This suggests a further rationale for his not treating temporary faith under this category; there cannot be 'the bestowing of any good' on the reprobate.

[2] Ibid. 123ff.

[3] Ibid. 125f. The unpardonable sin springs from 'malice' towards this illumination. Cf. *Conscience*, iv. 13, where he briefly discusses the nature of apostasy; while one may fall 'from the truth of the Gospel to Popery', there is no hint of any piety before apostasy.

[4] *Marrow*, 8. Ames's doctrine of temporary faith is largely confined to what he

in Ames's writings that a temporary believer may look like a real Christian. In the case of his mention of an enlightening 'sometime, and in a certaine manner' in the non-elect, Ames does not tell us more. It is the nearest he comes even to a tacit acknowledgement of the theological merit of the idea of temporary faith. He has succeeded in remaining 'sound', as it were, without having to face the serious problems that the teaching may precipitate. Ames cannot have avoided knowing of its prominence in Perkins's writings. But most important is his theological consistency. He is convinced that the will to be godly can only exist in the elect. Indeed, by omitting any threatening teaching of temporary faith from his system, Ames has left the road clear of any debris that could inhibit the sincere seeker's willingness to obey the Lord. In Ames's system there is no hint that a person could imagine that his sanctification is but the temporary flourishing of the reprobate.

Moreover, Ames shows us clearly that he has thought the matter through, i.e. sanctification and temporary faith must not mix. If sanctification is to be the sure evidence of election, then the reprobate can never have sanctification. Whatever else characterizes the reprobate, sanctification does not. For 'sanctification is a certaine effect and signe' of our election.[1]

Because sanctification is, as it were, actuall election: for as by the election of God, the heires of salvation are distinguished from others in God Himselfe, or in His intention and counsell; so also by regeneration and sanctification are they distinguished from others in themselves. For to sanctifie . . . is to set apart to some use.[2]

Ames shows here he is convinced of two things: (1) God never intended that any but His elect will be sanctified, and (2) we may know in ourselves that sanctification is what sets us apart from others. And lest one doubt what is behind Ames's assertion he proceeds to three 'uses' of this doctrine. The first is in all probability an allusion to his mentor:

Use 1. This may serve to refute those men that make sanctification the common possession of those that are not elect.
    2. To comfort all those that are partakers of true sanctification: because there by they may [be] the more assured of their election.
    3. To exhort us to be very carefull to encrease our sanctification.[3]

calls the papists' faith. A knowledge without 'affiance' is found in devils and 'in them [e.g. papists] that have no part of spiritual life'. *Svbstance*, 53.

[1] *Peter*, 4.   [2] Ibid.   [3] Ibid. 4–5.

It may now be seen more clearly why Ames puts considerable stress on the role of the human will. It is his conviction that only efficacious grace will move the will to choose the good; hence he focuses his attention upon the will. Indeed, in the *Marrow* Ames does not wait until the discussion of faith (Chapter 3) to disclose how strongly he intends to emphasize the will. In the discussion of the 'Nature of Divinity' (Chapter 1) he comes quickly to the point: 'Moreover seeing this life [of 'living to God'] is a spirituall act of the whole man, whereby he is carried on to enjoy God, and to doe according to his will, and it is manifest that those things are proper to the will, it followes that the prime and proper subject of Divinity is the will.'[1]

Ames believes, then, that if he can lead a soul to a willingness to serve God, he has fulfilled the central task of divinity. The human will is the key. It cannot choose the good without grace, but if it does choose the good it is because grace caused it. Ames has no fear of causing a reprobate to manifest sanctification, for such consecration is outside the will of a reprobate. Thus if sanctification is there, such a person is bound to be elect.

Ames's contribution is his consistent argument that faith cannot be anything but an act of the will, and he builds this theology upon the framework he inherited from Perkins. He simply calls a spade a spade. His theology is the eventual product of the Beza–Perkins tradition; it is 'Arminian' in every way but in the theoretical explanation that lies behind the actual practice of the believer (or unbeliever).

Ames insists, however, that faith always presupposes 'a knowledge of the Gospell'. But 'there is no saving knowledge in any . . . but what followes this act of the will'. Indeed, saving knowledge 'depends on it'.[2] Ames defines faith as 'a resting of the heart on God',[3] or 'that act of the will or heart, which properly is called election or choyse; whereby we rely upon Christ, repose and rest on him'.[4] He is very worried, moreover, about a faith that is seated in the understanding.

But the act of the understanding properly and immediately doth not transfer the whole man, but the act of the will, which alone therefore is called the act of the whole man: Nor can it be heer answered that Faith is an aggregate thing, consisting partly of knowledge, and partly of affiance; because unto such aggregate things, single and distinct operations can not be attributed, as are attributed to Faith.[5]

---

[1] *Marrow*, 3.   [2] Ibid. 6.   [3] Ibid. 5.   [4] *Svbstance*, 50.   [5] Ibid. 53.

It will be recalled that Perkins thinks faith is seated in the mind because faith must reside in one faculty.[1] Ames agrees but thinks that the one faculty is the will. Ames is therefore found also differing from his friend Paul Baynes[2] when Baynes asserts that faith resides in both the mind and will: 'Now whereas true Faith is of some placed partly in the understanding, and partly in the will, that is not so accurately spoken, because it is one single vertue, and doth bring forth acts of the same kinde, not partly of Science, and partly of affections.'[3]

Ames recognizes that in Scripture faith is often equated with knowledge, particularly when there is a 'speciall assent' that God is ours. But he claims this 'is not the first act of Faith, but an act flowing from Faith'.[4] Ames is unhappy with the idea that faith is knowledge. True faith is the act of the will; the knowledge of faith is but 'that reflex act, which is proper to man, whereby he hath a power, as it were to enter into, and perceive what he is in himselfe'.[5] Faith itself is not '*γνῶσις*, but *ἐπίγνωσις*, that is, an acknowledging'.[6]

Now faith is signified [in Scripture] by the name of knowledge, because by the hearing and knowledge of the word it is usually begotten in us. And faith is called the instrument of grace, not as it is in God himselfe ... but as the sense, fruit and knowledge of this grace communicated unto us.[7]

Ames is therefore consistent within the voluntaristic frame of reference he has adopted. Faith is not knowledge but an acknowledging; the knowledge of faith itself is in the understanding by the reflex act.

While Ames inverts the meaning Calvin intended by making faith an 'instrument', he rejects Calvin's teaching of implicit faith entirely. It will be recalled that Perkins thinks he follows Calvin by espousing an implicit faith as weak but still saving.[8] Ames holds that 'implicite faith is good and necessary, but it is not of it selfe sufficient to salvation'. While Perkins claims that implicit faith is the will to believe, Ames argues that 'it cannot be that the will be effectually affected, and embrace that as good, which it doth not at all distinctly know'.[9] Ames is not merely rejecting the papist view of implicit faith; he also rejects an implicit faith that is said indistinctly to grasp the contents of Scripture,[10] the principle Calvin endorses as valid.[11]

[1] Cf. *supra*, p. 62 n. 3.   [2] Cf. *supra*, p. 102 n. 3.   [3] *Marrow*, 9.
[4] Ibid. 8.   [5] *Conscience*, ii. 3.   [6] *Peter*, 134.
[7] Ibid.   [8] Cf. *supra*, p. 65 n. 6.   [9] *Marrow*, 256.
[10] Ibid. 255.
[11] An example of implicit faith, Calvin says, is when 'in our daily reading of

Saving faith, then, is 'Explicite Faith', that 'whereby the truths of Faith are believed in particular, and not in common only'.[1]

Explicite Faith must necessarily be had of those things which are propounded to our Faith as necessary meanes of salvation . . . repentance from dead workes and of Faith in God . . . The outward act of Faith is confession, profession, or manifestation of it, which in its order, and is necessary to salvation, Rom. 10. 9. 10. Namely in respect of the preparation and disposition of minde alwayes necessary.[2]

Not only is Ames making preparation and a right kind of disposition prerequisites to saving faith, but he makes it clear that the concept he is rejecting is precisely what he thinks breeds 'Infidelity, Doubting, Error, Heresie, Apostacie'.[3] These he thinks flow from an implicit faith that resides in the understanding, and make manifest that they did not spring from that faith 'which is in the will'.[4] Ames therefore departs not merely from Calvin but Perkins as well. Yet Ames demonstrates what Perkins's system ought to have looked like, given the structures Perkins chose to build upon.

We must now examine the way in which Ames seems to have profited from Arminius's correction of Perkins's doctrine of faith. What Perkins calls two works of grace Ames calls two kinds of receiving of Christ: a passive and active. Ames understands *implicit* faith to be a 'passive' receiving of Christ, an enlightening of the mind.[5] But Ames avoids the mistake which Arminius exposed in Perkins; he is careful not to assign any saving merit to the passive receiving of Christ, which is the same thing as Perkins's first work of grace. Since 'the will is the most proper and prime subject of this grace', there must be an 'active' receiving of Christ.[6] The passive receiving may be had without repentance. But, 'With this Faith wherewith the will is turned to the having of the true good, there is always joyned repentance, by which the same will is turned also to the doing of the true good, with an aversnesse, and hatred of the contrary evill, or sinne'.[7] Because there is no repentance joined with the passive receiving of Christ one may also see why a teaching of temporary faith is remote in his system. Such may be inferred, for presumably if the passive receiving does not issue in an active receiving, the grounds for a temporary faith are present. But Ames

Scripture we come upon many obscure passages that convict us of ignorance'. Christ's disciples moreover 'had faith in the words of Him Whom they knew to be truthful'. *Inst.* III. ii. 4.

[1] *Marrow*, 256. [2] Ibid. [3] Ibid. 257. [4] Ibid.
[5] Ibid. 126 f. [6] Ibid. 127. [7] Ibid.

is careful not to get involved with this. The important thing is that saving faith is seated in the will alone; the *active* receiving corresponds to *explicit* faith, or Perkins's second work of grace. Faith is not saving until it is an act of the will.

But Ames has created a new problem to be reckoned with. He makes faith and repentance effectively the same thing. This is because he places repentance before faith in his *ordo salutis*. Ames is clearer than any divine in the experimental predestinarian tradition examined above in making repentance precede faith. While repentance is indeed an 'effect' of faith, 'Repentance in respect of that carefulnesse, and anxiety & terror arising from the Law which it hath joyned with it, doth goe before Faith, by order of nature, as a preparing and disposing cause'.[1]

However, while Ames is remarkably consistent within the structures of his voluntaristic system, he fails to show that there is any real difference between faith and repentance. He effectively equates the two, and it is strange that he does not come to grips with this. He seems implicitly to realize this, however, when he says that repentance 'hath the same causes and principles with Faith' inasmuch as 'both have their seat in the heart or will of man'.[2] Ames would have been clearer had he said that the distinction (which he implies) that lies between repentance and faith is really between faith/repentance and assurance. He makes the term faith redundant. He explains, however, that faith and repentance have different 'objects': repentance is towards God and faith is towards Christ (Acts 20: 21); it was God, moreover, who was first offended by sin. He also claims that faith and repentance have different 'ends': faith seeks reconciliation with God, repentance 'a sutablenesse to the will of God'.[3]

However, this theoretical distinction does not explain the obvious fact that, in so far as the role of believer is concerned, they are effectively the same thing. But Ames does not want to call faith assurance as this would clash with all else he espouses. Yet he says: 'Repentance is wont to be perceived before Faith: because a sinner cannot easily perswade himselfe that he is reconciled to God in Christ, before he feele himselfe to have forsaken those sins which did separate him from God.'[4] What Ames means here is that repentance is grasped before there is *assurance* of faith. Faith is an act of the will and repentance is an act of the will, but we know that we have faith only when we can reflect on the fact we have repented.

---

[1] *Marrow*, 128.   [2] Ibid. 127–8.
[3] Ibid. 128.   [4] Ibid. 129.

In Ames's system, then, faith is a misnomer. By faith he can only mean repentance. Assurance is not of the essence of faith, but repentance is. For if repentance as a disposition precedes faith and if repentance as forsaking sin follows faith (and shows that we have faith), when does faith by itself truly get into the morphology of conversion?

It appears then that we can only know that faith *has* occurred, and that by our works. We can only know our election by having faith; we can only know our faith by having works. It seems that Ames makes faith as secretive as election itself; both remain hidden until there are works that one can see.

The whole order therefore of this consolation, whereby we may be certain of salvation, is as followeth: in such a Syllogism (wherein both will and understanding have their parts) whereof the proposition stands in the assent of the understanding, and makes up a dogmatical Faith. The assumption is not principally in the compounding understanding, but in the single apprehension and will, so as to make it true and of force to infer the certainty in the conclusion; which the heart doth by this act of affiance, that being the property of justifying Faith, and this existing in the heart. The conclusion is also principally & ultimately in the single apprehension and will, or in the heart, by the grace of hope; and both it, and the experimental reflexion joyn'd with it (which is in the understanding, and the other also, by this reflexion) are the effects of the experimental knowledge and reflexion of our understanding, in the assumption upon the true existence of the single term in the heart or will, which bears the whole burthen of the assurance.[1]

The 'whole burthen of the assurance' is grounded in our works. Indeed, 'An endeavour to abound in vertue, and to do good workes, is the only meanes to make our calling and election sure'.[2] For good works are 'the causes of that knowledge which we have of our calling and election'.[3]

For the knowledge and assurance of these things depends upon the reflex act of our understanding, whereby we see in our selves the markes and signes of effectuall calling, and consequently of eternall election. Hence this assurance increaseth and decreaseth in us, according as our endeavour to abound in vertues, and so do good workes is greater or lesser.[4]

However, Ames, like Hooker, does not intend that assurance come easily. 'What ought a man to do', Ames asks, 'that he may be translated out of a state of sin, in to the state of grace?'[5] He answers

---

[1] *Svbstance*, 55 f.   [2] *Peter*, 164.   [3] Ibid. 165.
[4] Ibid.   [5] *Conscience*, ii. 8.

in seven propositions: (1) a man must 'seriously looke into the Law of God, and make an examination of his life'. (2) There must follow a 'conviction of Conscience', (3) a despair of saving ourselves, and (4) a true humiliation of heart. But the latter comes only by (5) 'a distinct consideration of some particular sins', if not (6) 'by the sight of some one sin'. This humiliation (7) is 'helped forward oft times by some heavy affliction'.[1]

This doctrine of preparation is in essential agreement with Hooker's more detailed scheme. Ames's writings are not sermons, as Hooker's are, but come directly from his pen. He therefore does not take months and months to move from 'contrition' to 'humiliation' as Hooker does. Ames is summarizing his doctrine of preparation as a whole. But it may nevertheless be gathered that he does not expect assurance to come readily. For he comes next to the question, 'what a man ought to do that he may be partaker of his grace?'. Ames gives a fourfold answer to show there are 'diverse duties, which ly upon a man about his vocation, and which both ought, and are wont ordinarily to be performed before the certainty of this grace can be gotten'.[2] (1) One must have an estimation of God's word 'above all riches'. (2) One must 'imploy his greatest care labour and industry, about this businesse'. (3) He must 'with all diligence, care, and constancy, apply himselfe to the use of all those meanes' which God hath provided. And (4) one must 'sell all that he hath to buy this pearle'.[3]

Obviously this fourth statement suggests that we bargain with God in order to obtain grace. Ames realizes what is implied in these lines, and comments:

For although God doth freely bestow life upon us, and receive nothing at our hands in lieu of it . . . Yet we ought to forsake all unlawfull things actually, and all externall and naturall goods also, in the purpose, and disposition of our minds, else we cannot obtaine the grace of God.[4]

One may thus see how far the experimental predestinarian tradition has come towards an anthropocentric doctrine of faith. William Ames has taken the voluntarism that was begun in Beza's theology and popularized by Perkins, and brings it to a logical conclusion. Man is thus seen earning God's grace by a willingness to consecrate

---

[1] *Conscience*, ii. 8–9.   [2] Ibid. 11.   [3] Ibid.
[4] Ibid. Ames makes extensive use of the motif of the covenant of works and covenant of grace. His exposition, however, is not relevant to this study. Cf. *Marrow*, 114ff.

himself to a godly life. The irony is that this theology purports to lie in a thoroughly predestinarian system.

Ames even raises the question 'by what motives a man may be stirred up to embrace the call of God'.[1] He has a sevenfold answer: one must consider (1) 'who it is that calls him' (God); (2) 'what it is to which God calls him' (eternal happiness); (3) 'what that is out of which he is called' (sin and death); (4) 'what the cause is that moves God to call him' (mercy); (5) one should 'humbly compare himselfe with others, to whom this grace of vocation is denied'; (6) recognize 'how hainous an offense it is to neglect this call of God'; and (7) consider 'that misery, which he doth by the Law of equity bring upon himselfe by this sin' (God's punishment).[2] In appealing to man's will in this way, Ames actually goes beyond anything Arminius had published. Ames does not explicitly state that he is addressing the natural man, but this is implied. Otherwise his counsel urging men to get themselves under the Law of God as the first step to preparation seems superfluous. On the other hand, so is his predestinarianism as a whole in the light of these pleadings to man's will; but it must not be forgotten that Ames thinks only the elect will heed his warnings.

Ames devotes a chapter in *Conscience* to 'putting off ones Conversion'.[3] He argues that 'it is not lawfull to make the least delay at all in our conversion unto God'. For the 'delay of Repentance increaseth hardnesse of heart' and 'the number of sinnes, our guilt'. Furthermore, 'the duration of our life is altogether uncertain' and 'late repentance is very seldome true, and almost alwayes suspitio[u]s'.[4]

If one accepts Ames's view of faith, the essence of which is repentance, the only way one has to become certain of his own election is to check his religious pulse. Such is subjective and introspective. Moreover, a conscience 'admits of degrees', and can be weak or strong. But a 'good conscience is maintained' by these four things: (1) that the fear of God be lively and fresh in our hearts; (2) that we meditate on God's Law day and night; (3) that we examine our ways with 'quick and sharpe judgement'; and (4) 'by dayly repentance and renewing of Faith, we wash off the filth that we contract . . . For therein lyes the strength of the conclusion or

---

[1] *Conscience*, ii. 11. [2] Ibid. 11–12. [3] Ibid. 6.

[4] Ibid. 6–7. It is with regard to the nature of conscience that Ames most explicitly recognizes his need to correct Perkins. His treatment of the conscience is subservient to the will. In any case Ames retains the practical syllogism. Ibid. i. 1 ff.

judgement of Conscience'.[1] Thus we are back to repentance in the end to judge whether or not we have faith. With Perkins the test is whether we have a temporary faith or a saving faith; with Ames the test is whether or not we have faith.

Ames's voluntarism, while eliminating the worry about temporary faith, seems to lead him to a quasi-perfectionism. While he admits that none is without sin in this life, he still claims that 'all that are truly sanctified doe tend unto perfection'.[2] Throughout his exposition in *Peter* Ames employs the terms 'piety' and 'godliness' to denote (1) what must characterize professing Christians and (2) what makes us certain that we have faith. He also makes repeated use of the word 'condemne' when coming to the 'uses' of doctrine, for example, 'This may serve to condemne those, which deferre and put off the time of amending their lives, as if they had not yet sinned enough'.[3]

If ever a man deserves the name of 'Puritan', it is William Ames. Apart from his keen interest in ecclesiological matters, his soteriology alone, which pre-eminently stresses purity of life, bears out all that this word has implied. Indeed, considering the stature he had in Massachusetts Bay, whose early residents gave America her soul, much of what became identified with the legalism and stringency of the early New England way is to be imputed largely to William Ames.

In *Conscience* Ames deals with heresies: what makes heretics, and whether papists, anabaptists, Lutherans, and Arminians are heretics. While some of Ames's most intense debates were with the Arminians, Arminianism 'is not properly an heresie, but a dangerous error in the Faith' since it denies effectual calling.[4] If Ames is conscious of the fact he has much in common with the Arminians, he does not say so.

Ames's friends reported that he died as he had lived, firm in his faith and triumphant in his hope.[5]

[1] *Conscience*, i. 38. [2] *Marrow*, 145. [3] *Peter*, 91.
[4] *Conscience*, iii. 12. [5] Sprunger, *The Learned Doctor William Ames*, 247.

PART FIVE

THE WESTMINSTER ASSEMBLY OF DIVINES

12

JOHN COTTON AND THE ANTINOMIAN CONTROVERSY IN AMERICA (1636-1638)

[This] may give light touching a controversie, if it be stirring in the Country, I know not whether it be, I fear it is, and yet hope that if matters were rightly understood, there would be no material difference: for if the Question be not about grace, but about the discerning of grace . . . [the difference regarding the latter] will be of much less dangerous consequence [than the former]. . . . How far there is difference in the Country, I cannot give an account; but I desire that you may all understand what I say.[1]

ON 12 June 1643 Parliament called for 'an Assembly of Learned, Godly and Judicious Divines' to be consulted with by Parliament for the settling of the government and liturgy of the Church, and 'for the vindicating and clearing of the Doctrine of the Church of England from all false Calumnies and Aspersions'.[2] The historic Assembly of Divines convened for the first time on 1 July 1643;[3]

[1] J. Cotton, *A Treatise of the Covenant of Grace* (1659), 146. This appeared as *The New Covenant* (1654) and *The Covenant of Gods Free Grace* (1655). All are endorsed by the Westminster divine Joseph Caryl. (These are not to be confused with *The Covenant of Gods Free Grace* (1645).) The 1659 edition (reissued in 1671) is based upon 'a Copy far larger than the former; and Corrected by the Authors own hand'. The preface states that this edition was 'corrected also in some places by the Authors own hand before his death'. Larzer Ziff, *Career of John Cotton*, 265, and E. H. Emerson, *John Cotton*, 164, agree that this work contains the sermons Cotton preached in about 1636.

[2] *Journals of the House of Lords* (n.d.), vi. 93. As early as 19 Apr. 1642 the House of Commons ordered that 'the Names of such divines as shall be thought fit to be consulted with, concerning the Matter of the Church, be brought To-morrow Morning'. *The Journals of the House of Commons* (1803), ii. 534. One hundred and twenty-one divines were chosen for this task. Each member recommended two divines: two were appointed for each county in England, two for each university, two for the Channel Islands, one for each county in Wales, and four for the city of London. A. F. Mitchell, *The Westminster Assembly* (1883), 108.

[3] The first meeting was in the Chapel of Henry VII at Westminster Abbey. After 2 Oct. 1643 they began meeting in the Jerusalem Chamber of Westminster Abbey. The main work of the Assembly continued until 22 Feb. 1649, during which time it met 1,163 times. B. B. Warfield, *The Westminster Assembly and its Work* (1931), 3.

sixty-nine were in attendance.[1] Dr William Twisse, the moderator, preached a sermon on John 14: 18: 'I will not leave you comfortless; I will come unto you.'[2]

On 19 July 1643 the divines sent a petition to Parliament, urgently requesting 'That the bold venting of corrupt Doctrines, directly contrary to the sacred Law of God, and religious humiliation for sin, which open a wide door to all Libertinisme and disobedience to God and man, may be speedily suppressed every where . . .'.[3] Robert Baillie, commenting on the prevailing theological controversies during this period, writes: 'the Independent partie grows but the Anabaptists more; and the Antinomians most'.[4]

The only 'Antinomian' apparently to be invited to the Westminster Assembly was John Cotton, who, now in America, is found espousing radically different views from those he held in England. The invitation came in 1642 (by which time Cotton had endeared himself to the Independents), not because of his doctrine of faith but because of his congregational views.[5] Despite Cotton's stature on both sides of the Atlantic, it is highly unlikely that he would have been invited to the Westminster Assembly on the basis of his New England soteriology.[6] Cotton's doctrine of faith put a stigma upon him for a few years, but his popularity was somewhat restored by his ecclesiological views.

John Cotton arrived in America on 4 September 1633 and was

---

[1] A quorum of forty was required. Robert Baillie, a Scottish delegate, says that 'ordinarilie there will be present above three-score of their divines'. *The Letters and Journals of Robert Baillie* (1841–2), ii. 108.

[2] Mitchell, op. cit. 131.

[3] *A Copy of the Petition of the Divines of the Assembly, Delivered to both Houses of Parliament, July 19, 1643* (1643), 3.

[4] Baillie, op. cit. ii. 117.

[5] Ziff, op. cit. 178f.; Emerson, op. cit. 68. In 1642 Cotton published *The True Constitution Of A particular visible Church proved by Scripture*. The Westminster Assembly was basically comprised of three ecclesiological parties: the Presbyterians (the majority), the Independents, and the Erastians. Thomas Hooker was also invited.

[6] The present writer has examined most of the extant writings (to 1649) of nearly every Westminster divine who published (this includes 112 treatises of fifty-three divines). There is no variance among them on the nature of saving faith. In a word: every one of them who treats the subject accepts the practical syllogism. This includes Joseph Caryl, who endorsed Cotton's *A Treatise of the Covenant of Grace*. Cf. J. Caryl, *An Exposition with Practicall Observations Continued Vpon the Eighth, Ninth, and Tenth Chapters of the Book of Job* (1647), 479f.: 'The excellency of our condition consists in being godly . . . our justification may have a light or evidence in our sanctification . . . and they who reflecting upon their souls, see the image of Christ there, may be sure that Christ is theirs.'

made teacher of the Boston church on 10 October. Although the church seems to have grown rapidly after Cotton's arrival,[1] by 1636 it was in the middle of an intense controversy. The trouble which Cotton feared was 'stirring in the Country' in fact culminated in what became known as the Antinomian Controversy. This historic event was the result of Cotton's later theology plus the role of his admirer Mrs Anne Hutchinson, who embellished his views. Cotton in any case was quite likely the immediate cause of the affair as a whole. For the positions which he espoused in Massachusetts Bay, even apart from Mrs Hutchinson's opinions, proved too much to bear for his contemporaries.

Cotton is the first major figure to depart from the prevailing orthodoxy of the experimental predestinarian tradition, to which he himself had belonged. The increasing preoccupation with the conscience in the light of the Law continued 'till the strain proved too great, and Antinomianism set in'.[2] Whether Cotton's doctrine deserves to be called Antinomian is debatable,[3] but it was he who, standing largely alone, rose up hoping to reverse the tide. His efforts, for the most part, failed.

Cotton's views in 1636 and afterwards may be briefly summarized. (1) Faith alone is the evidence of justification. Cotton makes assurance the essence of saving faith. (2) There is no saving preparation for grace prior to union with Christ, nor is there anything man can do to hasten faith (or assurance). (3) Sanctification is no proof of justification. Behind this conviction lies the revival of the doctrine of temporary faith. Cotton holds that the reprobate, by virtue of temporary faith, may produce a 'real'

---

[1] 'More were converted and added to that church, than to all the other churches in the bay.' John Winthrop, *Journal* (New York, 1908), i. 116. In the six months following Cotton's admission to the church sixty-three persons (or nearly half the number of members acquired during the previous three years) joined it. Alexander Young, *Chronicles of the First Planters of the Colony of Massachusetts Bay* (Boston, 1846), 354-5. Cf. Boston Church Records, *Collections of the Colonial Society of Massachusetts*, xxxix. 12-18.

[2] G. F. Nuttall, *The Holy Spirit in Puritan Faith and Experience* (Oxford, 1947), 36.

[3] 'Antinomian' simply means 'against law'. The term emerged as a consequence of the views of the Lutheran divine Johann Agricola (d. 1566). Its use refers to the degree to which the Law applies to the Christian. Agricola dismissed its relevance. The term gradually came to be used pejoratively, and such seems to be true with regard to Cotton and the 'Antinomians' treated in Chapter 13. These divines were so nicknamed owing mainly to their insistence that assurance of salvation is to be had apart from experimental knowledge. This study will guardedly use the term Antinomian to describe these men, but, as will be seen below, the term 'experiential predestinarian' perhaps depicts their theology more accurately.

sanctification, and that conversely sanctification may be less discernible in true saints than in some hypocrites.

Precisely when Cotton came to hold these views is not known,[1] but preaching them in Massachusetts Bay got him into trouble with his peers, among whom were Thomas Hooker, Thomas Shepard (1605-49), and Peter Bulkeley (1583-1659).

To a remarkable degree Cotton revived Calvin. Indeed, Mather writes, 'Even such a Calvinist was our Cotton!'[2] But Cotton's Calvinism was not palatable to those ministers around him who were not prepared to discard the diet on which they had been nurtured. Hooker and his followers were committed to a system they believed was tried and proved. Cotton's Calvinism was threatening to those who had built their soteriology upon the assumption that man ought to prepare himself for saving grace and that sanctification proves election. Moreover, the doctrine of temporary faith had been brushed aside; William Ames buried it. Cotton came to grips with this doctrine, however, and refused to teach any longer that sanctification proves one's election.

However, to assume that Cotton captures the whole of Calvin's soteriology would be quite wrong. Cotton appears not to have grasped Calvin's view that Christ died for all and that Christ is therefore the pledge of our election. Moreover, as will be seen below, Cotton is so enmeshed in the system of the covenant of works and the covenant of grace that he seems not to see that Calvin's doctrine cannot be neatly superimposed upon this motif.

[1] Cotton claims to have preached these views in England. In a letter to Thomas Shepard (1636) he refers to 'this manner of holding out Christ, which I have applyed my ministery unto these many yeares in old Boston, and in New'. David D. Hall (ed.), *The Antinomian Controversy, 1636-1638: A Documentary History* (Middletown, Conn., 1968), 33. The letter is printed in full here (29-33). Hereinafter called *Antinomian Controversy*, this work includes every major treatise of Cotton necessary to construct his soteriological views in America, save for *A Treatise of the Covenant of Grace*. Cotton's statement to Shepard is confusing, however, since his earlier works give no hint of 'this manner of holding out Christ'. But since Cotton began preaching at St. Boltolph's in 1612, this allows plenty of room for a change of views, even though many works issued that reflected (apparently) his earliest ministry. Moreover, Mrs Hutchinson, who admired Cotton in old Boston, apparently 'could not be at rest' until she followed her beloved minister across the sea in 1634. *Antinomian Controversy*, 5. Since Mrs Hutchinson almost immediately began spreading her 'Antinomian' views, it is likely she held to them prior to her coming to America.

[2] Mather, op. cit. i. 274. 'Said he, "I have read the fathers and the school men, and Calvin too; but I find that he that has Calvin, has them all." And being asked, why in his latter days he indulged nocturnal studies more than formerly, he pleasantly replied, "Because I love to sweeten my mouth with a piece of Calvin before I go to sleep."'

As a consequence of this apparent failure fully to apprehend Calvin, Cotton remains quite subjective in his approach as a whole. He tends to make faith an experience—a subjective emotional feeling, as it were. While Cotton is like Calvin in contending that faith is but to grasp the promise of the Gospel, Cotton's lack of Christo-centrism appears to make one struggle painfully to grasp that promise. In any case, Cotton admirably manages to break out of the experimental predestinarian mould with regard to the issues of preparation for grace and the ground of assurance. On these points, given his acceptance of federal theology, he could hardly have come much closer to Calvin.[1]

Cotton's thesis in *A Treatise of the Covenant of Grace* is that Christ must be given to the soul 'before Faith can be there'.[2] He makes this point when addressing the question of the 'order the Lord giveth the Covenant, and the blessings of it: whether Faith before them, or those Blessings before Faith be able to apply them?'[3] Cotton answers: 'He doth give himself to work Faith, before Faith can be there; for it is the Fruit of the Spirit that Faith is wrought in the soul.' For it is impossible 'to apply Christ, before we be in Christ', since 'man is as passive in his Regeneration, as in his first Generation'.[4] Moreover, since the 'first Gift' that the Lord gives to the elect is Himself,[5] it follows for Cotton that Christ is not given upon a conditional but only an 'absolute promise'.[6] For there is 'no condition before Faith'. Thus 'our first coming on to Christ, cannot be upon a condition, but upon an absolute Promise'.[7]

Cotton is manifestly aware that this teaching contradicts the prevailing concept of preparation for grace. 'Reserving due honour to such gracious and precious Saints, as may be otherwise minded, I confess I do not discern, that the Lord worketh and giveth any saving preparations in the heart, till he give union with Christ. . . .'[8] Cotton reasons that if the Lord gives 'any saving Qualification' before Christ is given to the soul, 'then the soul may be in the state of salvation before Christ' is given. Such a notion he believes is 'prejudicial unto the Grace and Truth of Jesus Christ'.[9] It follows that 'whatsoever work there be in the soul, it is not there before Christ be there'.[10]

---

[1] But it is hardly accurate to say that Cotton is 'the first consistent and authentic Calvinist in New England'. John S. Coolidge, *The Pauline Renaissance in England* (Oxford, 1970), 138.

[2] *A Treatise of the Covenant of Grace*, 41.   [3] Ibid. 40-1.   [4] Ibid. 41.
[5] Ibid. 39.   [6] Ibid. 42.   [7] Ibid.
[8] Ibid. 39.   [9] Ibid. 39f.   [10] Ibid. 40.

Without calling it such, Cotton takes a position that seems to be similar to Calvin's doctrine of implicit faith, which, as will be recalled, Calvin also calls a 'preparation of faith'. Cotton thinks there is 'a saving preparation' before our consolation, or 'manifestation *of* our gracious union with Him'.[1] But regarding the union itself, 'there are no steps unto that Altar'.[2] By 'manifestation' Cotton means the more explicit awareness that Christ *has* been given to a soul. His concern is that union with Christ, which seems to be unconscious to the believer, goes before faith. Any preparation is subsequent to that union but precedes our awareness of faith. As will be seen below, Cotton also calls this a passive receiving of Christ and it obviously parallels Calvin's view of implicit faith. It will be recalled that Ames grants a passive receiving, or implicit faith, but does not allow that it is saving.

Cotton labours to show the futility of man's will prior to union with Christ. While Calvin's word is 'effaced', Cotton's is 'subdued'.

Mind you; there is no promise of life made to such as wait and seek in their own strength, who being driven unto it, have taken it up by their own resolutions . . . but if ever the Lord mean to save you . . . he will pluck away all the confidence that you have built upon . . . Now when a mans will is thus subdued, that he hath no will of his own to be guided by, but the will of God, this is true brokenness of heart, when not only the judgement, but the heart and will is broken.[3]

By 'subdued' Cotton means that neither man's 'working, nor believing, or waiting, nor seeking as of himself will do him any good'.[4] Indeed, the same Cotton who once spoke of the soul's being 'fit for Christ' in the sense of being a worthy vessel now argues that man must be brought to the place that 'there is no mercy that he can challenge for any goodness sake of his own'.[5] Until one is brought to this point, 'the soul will alway think he can do something'.[6] Rather than positing a fitness in the sense of being worthy of Christ Cotton now says the soul before faith must be 'utterly void'.[7] By being 'void' Cotton does not mean the kind of contrition or humiliation that Hooker or Ames speaks of, but an emptiness so that man has nothing he can point to, or even reflect upon, including his preparedness.

In emphasizing this conviction further, Cotton deals with the subject of preparation by using the familiar 'Spirit of bondage'. His

---

[1] *A Treatise of the Covenant of Grace* (my italics).   [2] Ibid.
[3] Ibid. 144-4.   [4] Ibid. 145.   [5] Ibid.
[6] Ibid. 137.   [7] Ibid.

doctrine of faith may be said, however, to be constituted not of two but of three works of the Spirit—in this order: the Spirit of bondage, of burning, and of adoption. The Spirit of bondage is God's work to set home to the consciences of men 'the weight and danger of their sins, and bindeth under the sense of his wrath unto fear of Damnation'.[1] It is at this point Cotton makes abundantly clear that the Spirit of bondage *can* be aborted. Thus it is here that his doctrine of temporary faith also emerges. For the Spirit of bondage may be at work in the reprobate. Consequently one has no assurance in Cotton's scheme, unlike Hooker's, that all will be well in the end, even if he feels the change working in him via the terror of the Law. Cotton admits that the Spirit of bondage may produce such a change that will cause men to have hope. But he thinks this hope is indeed premature. The Spirit of bondage 'will marvellously prevail with the sons of men, to draw them on to strong works of Reformation, from whence they reap no small consolation'.[2] But such reformations may spring from a 'temporary Faith'.[3] Thus Cotton makes the Spirit of bondage, if it does not improve, reciprocal with temporary faith.

The Spirit of bondage must be followed by the 'Spirit of burning'. This Cotton likens to the ministry of John the Baptist. And it is possible to come under the Spirit of bondage and never graduate to the Spirit of burning.

Now there are many under a spirit of bondage, that never came under a spirit of burning; and they being convinced of sin, and of the danger thereof, yet hope to wrestle it out, and work it out by their own performances, till the spirit of Burning come and consume all that false confidence.[4]

The Spirit of burning 'burns up all that a man hath wrought, or can work'.[5] This comment is very likely aimed at those who think they can prepare themselves by striving after godliness. The Spirit of burning, Cotton thinks, is designed to blast away a feeling of any spiritual progress towards faith: 'when it cometh unto the goodliness of flesh, that is consumed by a spirit of Burning.'[6] 'The Lord by this spirit of burning, doth burn up all our branches also, how fair and green soever they have been; all our fastings, and humiliations, and almsdeeds, and prayers . . . these things are all burnt up.'[7]

The statement, however, which tops all others is Cotton's assertion

---

[1] Ibid. 16. [2] Ibid. 46. [3] Ibid. [4] Ibid. 17–18.
[5] Ibid. 18. [6] Ibid. 19. [7] Ibid. 131.

that the Spirit of burning must blast 'thy faith also' if that faith is but 'a resolution of thine own'.[1] This seems to be a clear denial of voluntarism. As long as the soul says to himself, 'though I cannot work, I will believe; and if I cannot believe, I will wait that I may believe', Cotton thinks 'still the root of Adam [is] left alive in us, Whereby men seek to establish their own righteousness'. Thus what Perkins calls the least measure of faith—the will to believe—Cotton attributes to man's effort to establish his own righteousness. 'For nature is fully possessed, that what God commandeth, I am able to do it: nature will not be perswaded to the contrary: If I hear God command any thing, I will do it, (saith a carnal heart) and if I cannot believe, I will wait that I may believe: this is still but nature.'[2]

Cotton is prepared to use the term 'fit' for Christ, but with two significant changes (compared to his earlier writings). First, that the fitness referred to is not feeling worthy but realizing we are *not* 'fit': 'till it come unto this, the soul is not fit for Jesus Christ'.[3] The second difference is that, in keeping with his denial of man's will in conversion, being 'fit' even by the Spirit of burning is no guarantee the Spirit of adoption will follow. Thus in the same manner that being under the Spirit of bondage is no guarantee that saving faith will eventually emerge, neither does being under the Spirit of burning issue in an assurance one is about to receive faith. For the Spirit of burning is not regeneration, and it too may disappear before the Spirit of adoption comes.

Thus the Spirit of God may work powerfully in the hearts of men, and burn up their root and branch: and this a spirit of burning may do, and yet leave the soul in a damnable condition, for ought I know; and such as many a soul may be in, and yet never come to enjoy saving fellowship with Jesus Christ.[4]

What Cotton seeks is a subjective, albeit passive, experience of faith alone. The Spirits of bondage and burning, though prerequisites to saving faith, are not states through which one passes with the conscious assurance that all will be well in the end. Since Cotton has utterly taken away any role of man's will in both preparation and faith, the soul could be more anxious than ever under his ministry, especially in the light of his doctrine of temporary faith.[5]

---

[1] *A Treatise of the Covenant of Grace*, 132.   [2] Ibid.
[3] Ibid. 134.   [4] Ibid.
[5] Cf. John Winthrop, *A History of New England* (Boston, 1825), i. 236. 'A woman

Cotton does not tell us *how* to obtain faith; he merely implies that if we have faith we know it. This is because he believes the Spirit witnesses immediately to the heart. There is no hint at all of any mediate witness, or reflex act, such as he had once espoused. Indeed, Cotton is the first in his tradition to allow for the immediate witness of the Spirit, by which he appears also to mean direct revelation from God—even 'for all ordinary Christians', not merely 'glorious and transcendent Christians, men of renown'.[1] For Christians ought 'not to be afraid of the word Revelation'.[2] Cotton acknowledges that 'many have attended to Revelations, that have been deceived: it is true; for the Devil himself, will transform himself into an Angel of light'.[3] But this potential danger of satanic delusions does not stop Cotton from maintaining an immediate revelation, as though apart from the Word:

But yet on the otherside, let not men be afraid, and say, That we have no revelation but the word: for I do believe, and dare confidently affirme; that if there were no revelation but the word, there would be no spiritual grace revealed to the soul; for it is more then the letter of the Word that is required to it: not that I look for any other matter besides the word. But there is need of greater light, then the word of itself is able to give . . .[4]

Cotton claims that the 'promises in Scripture' by themselves have not 'wrought any gracious change in any soul, or [are] able to beget the faith of Gods elect'.[5] For 'without the work of the Spirit, there is no faith begotten by any promise'.[6] He argues that 'neither word, nor work [i.e. of sanctification] can set on a promise' until 'the Holy Ghost confirm it; it is his immediate work'.[7] The Spirit 'doth set on a power above the word, and in that respect I call it *immediate*'.[8] This witness is 'by a testimony from it self, which it doth set on more clearly, then either of the former testimonies'.[9] When the Spirit comes, then, 'He comes with power, and speaketh peace more plentifully unto the soul'.[10] Thus Cotton claims that faith carries its own witness, or assurance. He rejects making sanctification the ground of assurance; the only valid ground is the Spirit's direct witness. 'The Spirit setteth on his testimony with more clearness,

of Boston congregation, having been in much trouble of mind about her spiritual estate, at length grew into utter desperation, and could not endure to hear of any comfort, etc., so as one day she took her little infant and threw it into a well, and then came into the house and said, now she was sure she should be damned, for she had drowned her child.' The child was rescued, however.

[1] *A Treatise of the Covenant of Grace*, 186.   [2] Ibid. 199.
[3] Ibid.   [4] Ibid.   [5] Ibid.   [6] Ibid. 199–200.
[7] Ibid. 214.   [8] Ibid.   [9] Ibid. 190–1.   [10] Ibid. 191.

power, certainty unto the soul; therefore he is called by unction by which the Saints know all things . . . by his testimony we have more full assurance of all things concerning our spiritual estate.'[1] Cotton grants that the witness of faith is mediated by the Word, but 'the word of God of it self, doth not testifie' unless 'the Spirit doth' accompany it.[2]

Cotton believes men may think they are under a covenant of grace when in fact they are under a covenant of works, in which 'there be a semblance of Justification, and Adoption, and a kinde of Sanctification, yet they endure but for a season'. Christ is but a 'conditional Redeemer' to such.[3]

Although the sanctification that is derived from being under a covenant of works is temporary, it is 'real' none the less.

There be that think there is no reality in hypocritical sanctification; but certainly it is a real work, the gifts be real, through common Graces; and not meer counterfeit pretences . . . They are enlightened . . . and are made of the holy Ghost, &c these things are real, and not imaginary.[4]

Indeed, 'so glorious may this common Sanctification be, that it may dazle the eyes of the best of Gods children, and especially of poor Christians, and almost discourage them, when they see such to fall away'. In any case, 'the Scripture doth call it Sanctification' (Hebrews 10: 29).[5]

Cotton acknowledges that it is 'an easie thing for Christians to mistake their evidence' by making sanctification the ground of assurance.[6] But this is to hope in but a conditional promise, and therefore be under a covenant of works, despite the fact that there may be a flourishing of sanctification. To tell the difference between the elect and the reprobate with temporary faith is 'a work fitter for Angels' than for 'the Ministers of the Gospel'.[7] In any case, Cotton insists that sanctification is not to be discerned until one is first convinced of his justification.[8]

Cotton argues that if justification is 'not wholly doubted of', then (but only then) it is 'of use to witness'.[9] At any rate there 'can be no true Sanctification, unless there be Faith whereby the person is

---

[1] *A Treatise of the Covenant of Grace*, 191.

[2] Ibid. 192. The word of promise is 'mediate'; the 'power above the word' is 'immediate'.

[3] Ibid. 33.   [4] Ibid. 54.

[5] Ibid. Conversely, 'true Christian sanctification' is 'many times dark to a sincere Christian'. Ibid. 55.

[6] Ibid. 43.   [7] Ibid. 44.   [8] Ibid. 40–2, 70, 194.   [9] Ibid. 42.

accepted'.[1] Thus in this regard Cotton is the first in his tradition to take seriously the point Calvin stresses, viz. that faith must precede repentance in the *ordo salutis*. Cotton cites Calvin in defence of his view that faith closes upon a free, unconditional promise of grace, not upon a conditional promise.[2]

Cotton insists that Christ performed 'all things needful for the Application of this Redemption unto our souls' and this means He 'performeth all those conditions that are required on our parts'.[3] The Law itself is 'fulfilled in me so farre as Christ is in me'.[4] While Christians 'in some sence' are 'wholly freed from the Law', they are also 'in some sence' under it.[5] And the Spirit is given to God's servants 'enabling them to keep it'.[6] When they transgress the Law they 'feel the fatherly displeasure of God',[7] and when they are in obedience to the Word they sense 'Gods gracious acceptance of their waies'.[8] But even here they do not deduce 'the assurance of their justified state'.[9] Perhaps the most 'antinomian' assertion is this:

As a Christian looketh not for salvation by his obedience to the Law, nor feareth condemnation by his disobedience: so neither doth he seek for any blessing from his obedience, nor fear any curse from his disobedience . . . he expecteth all his blessing from free justification, and union with the Lord Jesus Christ . . .[10]

As to the charge he is propounding Antinomianism, Cotton retorts that such a notion is an 'aspersion' and 'false'.[11] He does not think that any under a covenant of grace 'dare allow himself in any sin', but if one did, God would 'school him thoroughly'.[12]

There has never been a hint of any licentious living surrounding Cotton or the Boston church. Moreover, Cotton's doctrinal development might have gone largely unnoticed had it not been for Mrs Anne Hutchinson. Mrs Hutchinson, the daughter of an Anglican clergyman, had endeared herself to the entire population of Massachusetts Bay by her works of mercy, particularly as a midwife. Her nursing skills gained her a ready entrance to many homes, and when she found individuals suffering from an overdose of 'works-preaching', she was ready to assuage their doubts and confusion concerning the matter of assurance. In addition to her influence in many homes she held informal meetings in her own home after the Sunday and Thursday services, to discuss the

---

[1] Ibid. 56.
[2] Ibid. 23. Cotton cites *Inst.* III. ii. 29.
[3] *A Treatise of the Covenant of Grace*, 28.
[4] Ibid. 75.
[5] Ibid. 82.
[6] Ibid. 84.
[7] Ibid.
[8] Ibid. 86.
[9] Ibid.
[10] Ibid. 92–3.
[11] Ibid. 97.
[12] Ibid. 98.

sermon. Among other things Mrs Hutchinson allegedly declared that all the ministers in Massachusetts Bay, save Mr Cotton, were preaching a covenant of works.[1]

At some time before June 1636 Thomas Shepard, pastor in New-town (now Cambridge), wrote a letter to Cotton requesting that the latter clarify his views—'give us satisfaction by way of wrighting rather than speech'.[2] Thomas Hooker also appears to have been with Shepard at this time.[3] The burden of Shepard's letter is whether the believer must await the revelation of the Spirit before closing with Christ's promise, and whether 'this revelation of the spirit, is a thing beyond and above the woord'.[4] Cotton responds, defends the general position outlined above, and concludes: 'I would not wish christians to build the signes of theire Adoption upon (any) sanctification, But such as floweth from faith in christ jesus.'[5]

In the summer of 1636 Cotton had an exchange with Peter Bulkeley.[6] The central issue is union with Christ, whether man's faith is any way a cause of that union. Bulkeley's position is that faith is the cause of that union.[7] Cotton's view is that 'this union is made before Faith worketh, and the worke of this Fayth is but an effect of the union, and not any Cause of it'. Cotton insists that this union is a passive reception in the believer and cites William Ames's view of the passive reception of Christ.[8] What Cotton does not apparently recognize is that Ames does not consider this passive reception saving until the believer rests on Christ through an act of the will. Cotton considers the passive reception saving.

The following December the elders of Massachusetts Bay drew up sixteen questions which they put to Cotton.[9] Most of the sixteen

[1] For the details of the Antinomian Controversy see *Antinomian Controversy*, *passim*; Ziff, op. cit. 106–49. The original account is in John Winthrop, *A Short Story of the Rise, reign, and ruin of the Antinomians, Familists & Libertines* (1644).

[2] *Antinomian Controversy*, 25. Thomas Shepard, born at Towcester, Northampton-shire, was admitted to Emmanuel College, Cambridge, as a pensioner, taking his BA in 1623 and MA in 1627. He was converted by John Preston. He became Hooker's son-in-law. After a brief ministry at Earles-Colne he was suspended by Laud. He came to America in 1635 and became pastor at Newtown in February 1636.

[3] Ibid. 24, 33.   [4] Ibid. 25 ff.   [5] Ibid. 32.

[6] Ibid. 34. Peter Bulkeley was born in Cheshire. In 1599 he went to St. John's College, Cambridge. He took the MA in 1608. In 1620 he succeeded his father to the living at Odell. He was suspended by Laud in 1635, and headed for America in 1636, settled at Concord, and founded the twelfth church in the colony.

[7] Ibid. 34 f.   [8] Ibid. 36–7.

[9] Ibid. 46–59. This was published as *Sixteene Questions of Serious and Necessary Consequence, Propounded unto Mr. John Cotton of Boston in New-England, Together with His Answers to each Question* (1644).

questions revolve around the issue of the ground of assurance.[1] Cotton gives his reply to each question. His position remains essentially the same. He says that the testimony of the Spirit is 'so cleare, as that it may witnesse immediately' although it is never without sanctification.[2] But if justification 'lyeth prostrate (that is, altogether dark and hidden from me) I cannot prove my selfe in a state of Grace by my Sanctification'.[3] Cotton notes that this issue is that of the 'greatest Agitation' in the colony.[4] He reminds his fellow ministers that the figure described with reference to the stony ground and thorny soil in the Parable of the Sower 'may find comfort', but 'in truth, in so doing he buildeth upon such a Sanctification which is indeed a sanday Foundation'.[5]

Thus Cotton by this assertion has brought into the open what many divines in his tradition had sought to sweep under the carpet: the doctrine of temporary faith. But Cotton does not dwell on this. This to him is not the only reason for rejecting sanctification as the ground of assurance. He believes the witness of the Spirit alone is to be sought and that it by itself is sufficient to give full assurance. He allows that the practical syllogism is acceptable—if 'the Reason be not carnall but spirituall'.[6] But by this he means that the person first has received the witness of the Spirit; the 'experimental observation of a good Conscience' is to be admitted if the conscience has been 'established by the Witnesse of the Spirit'.[7] Here Cotton is consistent with his point seen above that sanctification is 'of use to witness' if the absolute promise has been grasped first.

The elders gave a reply to Cotton's sixteen answers. They remain quite unhappy with most of his defence. One interesting matter in the reply of the elders is that they accuse Cotton of charging none other than the Apostle Peter with going 'aside unto a Covenant of works'.[8] The biblical banner for the experimental predestinarian tradition, 2 Peter 1: 10, emerges in the Antinomian Controversy. For Peter, they say, exhorts us 'to use all diligence, adding one grace to another thereby to make our calling and Election sure'.[9]

---

[1] It is interesting that the issue of preparation is scarcely mentioned, although such is always implied when sanctification is the ground of assurance. Pettit, *The Heart Prepared*, 144, is correct to note 'how sensitive the preparationists had now become to the vulnerability of their doctrine'.

[2] *Antinomian Controversy*, 49.   [3] Ibid. 52.

[4] Cotton wavers on one question: whether a weak believer may not wait on God and derive some comfort from this, viz. 'that he doth waite'. Cotton concedes that one may. Ibid. 50.

[5] Ibid. 54.   [6] Ibid. 58.   [7] Ibid.   [8] Ibid. 60-7.   [9] Ibid. 72.

Cotton gave a rejoinder to the elders' reply, a very lengthy defence.[1] His position remains the same: union with Christ must precede faith. For 'all conditions before union with Christ are corrupt and unsavoury' and all conditions after that union 'are effects and fruits of that union, and that of Faith which floweth from that union'. Otherwise we may bring forth 'good fruit before union with Christ which the Gospel accounteth impossible'.[2]

As for 2 Peter 1: 10, Cotton claims that becoming assured by good works is but a papist position.[3] He casts his lot with John Calvin, who 'maketh the free promise the foundation of faith or assurance'. For Calvin says 'a conditional promise whereby we are sent to Works, doth not promise life but as we see the condition found in ourselves'.[4] Furthermore, in his contention that sanctification must not be the ground of assurance, he drops this comment: 'I hope it will be no offence to you, no more than to myself, if we borrow light from Calvin to clear the meaning of the Holy Ghost.'[5]

It appears therefore evidently by the Judgment of Calvin, That these places which give signs of our good estate from Sanctification, were not given at all to such Christians as are doubtfull of their estates, from thence to gather the first Assurance of their good estates: but to such only as are formerly assured of their good estates . . .[6]

Cotton repeatedly appeals to Calvin in this controversy,[7] and takes Calvin's line with regard to 2 Peter 1: 10. Cotton states that Peter exhorts men to be fruitful, but 'not thereby, as by Effectual means, nor thereby as by the full end of their way to make their calling and Election sure'.[8] As for Calvin's view of 2 Peter 1: 10, Cotton follows him entirely and points out that Calvin does not refer this matter to the conscience; moreover, 'so loath he is to allow the Assurance of faith of our good estates to arise from our Sanctification'.[9] But Cotton does not appear fully to understand *why* Calvin takes this position, viz. because Christ alone is our pledge.

Finally, when giving more detail regarding the practical syllogism, Cotton deals with that seen so often in Perkins:

He that Repenteth and beleeveth the Gospel shall be saved.
But I repent and beleeve the Gospel
Therefore I shall be saved, (and consequently am justified).[10]

---

[1] *Antinomian Controversy*, 78–151.   [2] Ibid. 92.   [3] Ibid. 93.
[4] Ibid.   [5] Ibid. 105.   [6] Ibid. 106.
[7] See ibid. 117, 121, 125, 129–30, 140, 145. The issue is the same: sanctification is not to be the ground of assurance.
[8] Ibid. 124.   [9] Ibid. 125.   [10] Ibid. 148.

Cotton thinks that the conclusion is 'safe' if the 'minor proposition be true'. But the minor proposition is only true if the Gospel has been 'applied to that Soul, not only by outward ministry of the Word but by the Spirit of God himself, revealing the grace of Christ therein'.[1] Hence the practical syllogism is not to be applied by the doubter.

Cotton's rejoinder to the elders seems to have ended the written exchange between himself and them. However, at some time between May and August 1637 there was a conference between Cotton and the elders.[2] In this conference 2 Peter 1: 10 again emerges, and on this controversial Scripture Cotton yields to his venerable hero: 'Let Calvin answer for me.' Cotton thus reminds his opponents again of Calvin's view: 2 Peter 1: 10 'is not in my judgement to be referred unto conscience'.[3]

There was singularly little meeting of minds between Cotton and his fellow pastors. This is hardly surprising in the light of the long tradition that began with Perkins; the greatest surprise is the change of Cotton himself. The difference between Calvin and Beza is largely repeated in the Antinomian Controversy when Cotton encounters the heirs of the Beza–Perkins tradition.

Thomas Shepard suggested that the only way to deal with the matter was to confront Anne Hutchinson. The meeting of the elders in the late summer of 1637 is now called the Hutchinson Synod. The details of this trial are interesting but cannot be dealt with here. Cotton stood by her until the bitter end, when she claimed direct revelations from God as the determining factor in conduct. His standing by her for so long suggests that Cotton knew that his own preaching was in some measure responsible for her claim. But now Cotton backed down from defending her in the presence of his fellow pastors. The trial itself was held in Shepard's church. Thomas Hooker often moderated and Peter Bulkeley was present as well. Here is a portion of the trial's proceedings:

> Mr. Nowell. How do you know that that was the spirit?
> Mrs. H. How did Abraham know that it was God that bid him offer his son, being a breach of the sixth commandment?
> Dep. Gov. By an immediate voice.

[1] Ibid.
[2] Ibid. 175–98. This was published as *A Conference Mr. John Cotton held at Boston With the Elders of New-England* (1646), and reissued the same year as *Gospel Conversion*.
[3] *Antinomian Controversy*, 185.

Mrs. H. So to me by an immediate revelation.
Dep. Gov. How! an immediate revelation.
Mrs. H. By the voice of his own spirit to my soul . . .[1]

Mrs Hutchinson was condemned by the court and her sentence was banishment from Massachusetts Bay.[2] Four years later, in Rhode Island, she was killed by Indians.

Once the controversy had subsided Cotton considered moving to New Haven. He wanted to 'preach as he pleased to whom he pleased'.[3] Moreover, 'it was hard for him to remain in a situation where respect for his doctrine had been considerably diminished'.[4] Indeed, Shepard suspected the controversy had little effect in altering Cotton's views; he wrote in his diary: Cotton 'repents not: but is hid only'.[5] Winthrop wanted Cotton to stay in Boston, thinking that Cotton's departure would be a signal to England that all was not well.[6] Cotton remained in Boston until his death.

Cotton's stature increased, however, in a few years. In 1644 *The Keyes of the Kingdom of Heaven*, his strongest defence of congregational ecclesiology, was published with the endorsement of the Westminster divines Thomas Goodwin and Phillip Nye. Neither Cotton nor Hooker accepted their invitations to attend the Westminster Assembly.

Hooker died in 1647 and Cotton wrote a poem in his honour. Shepard died in 1649, Bulkeley in 1659. Cotton himself died on 23 December 1652. John Wilson (d. 1667), pastor of the Boston church, was at Cotton's side in his last moments, and prayed that God would lift up the light of His countenance upon the dying man and shed love into his soul. Cotton's last words were, 'He hath done it already, Brother'.[7]

John Cotton was the only major figure in his tradition to break out of its mould, and did so in the direction of Calvin. Calvin was clearly his guide, and there is no doubt that Cotton succeeded to a large degree in bringing Calvin's doctrine of faith into his scheme. Rather than an experimental predestinarian Cotton might best be called an experiential predestinarian.

There is one interesting footnote. Cotton curiously does not appear to use Calvin's term 'persuasion' with regard to his descrip-

---

[1] *Antinomian Controversy*, 337.   [2] Ibid. 348.   [3] Ziff, op. cit. 109.
[4] Pettit, *The Heart Prepared*, 155f.
[5] T. Shepard, *Autobiography* (Boston, 1832), 386.
[6] Ziff, op. cit. 146.   [7] Ibid. 255.

tion or definition of faith,[1] although such is apparently his meaning. The explanation in part may lie in Thomas Shepard's reasoning. 'Some run to the other extreme', Shepard writes, 'and make faith nothing else, but a perswasion or assurance that Christ dyed for me in particular, or that he is mine.' Shepard judges, 'That which moves some thus to think, is the universall redemption by the death of Christ, they know no ground or bottome for faith but this Proposition, Christ dyed for thee, and hence make Redemption universall.' Shepard also thinks faith as a persuasion fits best with Arminianism.[2]

Shepard's statement further suggests that Arminius has indeed stolen from Reformed theology Calvin's conviction that Christ died for all men. Whether Cotton's further reading of Calvin ever brought him to see this was Calvin's own view, one cannot say. Had he seen it, the need for a subjective experience of the Spirit could have been avoided. But had Cotton preached it, he would probably have been in greater trouble than ever. To assert that Christ died for all would have brought more controversy than ever to Massachusetts Bay, a community that seems not to have realized that their own views were quite close after all to those of Arminius.

---

[1] Cotton does not define faith in *A Treatise of the Covenant of Grace*. In 1634 he defined faith as 'a work of God's Almighty Quickning Power, wrought by the Ministry of the Word and Spirit of God, whereby the Heart is weaned from all Confidence in the Flesh, and believeth in God and the Lord Jesus Christ to Righteousness'. *A Treatise of Faith* (1713), 3. In his catechism he defines faith as 'a grace of the spirit; whereby I deny my selfe: and believe on Christ for righteousnesse and salvation'. *Milk for Babes* (1646), 11.

[2] T. Shepard, *The Sound Beleever* (1645), 161.

13

THE WESTMINSTER DIVINES AND THEIR SOTERIOLOGICAL UNITY

In a sermon before the House of Commons in 1641, Edmund Calamy (d. 1666) urged Parliament not only to 'root out Arminianism' but to settle the Church's doctrine so 'that there may be no shadow in it for an Arminian'.[1]

When the Westminster divines were chosen in 1642 there was a soteriological consensus among them; this was guaranteed by Parliament's careful selection. The Arminian threat from within was therefore regarded as having been eliminated before the divines began their initial deliberations. While there was ecclesiological diversity, there was soteriological unity. Ecclesiological issues dominated the proceedings; 'doctrinal matters lay wholly in the background', for the divines were in 'complete fundamental harmony' concerning things soteriological.[2] There is no hint, either from the minutes of the Assembly's proceedings or from the various writings of the divines themselves, that any member espoused an Arminian doctrine of predestination. Moreover, there is no indica-

---

[1] E. Calamy, *Gods free Mercy to England* (1642), 20.

[2] B. B. Warfield, *The Westminster Assembly and its Work*, 12, 55. Two exceptions to this are to be noted. First, there seem to have been 'long and tough debates about the Decrees of election'. Baillie, *Letters*, ii. 326. The issue was over the order of the decrees. However, the Assembly seems to have taken the advice of Edward Reynolds: 'Let not us put in disputes and scholastical things into a Confession of Faith.' *Minutes of the Sessions of the Westminster Assembly of Divines* (1874), 151. The final wording in the Confession avoids a supralapsarian preciseness and can be endorsed by either a supra- or infralapsarian. Cf. Warfield, *Westminster Assembly*, 56. Secondly, it seems the views of the French theologian Moise Amyraut (d. 1664) were brought into the debate. Amyraut claims to have followed Calvin in holding that Christ died for all men. Brian G. Armstrong, *Calvinism and the Amyraut Heresy: Protestant Scholasticism and Humanism in Seventeenth-Century France* (Madison, 1969), 130–60. 'Unhappilie Amiraut's Questions are brought in our Assemblie. Many more loves these fancies here than I did expect.' Baillie, op. cit. ii. 324. Edmund Calamy holds to a universal redemption, but not 'in the Arminian sense'. *Minutes*, 152. Three joined in the debate on Calamy's side: Lazarus Seaman, Stephen Marshall, and Richard Vines. Ibid. 152 ff. Cf. Warfield, *Westminster Assembly*, 56. In any case, the doctrine of limited atonement won out. Cf. *infra*, p. 199 n. 3.

tion of a divergence of opinion among any of them on the nature of saving faith.[1]

THE 'ANTINOMIAN' THREAT

The greatest threat that seems to have emerged from within the predestinarian family generally came from some 'Antinomians'. Shortly after the divines sent a petition on 19 July 1643[2] came their more specific 'petition against the Antinomians' on 10 August 1643. This petition names three treatises as exemplifying Antinomianism: *The Honey-combe of Free Justification by Christ Alone* (1642), by John Eaton; (2) *Christ Alone Exalted* (1643), by Tobias Crisp; and *The Doctrine and Conversation of John Baptist* (1643), by Henry Denne.[3]

While the issues raised by these writers often overlap with those of the Antinomian Controversy in America, there is no evidence that these divines, or those treated below, were influenced by John Cotton. But it is almost certainly true that the Westminster divines were fearful that men of the stature of Cotton might emerge at any time during the disturbed years of the 1640s. In any case, Westminster theology must be viewed not only in the light of the experimental predestinarian tradition preceding it but also in view of the Antinomian threat. This threat was nearing a peak while the divines were drawing up their documents. As will be seen below, some assertions in the documents speak directly to men like Tobias Crisp. But it will also be seen that various replies to 'Antinomianism' are but a repeat of experimental predestinarian theology.

John Eaton (1575-1641)

Eaton was born in Kent, and was educated at Trinity College, Oxford, receiving the BA in 1595, the MA in 1603. In 1635 he became vicar at Wickham Market, Suffolk, where he remained to the end of his days.[4]

The 'very essence' of true faith, Eaton says, is to 'beleeve the cleane contrary to our sense and feeling' (i.e. feeling we are sinful), and believing rather 'that wee have no sin in the sight of God: this is

---

[1] Cf. *supra*, p. 168 n. 6.   [2] Cf. *supra*, p. 168 n. 3.

[3] *The Journal of the Proceedings of the Assembly of Divines* (1824; this is volume xiii of *The Whole Works of the Rev. John Lightfoot, D.D.*), 9, 12.

[4] Besides *The Honey-combe of Free Justification* (hereinafter called *Honey-combe*), this study will draw from Eaton's *The Discovery of the most dangerous Dead Faith* (1641), hereinafter called *Dead Faith*.

true faith'.[1] But 'where there is reasoning from sense and feeling, there is not faith'.[2] In this latter statement Eaton means deducing assurance by sanctification and also feeling a sense of despair because of the lack of sanctification. We must believe 'that God is able above our reason, sense, and feeling by his Sons blood and righteousnesse utterly to abolish out of his own sight all our sins'.[3]

Eaton attacks the voluntarism that is characteristic of the experimental predestinarian tradition:

Such Preachers teach but the light of nature, the pride of workes, and vaine-glory of man; and so doe withdraw people from Christ to hang upon their own works and doings, by resting upon the popish rotten pillar that God accepts the will for the deed, and do drowne Christs glory, free Justification, do destroy faith, waste and consume the Church of Christ, teach a false bastard sanctification . . .[4]

Indeed, Eaton calls such preachers 'the wolves whereof S. Paul gave warning' who call more 'for workes and a good life' than 'assurance of the sound faith of their free Justification' in Christ alone.[5]

In *Honey-combe* Eaton works out his doctrine of justification in scholarly fashion, aligning himself with the mainstream of Protestant thinkers. While he quotes Perkins twice, Beza three times, and Zanchius twelve times,[6] he quotes Calvin forty-one times and Luther 106 times![7] His theme is that our consciences are 'made good to God-ward by Justification' and 'to menward by Sanctification'.[8] Justification is perceived 'by faith only; Sanctification is perceived by sense and feeling'.[9] And while justification is 'meritorious of all the favour and blessings of God: Sanctification it selfe merits nothing at all'. God leaves our sanctification so imperfect in this life, that 'all our rejoycing, and joy unspeakable and glorious may be in Justification'.[10]

Tobias Crisp (1600–43)

Crisp was born in London of a wealthy family. He attended Eton, then Cambridge, where he received the BA, and moved to Balliol College, Oxford, in 1626, graduating MA. Years later he received the degree of DD. From 1627 to 1642 he was rector of Brinkworth,

---

[1] *Honey-combe*, 48, 50.   [2] Ibid. 50.   [3] Ibid.
[4] *Dead Faith*, 62–3.   [5] Ibid. 66–7.
[6] These quotes are with regard to the imputation of Christ's righteousness by faith.
[7] Luther's *Galatians* and Calvin's *Institutes* are quoted most often to support Eaton's claim that justification is given without conditions.
[8] *Honey-combe*, 91.   [9] Ibid. 459.   [10] Ibid.

Wiltshire. At Brinkworth he was suspected of Antinomianism, and after he moved to London in 1642 he was bitterly attacked by some fifty-two opponents. Crisp was once an Arminian and was given to 'the legal way of preaching', but, 'changing his opinion, he ran into the contrary extreme of antinomianism'. Being shocked with his former views, 'he seems to have imagined that he could never go far enough from them'. Yet he was 'unblamable in his life and conversation'.[1]

Of the seventeen sermons in *Christ Alone Exalted* fourteen are based upon Isaiah 53: 6—'The Lord hath laid on him the iniquity of us all.' Crisp's main point is that saving faith is the realization in time of what has already happened in eternity, viz. justification had been accomplished in Christ: 'The Lord hath done it already.'[2] Crisp actually holds to a three-tiered justification: (1) eternal justification (the elect were already justified in eternity once God committed Himself to lay the elect's iniquities on the Son); (2) virtual justification (when Christ died and rose again); and (3) actual justification (when the elect in time discover they have already been justified).[3]

The discovery that we have been justified already is what Crisp means by saving faith. Like Cotton, Crisp tends to make faith an emotional experience. Moreover, Cotton's insistence upon union with Christ before faith is parallel with Crisp's idea of eternal justification. When Christ applies to our souls what He has done already He 'doth but introduce the knowledge of that which the Lord hath done before'.[4]

Faith is 'the Conduit pipe through which the Lord is pleased' to convey the knowledge of justification.[5] This knowledge is full assurance. Indeed, 'the Apostle doth not onely appropriate assurance, but even fulnesse of assurance to faith alone'.[6] Therefore 'faith is sufficient to resolve a soul of its interest in Christ'.[7]

In any case, Crisp vigorously rejects sanctification as a ground of assurance.

I mean briefly and plainly thus; the common way of people is to try themselves by signes and marks, and as signes and marks drawne from their sanctification and performances, will make up the conclusion they desire; so they sit down satisfied with their condition.[8]

---

[1] Benjamin Brook, *The Lives of the Puritans* (1813), ii. 472 ff.; Daniel Neal, *The History of the Puritans* (1822), iii. 16 f.

[2] *Christ Alone Exalted* (1643; with seventeen sermons), 262.

[3] Ibid. 264 ff.   [4] Ibid. 240   [5] Ibid. 509.

[6] Ibid. 510.   [7] Ibid. 513.   [8] Ibid. 431.

Indeed, to 'resolve the spirits of men' by holding sanctification as the sign of justification is a 'litigious and doubtful' course.[1]

Crisp also observes that it is common to say that sincerity takes the place of exactness of performance. 'But I answer, That if sinceritie and singlenesse of heart be made a mark and signe of interest in Christ, at last it will faile a person as well as universall obedience. . . . [and] whosoever builds upon it, may deceive himselfe . . .'[2] For there is 'not one fruit of sanctification, if it speaks as the Lord hath given to it to speak, that can speak peace to the soule'.[3]

Henry Denne (d. 1660?)

Denne was educated at Cambridge and was ordained in 1630. He was made curate of Pirton, Hertfordshire, and was there about ten years. Denne became convinced that infant baptism was unscriptural and was baptized by immersion in 1643, joining a congregation in Bell Alley. He was regarded as an Antinomian, but it seems he was often persecuted for his views on baptism.[4]

Denne takes the line that 'Christs righteousnesse is made ours' by imputation 'before the act of our Faith, and therefore necessarily without it'.[5] Not to take this view Denne thinks is to set Christ forth 'upon some conditions', and those who set Him forth this way do not 'deserve the name of Protestants'.[6] It is not faith but Christ who truly justifies; we are, however, justified by faith 'declaratively in our Consciences'.[7]

Such an act, then, 'is a consequent of our justification, and not an intercedent', since we 'must be grafted into Christ Jesus before we can believe, Therefore we must be justified before we can believe'.[8] Faith itself is 'beholding the glorious object [Christ], and so we are assured of our justification'.[9]

What Denne is particularly against is the idea 'that a desire to believe is faith it selfe'.[10] As 'all that desire to be rich, are not Rich; so all that desire to believe, do not believe'.[11] Moreover, to have 'a care to keep Gods Law, to do all things commanded, and to shun all things forbidden' is not the evidence of faith, for once an unjustified

---

[1] *Christ Alone Exalted* (1643; with seventeen sermons), 431.
[2] Ibid. 444.   [3] Ibid. 460-1.
[4] This study will draw from *The Doctrine and Conversation of John Baptist* (1643; hereinafter called *John Baptist*); and *A Conference Between a sick man and a Minister, shewing the nature of Presumption, Despair, and the true living Faith* (1643; hereinafter called *Conference*).
[5] *John Baptist*, 25.   [6] Ibid.   [7] Ibid. 26.   [8] *Conference*, 14–15.
[9] Ibid. 18.   [10] Ibid. 2. Cf. *John Baptist*, 51 f.   [11] *Conference*, 2.

man said: 'All these things have I kept from my youth' (Mark
10: 20-1).[1] Thus if the person is not first accepted, 'the will cannot
be accepted for the deed: before you can assure your self by this
will; you must see that your person is accepted'.[2] Furthermore,
repentance is no proof of saving faith; a reprobate may 'sorrow
heartily' for his sins.[3]

SOME REACTIONS TO 'ANTINOMIANISM'

Early in the proceedings of the Assembly of Divines the Antinomian
threat was being dealt with. In addition to the aforementioned
petitions, some divines published treatises; some endorsed treatises
of other divines who attacked the 'Antinomians'.

In 1643 John Sedgwick published *Antinomianisme Anatomized,
or, A Glasse for The Lawlesse: who deny the Ruling use of the Morall
Law unto Christians under the Gospel*. This was endorsed by the
Westminster divine Edmund Calamy as 'very necessary for these
times'.[4] The treatise attacks Eaton's two books, *Honey-combe* and
Dead Faith. *Antinomianisme Anatomized* is based upon three characters: the 'Nomist' and the 'Antinomist' on opposite sides, with
'Evangelist' (purportedly the correct position) in between. This
work stresses the Moral Law in the Christian life, including
'universall obedience'.[5] Sedgwick raises 2 Peter 1: 10 and states that
while works do not justify, 'yet they justifie faith to a mans own
conscience'.[6]

The Marrow of Modern Divinity (1645)[7] emerged when the Westminster Assembly was reaching its height of deliberations, and it
came with a warm endorsement by Joseph Caryl. Caryl finds the

---

[1] Ibid. 3.   [2] Ibid. 4.
[3] Ibid. 5f. Two other prominent 'Antinomians' are John Saltmarsh (d. 1647) and
William Dell (d. 1664). These men became chaplains in Oliver Cromwell's New
Model Army. See Saltmarsh, *Sparkles of Glory* (1647) and *Free-Grace* (1646); and
Select Works of William Dell (1773). For a further study of the Antinomian
controversies in England see Gertrude Huehns, *Antinomianism in English History*
(1951), 37–88; Leo F. Solt, *Saints in Arms* (1959), 6–42, 68–9. Cf. Ernest F. Kevan,
The Grace of Law (1964), *passim*.
[4] *Antinomianisme Anatomized* (1643), facing p. 1. Calamy was appointed chairman
of a committee on 'Antinomianism' in the Assembly on 14 Sept. 1643. C. A. Briggs,
'The Documentary History of the Westminster Assembly', *Presbyterian Review* (New
York, 1880), 142.
[5] *Antinomianisme Anatomized*, 44.   [6] Ibid. 24.
[7] Written by E. F., Edward Fisher, an unlettered but hardly illiterate London
barber. See J. M. Hagans, '*The Marrow of Modern Divinity* and the Controversy
Concerning it in Scotland' (BD thesis, Trinity College, Dublin, 1966), 12 ff.

treatise 'tending to Peace and Holinesse' and says that the author endeavours 'to reconcile and heale those unhappy differences which have lately broken out afresh amongst us'.[1]

Fisher takes the characters in *Antinomianisme Anatomized* and adds a fourth: Neophytus, a young Christian who wants to know the way of salvation. Evangelista has the truth, but neither Nomista nor Antinomista are happy with the 'middle path' of Evangelista[2] — that is, until the last, when all four are in apparent agreement. Along the way in any case both Nomista and Antinomista are often rebuked by Evangelista. Antinomista thinks he has been vindicated by Evangelista's rejection of Nomista's contention that the want of perfect righteousness 'shall be made up' by Christ's.[3] Evangelista rather holds that God accepts only Christ's righteousness.[4] Antinomista therefore rejoices:

O sir, you do please me wondrous well in thus attributing all unto Christ, I see you are the same that you were when I used to heare you . . . I thanke God, I have continued believing unto this day, being confident that I am so clothed with the perfect righteousnesse of Jesus Christ, that God can see no sin in me at all, but beholds me without spot or blemish.[5]

But Antinomista's delight is premature:

Evan. There is in this City at this day much talke about Antinomians; And though I hope there be very few that doe justly deserve that title, yet I feare . . . Surely thou art one of them, for thy speech bewrayeth thee. And therefore to deale plainly with you, I question whether you have as yet truly beleeved on the name of Jesus Christ, for all of you are so confident.[6]

Thus Fisher, or Evangelista, seeks to maintain a position that is neither legalistic nor 'Antinomian'. Fisher shows a familiarity with many writers. He quotes Luther, Calvin, Beza, Ursinus, Greenham, Perkins, Sibbes, Preston, Ames, Hooker, and many more. But he is highly selective with his sources and only uses them when they say something to support his case.

Evangelista warns Nomista against making 'the change of your life the ground of your Faith', as faith must precede holiness of life.[7] However, if one looks upon these evidences 'with reference to Jesus Christ, then they are not deceitfull, but sure evidences and demonstrations of faith in Christ'.[8] It is here that Fisher betrays that his sympathies are on Nomista's side, providing one looks at the signs

---

[1] *The Marrow of Modern Divinity* (1645), facing title-page.   [2] Ibid. 188.
[3] Ibid. 85.   [4] Ibid. 86f.   [5] Ibid. 88–9.
[6] Ibid. 90.   [7] Ibid. 135.   [8] Ibid. 155.

with reference to Christ. His view of faith, moreover, is essentially voluntaristic. Evangelista says to Nomista: 'Are you resolved to put forth the utmost of your power to believe, and so to take Christ?' Then 'you may without doubt conclude that the match is made'.[1]

Fisher explicitly makes it known he is rejecting the 'Antinomianism' of Crisp and Eaton.[2] In 1646 a second edition of *The Marrow of Modern Divinity* appeared, this time with a further recommendation by the Westminster divine Jeremiah Burroughes. In this edition Fisher also credits Thomas Hooker with his own conversion of some years before.[3]

In June 1645 the Westminster divine Simeon Ashe published a treatise by John Ball (d. 1640), *A Treatise of the Covenant of Grace*. In addition to Ashe's preface, a separate endorsement came from five other Westminster divines: Edward Reynolds, Daniel Cawdrey, Thomas Hill, Anthony Burgess, and Edmund Calamy.[4]

Ball's theology is essentially no different from the prevailing orthodoxy of the experimental predestinarian tradition. Indeed, he states that 'no remission is promised to be enjoyed but upon condition of repentance', so that 'repentance goeth before pardon'.[5] Consequently repentance 'must goe before justifying faith'. Faith, Ball says, is 'whereby we believe, that if a man performe the condition, he shall possesse the promise'.[6]

Three Westminster divines took pen in hand to deal with the growing threat of Antinomianism: Samuel Rutherford, Samuel Bolton, and Thomas Gataker.

Samuel Rutherford (d. 1662)

Rutherford, a powerful Scottish delegate, was a graduate of Edinburgh University. In 1638 he was appointed professor of divinity at St. Mary's College, St. Andrew's.[7]

---

[1] Ibid. 111.   [2] Ibid. 166, 168.

[3] *The Marrow of Modern Divinity* (1646), Preface.

[4] J. Ball, *A Treatise of the Covenant of Grace* (1645), To the reader. The divines also refer to Ball's *A Treatise of Faith* (1631), which Sibbes had recommended. Cf. *supra*, p. 104 n. 2. They believe Ball's works tend 'to reconcile the differences of these times'. Ball's works may have had some influence upon the final shaping of Westminster theology. Mitchell, *The Westminster Assembly*, 377. Cf. Warfield, *The Westminster Assembly*, 57.

[5] Ball, *A Treatise of the Covenant of Grace*, 349.   [6] Ibid.

[7] Fuller titles are given of the following works to show Rutherford's deeper motives in writing them: *The Tryall & Trivmpth of Faith: . . . Some speciall Grounds and Principle of Libertinisme and Antinomian Errors, discovered* (1645); *A Survey of the Spirituall Antichrist. Opening The secrets of Familisme and Antinomianisme in the*

Rutherford attacks the idea that faith must be a persuasion. It 'may be a perswasion in some sense', but 'no divine' could deny that 'a direct act of faith' without a 'reflex act' can of itself be known to be 'true, not counterfeit'.[1] This was Ames's position in a word. But the 'keeping of the Commandements, and the word of Jesus', which is the reflex act, 'is infallible in it selfe'.[2] Such keeping of the Word and 'holy walking' are 'infallible signes'.[3]

Moreover, 'I see no reason to call the workes of Sanctification inferior helps in the Manifestation, more then the voice of the Beloved'.[4] For both with the Spirit 'infallibly perswade'.[5] Rutherford insists that many weak Christians, however, 'cannot come up to an assurance of perswasion' although 'they are chosen to life, and have faith'.[6] Behind this assertion lies Rutherford's belief that 'a desire of grace' is grace,[7] the very view Eaton and Crisp had rejected.

However, Rutherford wants it understood that this desire pre-supposes that one has already been converted.[8] He seems sensitive to the charge of Arminianism, and states in this connection: 'We hold no morall preparations with Pelagians, Papists, and Arminians going before conversion.'[9]

We teach not, which Saltmarsh falsely chargeth us, that Vowes and under-takings never ascending to Christ, fit us for conversion . . . we deny, against Antinomians and Arminians any such Gospel-promise; he that doth this and this, and is so, and so fitted with such conditions, quallifications, as money and hire in hand, shall be converted as a reward of his worke.[10]

For 'no man but Pelagians, Arminians, and such do teach, if any shall improve their natural habilities to the uttermost' they shall be saved.[11] For all preparations 'before conversion' are 'no formall part of conversion' and cannot please God.[12] The implications of having been charged with Arminianism are apparent in Ruther-ford's rejoinder, and this may account in part for the absence of the kind of preparationism seen in some of the writers above.

Antichristian Doctrine of John Saltmarsh, and Will. Del, the present Preachers of the Army now in England, and of Robert Town, Tob. Crisp, H. Denne, Eaton, and others (1648) (in two parts, hereinafter called *A Survey*); and *Christ Dying and Drawing Sinners to Himself. . . . Where also are interjected some necessary Digressions for the times, touching divers Errors of Antinomians* (1647), hereinafter called *Christ Dying*.

[1] *Christ Dying*, 98.   [2] Ibid.   [3] Ibid. 98–9.
[4] Ibid. 99.   [5] Ibid.   [6] *A Survey*, ii. 235.
[7] Ibid. 4.   [8] Ibid.   [9] Ibid. 2.
[10] Ibid. 3.   [11] *Christ Dying*, 239 f.   [12] Ibid. 240.

Rutherford also rejects the idea that 'from eternity we were justified'.[1] In this instance he cites Crisp, and argues that 'justification in Gods decree and purpose from eternity, is no more justification then Creation, sanctification, glorification, the crucifying of Christ, and all things that fall out in time; for all these were in the eternall purpose of God'.[2]

Rutherford takes note of Mrs Anne Hutchinson, 'the American Jesabel', who he says held to many of the views he rejects.[3] He also notes her death, that the Indians 'slew her and her daughter', and 'some say the Indians burnt her house, and all she had'.[4]

Samuel Bolton (*1606–54*)

Bolton was educated at Christ's College, Cambridge. He ministered in London for several years and was made Master of Christ's College in 1645. He published *The Trve Bovnds of Christian Freedome* (1645). While he desires to answer Crisp,[5] his concern mainly is to defend the validity of the Moral Law in the Christian life. But he speaks to the issue of preparation for grace and defends the view that preparation for grace is necessary to the degree that means are necessary.[6]

Bolton's doctrine of justification may be summarized: (1) we are justified 'in decree, and so we are justified from everlasting'; (2) we are justified 'meritoriously' by Christ's death; (3) we are justified 'actually' only when we believe; (4) we are justified in the 'court of conscience' when we are assured; and (5) we are justified 'perfectly' when we are glorified.[7]

Thomas Gataker (*1574–1654*)

Gataker was born in London, and came up to St. John's College, Cambridge, in 1590, graduating MA, and eventually took the BD. In 1611 he was made rector of Rotherhithe, Surrey.[8]

Gataker was apparently drawn into the Antinomian controversies because John Saltmarsh had allegedly cited him as 'giving some

---

[1] *A Survey*, ii. 19.   [2] Ibid.   [3] Ibid. i. 176.
[4] Ibid. 182. In *An Antidote against Antinomianisme* (1643), 39, one D. H. refers to a book 'of our brethren of New-England, touching the tragicall effects of these [Antinomian] doctrines'.
[5] *Trve Bovnds*, 293.   [6] Ibid. 291.   [7] Ibid. 289.
[8] This study will draw from *Shadowes without Substance* (1646), a work that replies to Saltmarsh; and *A Mistake, or Misconstrvction, Removed. Whereby little difference is pretended to have been acknowledged between the Antinomians and Us* (1646) (hereinafter called *A Mistake*), also an answer to Saltmarsh.

Testimony to the Tenents of the Antinomian party'.[1] Gataker not
only rejects the claim but seems to have been driven to saying some
things even more explicitly than some of his colleagues.

Gataker defends not only the position that there are 'conditions'
by which one is saved but states that repentance precedes faith in
order. There are 'conditions, you see, reqired; and those not of
faith alone, but of repentance, and humiliation, and self-deniall, and
conversion, and renouncing of all, in disposition and purpose at
least'.[2]

Thus when Christ said that salvation is given to him who
'believes', it was 'not as if He required nothing els but *faith* of his
followers'.[3] For faith 'hath a peculiar office in that work that no
other grace hath; yet there is more then faith required unto
salvation'. Moreover, John the Baptist preached the pardon of sin
'upon the condition of faith and repentance, and newness of life'.[4]
Furthermore, Paul preached 'repentance towards God, and Faith
on Christ', putting repentance 'in the front'.[5] And in Matthew 4: 17,
Gataker asks, does not Christ 'command first to repent, and then to
beleev? for in that order his words run'.[6] The reason is that
'the commandement of repentance, and charity, and conversion,
and humiliation, [is] of the same nature with that of faith and
belief'.[7]

Gataker is thus found in the position of William Ames, who, as
will be recalled, does not clearly distinguish between faith and
repentance. They are, Gataker says, 'of the same nature'. What
Gataker opposes is assurance by an 'immediate voice'.[8] He believes
that the marks of faith—'repentance, selfdenyall, and obedience'—
are the 'grounds of assurances' which God's work allows.[9]

'FAITH' AND 'ASSURANCE'

On 20 August 1644 the Assembly appointed a committee to join
with the Scottish commissioners to draw up a Confession of Faith.[10]
Those originally appointed to draw up the Confession were nine

[1] *A Mistake*, To the reader. In *Free-Grace*, 224, Saltmarsh quotes Gataker in
support of his general theme, although the quotation itself is rather ambiguous.
[2] *A Mistake*, 10. [3] Ibid. 11.
[4] Ibid. Cf. *Shadowes without Substance*, 42. [5] *A Mistake*, 14.
[6] Ibid. 20. [7] Ibid. 21.
[8] *Shadowes without Substance*, 86. [9] Ibid.
[10] *Minutes*, lxxxvii.

divines: William Gouge, Thomas Gataker, John Arrowsmith, Thomas Temple, Jeremiah Burroughes, Anthony Burgess, Richard Vines, Thomas Goodwin, and Joshua Hoyle.[1] On 4 September 1644 Dr Temple, chairman of the Committee, requested that the same be augmented, and ten more were added: Herbert Palmer, Matthew Newcomen, Charles Herle, Edmond Reynolds, Thomas Wilson, Antony Tuckney, Brocket Smith, Thomas Young, John Ley, and Obadiah Sedgwick.[2] But on 12 May 1645 the *Minutes* states:

Report of the Confession of Faith read and debated. The first voted. Debate about the Committee for drawing up the Confession. The first draught of the Confession of Faith shall be drawn up by a Committee of a few.[3]

The 'Committee of a few' was comprised of seven: Reynolds, Hoyle, Herle, Gataker, Robert Harris, Temple, and Burgess.[4]

On 11 July 1645 it was ordered 'to divide the body of the Confession of Faith to the three Committees'.[5] This apparently means that the material prepared by the previous 'Committee of a few' should be handed over to larger committees, and be further discussed before being brought to the Assembly.[6]

In any case, these proceedings clearly show that no single divine, or even a minority, dictated the theology or wording of the Confession. But the most telling disclosure of the Assembly's *Minutes* as a whole is the apparently unquestioned acceptance of a distinction between faith and assurance; that 'Faith' should have one heading in the Confession and 'Certainty of Salvation' another.[7] This division between faith and assurance seems to have been accepted

[1] Ibid.   [2] Ibid.   [3] Ibid. 91.
[4] Ibid.   [5] Ibid. 112.
[6] Mitchell, op. cit. 358f. These three larger committees are probably three committees that had been originally chosen to undertake the revision of the Thirty-nine Articles. Ninety divines made up the original three committees. They are listed in Mitchell, op. cit. 145. On 16 July 1645 it was ordered that 'the first Committee' prepare the Confession 'upon these heads: God and the Holy Trinity; God's decrees, Predestination, Election, etc.; the works of Creation and Providence; Man's Fall. *Ordered*—The second Committee: Sin, and punishment thereof; Christ our Mediator. *Ordered*—the third Committee: Effectual Vocation; Justification; Adoption; Sanctification.' *Minutes*, 114.
[7] On 23 Feb. 1645 the heading 'Certainty of Salvation' was given to the Second Committee. On 19 Aug. 1646 it was resolved that 'These heads of Faith, Repentance, and Good Works shall be referred to the three Committees in their order to prepare something upon them for the Confession of Faith'. Ibid. 270. This seems to mean that those drawing up 'Certainty of Salvation' were not even on the same Committee that drew up 'Faith', since the Second Committee apparently was given 'Repentance'. On 21 Sept. 1646 it was resolved that 'The several heads of the Confession of Faith shall be called by the name of Chapters'. Ibid. 286.

implicitly from early on in the Assembly. There is no indication at all of any questioning of this significant division. Calvin's view that faith *is* assurance was thus rendered incapable of penetration into the Westminster documents from the start.[1] Beza won the day.

---

[1] On 14 Jan. 1646 it was decided that the 'Committee for the Catechism do prepare a draught of two Catechisms, one more large and another more brief, in which they are to have an eye to the Confession of faith'. Ibid. 321.

14

THE NATURE OF SAVING FAITH
IN THE
WESTMINSTER ASSEMBLY DOCUMENTS

This infallible assurance doth not so belong to the essence of faith, but that a true beleever may wait long, and conflict with many difficulties before he be a partaker of it . . . therefore it is the duty of every man, to give all diligence to make his calling and election sure . . .[1]

THE nature of saving faith in the Westminster Assembly documents is to be seen as the credal culmination of the experimental predestinarian tradition.[2] The biblical verse 2 Peter 1: 10, the Scripture to which William Perkins primarily appealed in *Whether a Man*, and understood by him and his followers as the formula for obtaining personal assurance of election, finds its way into the Confession of Faith at the most crucial point regarding the nature of saving faith.[3]

---

[1] *The humble Advice of the Assembly of Divines, Now by Authority of Parliament sitting at Westminster, Concerning a Confession of Faith, with the Quotations and Texts of Scripture annexed* (1647) (XVIII. iii), 31-2. Hereinafter called *Confession of Faith*; citations will refer to chapters and verses in parentheses, plus the pagination from this original edition of 1647. The reader is cautioned that not all subsequent editions of the Westminster Confession of Faith follow the original consistently.

[2] In addition to *Confession of Faith* this study draws from the earliest editions of each of the two catechisms: *The humble Advice of the Assembly of Divines, Now by Authority of Parliament sitting at Westminster, Concerning a Larger Catechisme* (1647) and *The humble Advice of the Assembly of Divines, Now by Authority of Parliament sitting at Westminster, Concerning a Shorter Catechisme* (1647). The former hereinafter will be called *Larger Catechism*, the latter *Shorter Catechism*. Unfortunately the Questions and Answers of these are not numbered, thus only the pagination can be given.

[3] 2 Pet. 1: 10 is cited seven times in the Confession. Besides its being in the margin of XVIII. iii it is given twice in the margin relating to predestination in III. viii, which says, 'that men attending the Will of God revealed in his Word, and yeelding obedience thereunto, may, from the certainty of their effectuall Vocation, be assured of their eternall Election [2 Pet. 1: 10]. So shall this Doctrine afford matter of praise, reverence, and admiration of God, and of humility, diligence, and abundant consolation to all that sincerely obey the Gospel [2 Pet. 1: 10].' It is cited twice in XVI ('Of Good Works'): (ii) 'These good works, done in obedience to Gods Commandments, are the fruits and evidences of a true and lively faith: and, by them, Beleevers manifest their thankfulnesse, strengthen their assurance [2 Pet. 1: 5-10]'; and (iii)

While Perkins had raised 2 Peter 1: 10 before men's eyes in the immediate light of his awesome teaching of temporary faith, this Scripture was no less retained by all experimental predestinarians as the formula for attaining to assurance, the eventual virtual demise of the doctrine of temporary faith notwithstanding.

Even if Perkins's followers preferred to treat the doctrine of the temporary faith of the reprobate with a benign neglect, Perkins's doctrine of faith as a whole was taken seriously. Few modifications pertaining to the nature of saving faith were to come after Perkins; he laid the foundations and his followers built their theology upon them. Perkins needed correcting at two points; Ames stated it best: (1) the seat of faith is the will not the understanding; and (2) the active receiving of Christ (which Perkins, following Beza, called the second work of grace) is saving, not the passive receiving (which Perkins called the first grace).

There was, however, an embellishment of Perkins's teaching that emerged after him but which the Westminster divines left largely untouched, namely, an explicit teaching of preparation for faith. Such a teaching reached its peak in the theology of Thomas Hooker; but the Westminster divines modified this concept to such an extent that it at first bears little likeness to the way he and others had expounded it. The most interesting omission in Westminster theology is an explicit doctrine of preparation for grace. It is possible that the awareness of the 'Antinomian' arguments served to render that teaching unsatisfactory for a creed that was to affirm man's utter inability to save himself. However, as will be seen below, there are lines in the documents none the less to which a preparationist might readily appeal.

Westminster theology may be briefly summarized: it is predestinarian, voluntaristic, and experimental.

PREDESTINATION AND FREE WILL

By God's decree some are 'predestinated unto everlasting life, and others fore-ordained to everlasting death'.[1] The number of both

---

'they ought to be diligent in stirring up the grace of God that is in them [2 Pet. 1: 3, 5, 10–11].' It is cited in XVII. i regarding the perseverance of the saints, and in XVIII. ii concerning assurance of grace: that assurance is grounded in 'the inward evidence of those graces unto which these promises are made [2 Pet. 1: 4–5, 10–11]'. *Confession of Faith*, 10, 28, 30, 31.

[1] *Confession of Faith* (III. iii), 9. Those not elected to eternal life God was pleased 'to passe by; and, to ordain them to dishonour and wrath, for their sin, to the praise

elect and reprobate 'is so certain, and definite, that it cannot be either increased, or diminished'.[1] A further statement, probably directed at the Arminians, is that God's decree is 'without any foresight of Faith, or Good works, or perseverance'.[2] Moreover, Westminster theology embraces a limited atonement:

> To all those for whom Christ hath purchased Redemption, he doth certainly, and effectually apply, and communicate the same, making intercession for them, and revealing unto them, in, and by the Word, the mysteries of salvation, effectually perswading them by his Spirit, to beleeve, and obey . . .[3]

This strong predestinarianism is accompanied by a strong assertion of man's total inability. Owing to man's 'original corruption', all are 'utterly indisposed, dis-abled, and made opposite to all good, and wholly inclined to all evil'.[4] As a result of the Fall, man 'hath wholly lost all ability of Will to any spirituall good accompanying salvation' and so 'is not able, by his own strength, to convert himself, or to prepare himself thereunto'.[5] This statement flies in the face of a theology like Thomas Hooker's, who explicitly stated that the natural man can, by virtue of common grace, get himself under the means, which, in turn, are effectual. Westminster theology thus stays clear of such a teaching.

However, the same God who appointed the elect to glory also 'fore-ordained all the means thereunto'.[6] Although God decreed 'all things [which] come to passe',[7] in 'ordinary Providence [He] maketh use of meanes' although He is free to work without them.[8] God effectually calls by 'his Word and Spirit',[9] and the Law of God is 'of great use' to the unregenerate, as it discovers 'the sinfull pollutions of their nature, hearts, and lives', increasing 'further humiliation for, and hatred against sin'.[10] This provides 'a clearer sight of the

of his glorious justice'. A similar statement is found in *Larger Catechism*, 4. The phrase 'to passe by' probably satisfied the infralapsarians, while the supralapsarians would not be likely to object either.

[1] *Confession of Faith* (III. iv), 9.   [2] Ibid. (III. v), 9.   [3] Ibid. (VIII. viii), 18.
[4] Ibid. (VI. iv), 14. Cf. *Larger Catechism*, 3.
[5] *Confession of Faith* (IX. iii), 20.
[6] Ibid. (III. vi), 9. 1 Pet. 1: 2, Eph. 1: 4–5, and Eph. 2: 10 are cited in the margin.
[7] Ibid. (v. ii), 12. 'He hath for his only glory, unchangeably, fore-ordained whatsoever comes to passe in time.' *Larger Catechism*, 3.
[8] *Confession of Faith* (v. iii), 12.   [9] Ibid. (x. i), 21.
[10] Ibid. (XIX. vi), 34. 'The Morall Law is of use to all men, to inform them of the holy nature and will of God, and of their duty . . . and thereby help them to a clearer sight of the need they have of Christ.' *Larger Catechism*, 24.

need they have of Christ'.[1] The *Larger Catechism* put a question:

Q. What doth God require of us that we may escape his wrath and curse due to us by reason of the transgression of the Law?
A. That we may escape the wrath and curse of God due to us by reason of the transgression of the Law, he requireth of us repentance toward God, and faith toward our Lord Jesus Christ, and the diligent use of the outward means whereby Christ communicates to us the benefits of his mediation.[2]

Because of the earlier assertion concerning man's inability to prepare himself for conversion, these statements must be taken to assume that the enquirer is already regenerate, although this is not made clear. Yet it seems that the divines are careful not to rule out the preparation process from being a vital part of the *ordo salutis*. For to those who enquire about their destinies preparation in some sense is apparently assumed. Indeed the Law precedes the Gospel in this process as also repentance precedes faith.

SAVING FAITH

The differences between Westminster theology and John Calvin are implicitly manifested above: the Law goes before the Gospel as repentance precedes faith. But on saving faith itself the differences are more obvious. While the idea of assurance of election itself may have come from Calvin, his theology concerning it seems never to have been considered by the Westminster divines. As the Arminian threat was nipped in the bud by the careful selection of the Westminster divines, so the possibility that pure Calvinism would be given credal sanction was extinguished once the decision was made to separate faith and assurance in the Confession.

Not once can there be found the synonyms for saving faith seen so often in Calvin—as assurance (or full assurance), persuasion, knowledge, apprehension, perception, or conviction. Instead Westminster theology manages consistently to use voluntaristic words: accepting, receiving, assenting, resting, yielding, answering, and embracing. There is no hint of man's will being effaced; it is rather renewed.

The Westminster description of effectual calling encompasses what Ames called the active and passive receiving of Christ. It will

---

[1] *Confession of Faith* (XIX. vi), 34.
[2] *Larger Catechism*, 44f. 'It is required of those that hear the Word preached, that they attend upon it with diligence, preparation, and prayer.' Ibid. 46. Cf. *Shorter Catechism*, 15.

be recalled that Ames insisted that both are a part of God's calling
but that faith is not saving until the *will* embraces the Gospel;
passive receiving is in the mind, active receiving is in the will.[1] The
Confession states that the elect are called when the Spirit and Word
work, 'inlightning their mindes, spiritually and savingly to understand the things of God; taking away their heart of stone, and
giving unto them an heart of flesh; renewing their wills . . .
effectually drawing them to Jesus Christ: yet so, as they come most
freely, being made willing by his grace'.[2] Man is thus enabled 'to
answer' the call, and 'to embrace' grace.[3]

'Saving Faith' itself is not only believing that God's word is true,
but 'yeelding obedience to the Commands, trembling at the threatnings, and imbracing the Promises of God for this life, and that
which is to come. But the principall Acts of saving faith, are,
Accepting, Receiving, and Resting upon Christ alone. . . .'[4] The
Larger Catechism describes justifying faith as when one 'not only
assenteth to the truth of the promise of the Gospel, but receiveth
and resteth upon Christ and his righteousnesse therein held forth'.[5]
The Shorter Catechism says that 'Faith in Jesus Christ is a saving
grace, whereby we receive, and rest upon him alone for salvation, as
he is offered to us in the Gospel'.[6]

The Confession says that faith is the 'instrument of Justification',[7]
which was Calvin's term. But for Calvin faith as an instrument is
God's act, opening blind eyes; for the Westminster divines, even
though in the context of God's prevenient grace, faith is *man's* act:
'Faith, thus receiving and resting on Christ, is the alone instrument
of Justification.'[8]

The Westminster divines conclude the chapter on 'Of Justification' by countering the 'Antinomians'. There can be no doubt that
they had men like Crisp in mind when they inserted these lines:

God did, from all eternity, decree to justifie all the elect, and Christ did, in
the fulnesse of time, die for their sins, and rise again for their justification:
nevertheless, *they are not justified*, untill the holy Spirit doth, in due time,
actually apply Christ unto them.[9]

[1] *Supra*, p. 159 n. 6.   [2] *Confession of Faith* (x. i), 21.
[3] Ibid. (x. ii), 21. The *Larger Catechism* adds that men are enabled 'to answer his call, and to accept and imbrace the grace offered' (15). Cf. *Shorter Catechism*, 5f.
[4] *Confession of Faith* (xiv. ii), 25f. 'Receiving' and 'Resting' are used twice also in xi. i, ii ('Of Justification'), 22.
[5] *Larger Catechism*, 17.   [6] *Shorter Catechism*, 14.
[7] *Confession of Faith* (xi. ii), 22.   [8] Ibid.
[9] Ibid. (xi. iv), 23. The following paragraph (xi. v) also is aimed at the

Saving faith at any rate is 'different in degrees, weak, or strong'; but it 'gets the victory; growing up in many to the attainment of a full assurance through Christ'.[1] The insertion of 'many' seems to allow that some may never attain to such assurance.

TEMPORARY FAITH

The scandalous doctrine of temporary faith is given but bare recognition in the Westminster documents. It is not called temporary faith nor are its possessors called temporary believers. It is at this point also that Westminster theology concurs with Ames's *Marrow*. It will be recalled that Ames retained an 'orthodox' stance on the matter of temporary faith but said singularly little about it.[2] The Westminster divines put this doctrine as if they had the *Marrow* at their fingertips: 'Others, not elected, although they may be called by the Ministry of the Word, and may have some common operations of the Spirit, yet they never truly come unto Christ, and therefore cannot be saved. . . .'[3] The Larger Catechism states: 'although others may be, and often are, outwardly called' by the Word, and 'have some common operations of the Spirit', they are 'justly left in their unbelief' owing to 'their wilfull neglect and contempt of the grace offered to them'. In a word: such 'never truly come to Jesus Christ'.[4]

There is neither an explicit nor implicit hint that these 'common operations of the Spirit' affect the will, much less produce sanctification. The Westminster divines, consciously or not, concur with William Ames, who saw that a robust teaching of temporary faith will not mix with a voluntaristic doctrine of faith, namely, a faith that is gathered to be saving only if there are also discernible graces of the Spirit.

'Antinomians', who, like Eaton, claimed that God did not see the sins of the justified: 'God doth continue to forgive the sins of those that are justified: and, although they can never fall from the state of Justification; yet, they may by their sins, fall under Gods fatherly displeasure, and not have the light of his countenance restored unto them, untill they humble themselves, confesse their sins, beg pardon, and renew their faith and repentance.'

[1] *Confession of Faith* (XIV. iii).

[2] Cf. *supra*, pp. 154f.

[3] *Confession of Faith* (X. iv), 21 f. This is dealt with under 'Of Effectuall Calling'. Ames treated this subject in a strikingly similar way, also under 'Calling', in the *Marrow*. See *supra*, p. 155 n. 3.

[4] *Larger Catechism*, 16.

THE POSSIBILITY OF ASSURANCE

Although hypocrites and other unregenerate men may vainly deceive themselves with false hopes, and carnall presumptions of being in the favour of God, and estate of salvation; which hope of theirs shall perish: yet, such as truly beleeve in the Lord Jesus, and love him in sincerity, endeavouring to walk in all good conscience before him, may, in this life, be certainly assured that they are in the state of grace, and may rejoyce in the hope of the glory of God, which hope shall never make them ashamed.[1]

By separating faith and assurance Westminster theology has restated, although not using the express language, what experimental predestinarians called the direct act (saving faith) and the indirect (or reflex) act (assurance). It will be recalled that John Dod made the distinction in terms of 'Moon-shine' and 'Sun-shine' assurance, and claimed that few attain to the latter. The statement above says that those who endeavour to walk in all good conscience 'may' be assured. Moreover, 'a true beleever may wait long, and conflict with many difficulties before he be partaker of it'.[2]

It seems then that a believer could die without assurance. While the Confession states that 'infallible assurance' does not belong to the essence of faith, the Larger Catechism asserts merely that 'assurance' is not of the essence of faith.

Q. Are all true beleevers at all times assured of their present being in the estate of grace, and that they shall be saved?
A. Assurance of grace and salvation not being of the essence of faith, true beleevers may wait long before they obtain it . . .[3]

While Westminster theology, having been written almost entirely by pastors, is no doubt designed to encourage weak Christians who fear they may not be elected to salvation, this language is incommensurate with Calvin's idea that 'the least drop of faith' firmly assures. Calvin stated that seeing Christ, although afar off, assures; Christ is the mirror of our election. But holding out Christ as the ground of assurance as a direct act seems not to have been regarded as an option by the Westminster divines. If such an idea was in their minds, there is no trace of it in the Westminster documents. As seen earlier in the case of Beza and Perkins, a limited atonement prohibits making Christ alone the ground of assurance—at least by a direct act of faith.

Nevertheless, the Westminster divines claim that there 'may' be

---

[1] *Confession of Faith* (XVIII. i), 31.   [2] Ibid.   [3] *Larger Catechism*, 19.

attained 'not a bare conjecturall and probable perswasion, grounded upon a fallible hope; but, an infallible assurance of faith'.[1] Such infallible assurance then is grounded in what appear to be three propositions: (1) 'the divine truth of the promises of salvation'; (2) 'the inward evidence of those graces *unto which these promises are made*'; and (3) 'the testimony of the Spirit of Adoption witnessing with our spirits that we are the children of God'.[2] The first proposition is to be understood in terms of the covenant of grace, a common assumption in experimental predestinarian thinking and taken over by the Westminster divines, to be dealt with below.

The second proposition is astonishing; although it parallels some of the strongest assertions found in the experimental predestinarian tradition. It will be recalled that John Preston made a similar statement.[3] Had the Confession merely stated that the promise of *assurance* is made to the evidence of graces—or even that assurance is grounded in the evidences to which the promises of salvation are *annexed* (as the Assembly had once agreed on), such theology would not have been surprising. But this statement makes the inward evidences virtually the ground not merely of assurance but of *salvation*.[4]

Had this claim been a single utterance in a sermon it could be dismissed as an unguarded comment. But this line, having been put into the historic Westminster Confession, is compelling evidence that, after all, the divines had departed from Calvin as much as had certain preparationists, who made 'fitness' tantamount to Christ's entrance into the heart. The absence of an explicit doctrine of preparation in Westminster theology is virtually compensated by this remarkable statement that holds out the promise of salvation to those who can discover inward graces in themselves. Moreover, this assertion seals the grave in which Perkins's doctrine of temporary faith has been laid; the promise of salvation is made to the 'inward evidence' of graces; the fear of being reprobate, if one finds these evidences, is answered.

[1] *Confession of Faith* (XVIII. ii), 31.

[2] Ibid. (my italics). But see *Minutes*, 260. There was a definite stage in the Assembly's proceedings at which it was resolved that these evidences were regarded as being 'annexed' to the promises. Along the way this word was curiously changed to 'made'.

[3] Cf. *supra*, p. 121 n. 11.

[4] Since this line is under the chapter 'On Assurance', it may be thought that the assertion only means promises of *assurance*; but 'these promises' refers to 'promises of salvation' in the first proposition.

As for proposition three, it is not explained. It will be recalled that Paul Baynes and Richard Sibbes stressed the witness of the Spirit of adoption, but both, using circular reasoning, finally turned to the various 'effects' to prove one had this witness of the Spirit. There is no indication that the divines meant what, say, John Cotton meant —an immediate witness—although they might have allowed this possibility. What the divines do affirm is that one 'may' know his election 'without extraordinary revelation' and that by the 'right use of ordinary means'.[1] Hence it is 'the duty of every man, to give all diligence to make his calling and election sure'.[2] Both the Confession and the Larger Catechism stress a good conscience in connection with obtaining assurance.[3] Westminster theology agrees with Sibbes's statement that assurance is the reward of 'exact walking'.

REPENTANCE: THE CONDITION OF THE NEW COVENANT

The Westminster divines do not explicitly state that repentance is the condition of the new covenant. But they should have; for this is virtually what they finally say. While the Westminster divines never intended to make works the ground of salvation, they could hardly have come closer. Since saving faith is defined as 'yeelding obedience' to God's commands, the 'principall Acts' of faith being of the *will*, this seems to make the claims of 'free grace' suspect.[4] This is best illustrated by looking at the federal theology of these documents.[5]

While the old covenant (of works) was promised 'upon condition of perfect and personall obedience',[6] the 'Covenant of Grace' is promised to sinners, 'requiring of them Faith'.[7] In the 'second Covenant' God 'freely provideth and offereth to sinners a Mediator'; the sole requirement: 'Faith as the condition.'[8] God requires 'nothing of them for their Justification, but Faith'.[9] But while this

---

[1] *Confession of Faith* (XVIII. iii), 31.   [2] Ibid. 32.

[3] Ibid. (XVIII. i), 31; *Larger Catechism*, 19: 'Such as truly beleeve in Christ, and endeavour to walk in all good conscience before him, may, without extraordinary revelation . . . be infallibly assured.'

[4] All three documents make a point of using 'free grace' with reference to justification. 'Justification is only of free grace.' *Confession of Faith* (XI. iii), 23. 'Justification is an act of Gods free grace unto sinners.' *Larger Catechism*, 16. Cf. *Shorter Catechism*, 6.

[5] The description of the covenant of works and covenant of grace is substantially a repeat of what may be found in Perkins, Preston, and Ames. *Confession of Faith* (VII. i–iv), 15 ff.   [6] Ibid. (VII. ii), 15.

[7] Ibid. (VII. iii), 16.   [8] *Larger Catechism*, 7.   [9] Ibid. 16.

faith is said to be God's gift,[1] we also know it is an act of the will. And since we may believe—indeed, wait long—without assurance that our faith *is* saving, we must still turn elsewhere before we know we have truly met the 'condition'. Thus 'free' justification has a price after all before it can be enjoyed: our perseverance in repentance and good works. The old covenant was promised upon the condition of 'perfect and personall obedience'; the new is promised upon the condition of faith—'yeelding obedience to the Commands'.[2] The difference seems to be that perfect obedience was required under the old covenant and doing our best is required under the new.

Indeed, although repentance is not the cause of our being pardoned, 'none may expect pardon without it'.[3] Being repentant means that one 'so grieves for, and hates his sins, as to turn from them all unto God, purposing and endeavouring to walk with him in all the wayes of his Commandements'.[4] Men should not be contented 'with a generall repentance, but it is every mans duty to endeavour to repent of his particular sins, particularly'.[5] Sanctification is described in much the same way, stressing mortification of lusts and the universality of sanctification 'in the whole man; yet imperfect in this life'.[6] Furthermore, 'good works' done in obedience to God's commandments 'are the fruits and evidences of a true and lively faith', and by them believers 'strengthen their assurance'.[7]

Although Westminster theology posits simply that 'faith' is the condition of the new covenant, by describing faith as an act of the will it comes quite close to making justification, or, at least, the knowledge of it, the reward for doing our best to be holy and good. While the predestinarian structures of Westminster theology are undeniable—making salvation utterly the gift of God—its doctrine of faith none the less tends to put the responsibility for salvation right back on to man.[8]

---

[1] *Larger Catechism*, 16.   [2] *Confession of Faith* (XIV. ii), 25.
[3] Ibid. (XV. iii), 26-7. Cf. *Larger Catechism*, 18, where the phrase 'new obedience' is added. Cf. *Shorter Catechism*, 14.
[4] *Confession of Faith* (XV. ii), 26.   [5] Ibid. (XV. v), 27.
[6] Ibid. (XIII. ii), 25.   [7] Ibid. (XVI. ii), 28.
[8] The retaining of a good conscience is ultimately connected to keeping the moral Law. The Law has promises annexed to it for the regenerate, showing them 'Gods approbation of obedience, and what blessings they may expect from the performance thereof'. Such uses of the Law 'sweetly comply' with the Gospel. Ibid. (XIX. vi, vii), 34. The *Larger Catechism* has an extended exposition of the moral Law (23-44). Cf. *Shorter Catechism*, 7-14.

Furthermore, once having obtained assurance, the believer may lose it.

True beleevers may have the assurance of their salvation divers wayes shaken, diminished, and intermitted; as, by negligence in preserving of it, by falling into some speciall sin, which woundeth the conscience, and grieveth the spirit; by, some sudden, or vehement temptation, by Gods withdrawing the light of his countenance, and suffering even such as fear him to walk in darknesse and to have no light . . .[1]

While such are 'never destitute of that seed of God',[2] inasmuch as believers 'can neither totally, nor finally, fall away from the state of Grace',[3] they seem to lose their assurance because it was grounded in a good conscience in the first place. Thus the loss of assurance is possible because the ground of assurance is not a solid rock but shifting sand; it may fluctuate in proportion to how one's conscience witnesses by reflection.

We are told, moreover, that our 'good works are accepted in Him',[4] not because they are perfect but because God 'is pleased to accept, and reward that which is sincere' for the sake of Christ.[5] This seems to bring us back to Perkins's idea that God accepts the will for the deed.[6] Assurance, then, is grounded in the reflection of our sincerity. This is the line so often seen in the experimental pre-destinarian tradition. Such a conclusion seems to be an inevitable consequence of imposing a voluntaristic doctrine of faith upon a theology of double predestination. On the other hand such a doctrine is likely indeed to be very far 'from inclining men to loosenesse'.[7] One of the offices of Christ the King is not only bestowing saving grace upon the elect but 'rewarding their obedience, and correcting them for their sins'.[8]

A good conscience, which must be maintained by good works, repentance, and perseverance, does not seem to be motivated by sheer gratitude to God for free salvation but by one's keen interest in salvation itself. While Calvin's doctrine of sanctification can be

---

[1] *Confession of Faith* (XVIII. iv), 32. Cf. Ibid. (XI. 5), 23. Cf. also Thomas Goodwin, *A Child of Light VValking in Darkness* (1643), 10, 17 ff., 29 ff., 43 ff. The 'immediate light of His countenance', which testifies we are His, may be 'utterly withdrawne', owing to the Spirit's own withdrawal, our own weakness, or Satan's temptation.

[2] *Confession of Faith* (XVIII. iv), 32.   [3] Ibid. (XVII. i), 30. Cf. ibid. (XII), 24.

[4] Ibid. (XVI. vi), 29.   [5] Ibid. (XVIII. iii), 32.

[6] Cf. *Larger Catechism*, 50: one who does not have assurance but who 'unfainedly desires to be found in Christ, and to depart from iniquity' should come straight to the Lord's Table.

[7] *Confession of Faith* (XVIII. iii), 32.   [8] *Larger Catechism*, 10.

seen as thankfulness, Westminster theology lends itself to making sanctification the payment for the promise of salvation. Presumably the loss of assurance means that the unhappy subject in such a time does not know but that he is reprobate after all. The only way to recover assurance is to till the ground—conscience—by measuring up to the Law.

There can be no doubt that Westminster theology, its failure to make Christ the ground of assurance notwithstanding, was written by serious men who desired supremely to glorify God. These divines firmly believed that the Church should be constituted of a holy people, and their doctrine of faith was intended to ensure such holiness.

But such insurance to protect the Church from Antinomianism and to preserve godliness costs, the cost that Calvin warned against —endless introspection, the constant checking of the spiritual pulse for the right 'effects', and, possibly, legalism. The Antinomian threat may have stopped the divines from inserting an explicit statement in behalf of preparation for faith, but it did little more; indeed, making the inward evidences of grace that to which the promises of salvation are 'made' is tantamount to a robust doctrine of preparation. Whatever else may be said about Westminster theology, one fact is plain: it is invulnerable to the charge of Antinomianism. The verse 2 Peter 1: 10 is seen not only as an encouragement to find assurance by a good conscience but warning against a life that does not experimentally prove one's calling and election.

Westminster theology, then, is experimental predestinarian. Its doctrine of faith is retroactive to Perkins and Beza, but not Calvin. Its actual theology is most akin to that of William Ames, who saw the need to correct Perkins, while retaining nearly all of his mentor's basic structures. Calvin's thought, save for the decrees of predestination, is hardly to be found in Westminster theology; only the notion of assurance itself seems traceable to Calvin. The Westminster divines retained the experimental way of thinking, which is more complicated than Calvin's simple idea, that 'Christ is better than a thousand testimonies to me'.

CONCLUSION

IN 1647, shortly after the Confession of Faith was completed, the Westminster divine John Arrowsmith told Parliament that 'the Crown and glory of England is, that she hath maintained the truth of Christ', and that the issue of the Confession 'will abundantly manifest to the world, that this crown is not wholly fallen from Englands head'.[1] It seems likely, moreover, that Edmund Calamy's hope that the Church's doctrine be settled 'that there may be no shadow in it for an Arminian'[2] was considered fulfilled by the emergence of this Confession.

But this must be questioned, not because the Arminians later (allegedly) held 'all the best bishoprics and deaneries' in England[3] but because of the crypto-Arminian doctrine of faith that pervades Westminster theology.

It was none other than Arminius himself who exposed the weaknesses of Perkins's theology. William Ames made some necessary corrections. Ames might have followed Arminius entirely, but he retained Perkins's predestinarian structures. Furthermore, correcting Perkins's doctrine of faith in the direction of Calvin would have required a radical alteration of the doctrine of atonement; but correcting Perkins within his own soteriological structures (which were also Ames's) required minor surgery.

When Ames made saving faith an act of the will, he solved the problem; he also effectively killed two Calvinistic notions: (1) faith as a persuasion, and (2) the doctrine of temporary faith. Perkins never should have made faith a persuasion in the first place, for he was really a voluntarist. He betrayed his voluntarism not merely by maintaining that one must 'apply' Christ to himself but by making faith a 'condition' of the covenant of grace; Arminius made faith an act of the will because he maintained that election itself was grounded in a 'condition'—faith. Moreover, Perkins ought never to have taken up Calvin's doctrine of temporary faith. He should have

---

[1] J. Arrowsmith, *A Great Wonder in Heaven* (1647), 30.

[2] Cf. *supra*, p. 184 n. 1.

[3] An old Arminian joke has it that when Bishop George Morley (d. 1684) was asked: 'What do the Arminians hold?', he replied: 'all the best bishoprics and deaneries'. Quoted in Carl Bangs, '"All the Best Bishoprics and Deaneries": The Enigma of Arminian Politics', *Church History* (1973), 5.

known that this would not mix with the view that sanctification is to be the ground of assurance.

Perkins's main problem apparently was that he could not see that Calvin and Beza were not alike. He may have assumed that Beza was but an extension of Calvin, and that Beza merely stated Calvin's theology better. Perkins's incorporation of the Heidelberg divines into the Bezan scheme was a good match; Ursinus and these men espoused a teaching that cohered well with Beza's thought, but not Calvin's. That these men retained faith as a persuasion (as well as the doctrine of temporary faith) seems due simply to their failure to be completely emancipated from the venerable Calvin to whom they owed so much. They were too close to their own theological enterprise to have sufficient objectivity to see that they were actually putting new wine into an old wineskin. This wineskin did not burst, however, until Arminius put his finger on Perkins's doctrine of faith. Ames provided a new wineskin for the Beza–Perkins theology, and the Westminster divines adopted a doctrine of faith and assurance which was everything Ames would have endorsed.

The architectural mind of Westminster theology, however, is Beza. Limiting the death of Christ to the elect robbed reformed theology of the simple idea that Christ alone is the mirror of election, hence the ground of assurance. Beza, moreover, was the first to use language that virtually made faith a condition that binds God to the promise;[1] the voluntarism of reformed theology centred on this concept, and things were never the same again. This voluntaristic seed grew into what we now know as federal theology. The voluntarism around which this scheme revolves began with Beza.

Faith for Calvin was never a 'condition'. In his words: faith is a passive work 'to which no reward can be paid'.[2] Concomitant with this was his view that the will is 'effaced' in conversion.[3] When Calvin set out to make salvation absolutely free, he succeeded—even making the gift of assurance as quickly attainable as the gift of Christ Himself; to Calvin they are the same. Calvin could not conceive of God giving His Son on the 'condition' of faith; for him the very seeing that God gave His Son *is* faith. Yet Calvin's pre-destinarianism is as inflexible as Beza's or Perkins's, except that he consistently maintained its hiddenness. That Christ had passed into the heavens to execute the secret decree was to Calvin the explanation for the way the secret testimony of the Spirit springs up in the hearts of the elect; but Calvin did not point men to the Spirit

---

[1] Cf. *supra*, p. 34 n. 3.   [2] Cf. *supra*, p. 20 n. 3.   [3] Cf. *supra*, p. 21 n. 1.

(Cotton's error) but to Christ's death—the 'pledge' from the Father that we are in fact chosen. Hence Calvin believed that the promise of salvation was 'made' (to use the Westminster phrase) to our *persuasion* that Christ died for us.

John Cotton is the only major figure in this study to take Calvin seriously; he read Calvin to understand what Calvin was really saying, something the experimental predestinarians apparently did not do. Cotton knew well where Calvin stood on most of the issues, and thought that, had Calvin been in New England in 1637, Calvin would have stood with him. And he would have, Cotton's failure to grasp Calvin's doctrine of atonement notwithstanding.

Westminster theology disowned thinking such as Cotton's. The Westminster divines seemed determined to produce a creed that left no room for Antinomianism or Arminianism. And they almost succeeded. But not quite; Arminius's doctrine of faith and assurance is so much like their own that it is remarkable that they seem not to have noticed it. The issue of the order of the decrees seems to have been more important to them; while the divines were quite anxious to retain the hardened predestinarianism of the Irish Articles to counter the Arminian view of predestination, they appear not to have noticed that Arminius's doctrine of faith was left untouched. Whether they would have reassessed their thinking had they noticed it is interesting but unprofitable speculation.

In any case, faith as an act of the will necessitates certain theological conclusions, all of which are those of Arminius: (1) the demise of faith as a persuasion; (2) the separation of faith and assurance; (3) the need for two acts of faith: the direct and reflex acts; and (4) assurance by the employment of the practical syllogism.

The question of perseverance remains. At first glance Westminster theology seems to have polarized itself against the Arminian hypothesis that the regenerate can fall. But not so; by taking back assurance from those who fall grievously into sin, the subject becomes suspect—both in his own eyes and in the eyes of others—in that he is back to zero, as it were, in his relationship to God. If he dies in a fallen condition, neither Westminster theology nor Arminius grant for sure that he is elected. Westminster theology theorizes that the fallen saint is never destitute of God's seed; but, like its predestinarianism as a whole, this is abstract and formal, and bears little connection to the concrete fact that the ground of assurance is godliness, and that that ground being removed removes hope.

It manifestly appears, then, that Westminster theology and Arminius agree that it is only the persevering believer after all who can be certainly said to be elected. If anything, Arminius might take the doctrine of temporary faith more seriously than Westminster theology. For it will be recalled that the Confession states that the promises of salvation are made to the evidence of graces, rendering groundless any fear of being reprobate; but the possibility of the ground of assurance being removed effectively puts one back into what Perkins would call temporary faith. However, the Westminster divines do not say this. Their solution probably would have been Perkins's, but they dare not raise that option openly in view of their statement that the promises of salvation are made to the evidence of grace; this kind of theology forced them to leave the matter of temporary faith alone.

Westminster theology is thus haunted with inconsistencies. These might have been largely resolved had they simply made Christ's death the ground of assurance.[1] But positing this would have ultimately forced them to the unversality of Christ's death, and Arminius had stolen that teaching from Calvinism long ago. They retained the Beza–Perkins theology with Ames's corrections. But their doctrine of faith is essentially no different from that of the man whose system they wanted to bury.

Westminster theology, then, represents a substantial departure from the thought of John Calvin. The fundamental shift, which owes its origin to Beza's equating the number of the elect with those for whom Christ died, centres mainly on the issue of faith and repentance in the *ordo salutis*. Westminster theology itself does not explicitly say that repentance precedes faith, but it obviously puts repentance before assurance, and that to Calvin reverses the order. For the promise of salvation, to Calvin, is made to the persuasion, or assurance, or faith, or knowledge, that Christ died for us. Repentance, or regeneration, is the inevitable consequence but never that to which the promise is made.

Westminster theology hardly deserves to be called Calvinistic—especially if that term is to imply the thought of Calvin himself. Perkins may not have been the first to assume that he upheld 'the

---

[1] See Karl Barth, *Church Dogmatics* (1957) (ii. 2), 338, who thinks that, whether reformed theology followed Calvin or merely went the way it went, 'it was a bad and unpleasant choice'; for 'how can [one] be assured of his election in this way when he is actually chosen by an absolute decree?' But Barth seems to underestimate Calvin's conviction that Jesus Christ is the 'pledge' of our election.

Calvinists doctrine', and Warfield certainly was not the last to think that Westminster theology was Calvin's,[1] but the time is surely overdue that historical theology present a more accurate picture of what really happened between Calvin's era and that which witnessed the emergence of Westminster theology. In the painting of that picture, this study hopes to be a beginning.

---

[1] B. B. Warfield, *Studies in Theology*, 148, thus errs when he says there is 'nothing' in the Westminster Confession 'which is not to be found expressly set forth in the writings' of Calvin. William Cunningham, *The Reformers and the Theology of the Reformation*, 125 f., is more guarded. While he thinks the authors of the Westminster documents held the Reformers' view (he includes others with Calvin) of faith and assurance, the divines 'did not distinctly embody them' in the documents themselves. As to Cunningham's statement (397) that 'no sufficient evidence has been brought forward that Calvin held that Christ died for all men, or for the whole world', this study has sought to produce the evidence.

BIBLIOGRAPHY

Publications are from London unless otherwise stated

PRIMARY SOURCES

AMES, WILLIAM, *An Analyticall Exposition of Both the Epistles of the Apostle Peter, Illustrated by Doctrines out of Every Text*, 1641.
—— *Conscience with the power and Cases thereof*, n.p. 1639.
—— *The Marrow of Sacred Divinity*, 1643.
—— *The Svbstance of Christian Religion: Or, a plain and easie Draught of the Christian Catechisme, in LII Lectures*, 1659.
—— *Technometra*, Amsterdam, 1631.
ANDREWES, LANCELOT, *Two Answers to Cardinal Perron and other Miscellaneous Works of Lancelot Andrewes*, Oxford, 1854.
ARMINIUS, JACOBUS, *The Works of Arminius*, 3 vols., 1875, 1828, 1875.
ARROWSMITH, JOHN, *A Great Wonder in Heaven*, 1647.
BAILLIE, ROBERT, *The Letters and Journals of Robert Baillie, A.M.*, 3 vols., Edinburgh, 1841.
BALL, JOHN, *A Treatise of the Covenant of Grace*, 1645.
—— *A Treatise of Faith*, 1631.
BALL, THOMAS, *The Life of the Renowned Doctor Preston*, 1885.
BAXTER, RICHARD, *Reliquiae Baxterianae*, 1696.
BAYNES, PAUL, *Briefe Directions vnto a godly Life*, 1618.
—— *A Caveat for Cold Christians*, 1618.
—— *Christian Letters of Mr. Paul Bayne*, 1620.
—— *Comfort and Instrvction in Affliction*, 1620.
—— *A Commentarie vpon the first and second chapters of Saint Paul to the Colossians*, 1635.
—— *A Covngerbane against Earthly Carefvlnes*, 1618.
—— *The Diocesans Tryall*, 1621.
—— *An Entire Commentary vpon the Whole Epistle of the Apostle Paul to the Ephesians*, 1647.
—— *An Epitomie of Mans Misery and Deliverie*, 1619.
—— *A Helpe to trve Happinesse*, 1618.
—— *Holy Soliloqvies*, 1620.
—— *A Letter Written by Mr. Pavle Bayne, Minister of Gods word, lately deceased*, 1617.
—— *The Mirrovr or Miracle of Gods Love vnto the world of his Elect*, 1619.
—— *The Trial of a Christians Estate*, 1618.
—— *Two Godly and Frvitfvll Treatises*, 1619.
BEZA, THEODORE, *A Booke of Christian Questions and answeares*, 1578.
—— *A briefe and piththie summe of the christian faith*, 1565?

—— *A Briefe Declaration of the chiefe points of Christian religion set forth in a Table*, 1613.

—— *A Discourse, of the true and visible Markes of the Catholique Churche*, 1582.

—— *A Little Catechisme*, 1578.

—— *Master Bezaes Sermons Vpon the Three First Chapters of the Canticle of Canticles*, 1887.

—— *The Treasvre of Trueth*, 1576.

BOLTON, SAMUEL, *The Trve Bovnds of Christian Freedome*, 1645.

BRADFORD, JOHN, *The Writings of John Bradford M.A.*, 2 vols., Parker Society, 1847, 1853.

BRADSHAW, WILLIAM, *A Plaine and Pithy exposition of the second epistle to the Thessalonians*, 1620.

—— *A Treatise of Ivstification*, 1615.

BUCER, MARTIN, *Common Places of Martin Bucer*, Abingdon, 1972.

BULKELEY, PETER, *The Gospel Covenant, or the Covenant of Grace*, 1646.

BULLINGER, HENRY, *The Decades of Henry Bullinger*, 4 vols., Parker Society, 1848-51.

CALAMY, EDMUND, *An Account of the Ministers, Lecturers, Masters . . .*, 2 vols., 1713.

—— *Gods free Mercy to England*, 1642.

CALVIN, JOHN. *Note.* CTS refers to Calvin Translation Society, Edinburgh, 1845- . The commentaries are not given in alphabetical order but the order in which the books appear in the Bible.

—— *Commentaries on the Four Last Books of Moses*, 4 vols., CTS.

—— *Commentaries on the Book of Joshua*, CTS.

—— *Commentary on the Book of Psalms*, 5 vols., CTS.

—— *Commentary on the Book of the Prophet Isaiah*, 4 vols., CTS.

—— *Commentaries on the Twelve Minor Prophets*, 5 vols., CTS.

—— *Calvin's Commentaries: Matthew, Mark and Luke*, 3 vols., Edinburgh, 1972.

—— *Calvin's Commentaries: The Gospel According to St. John*, 2 vols., Edinburgh, 1959, 1961.

—— *Calvin's Commentaries: The Acts of the Apostles 14-28*, Edinburgh, 1966.

—— *Calvin's Commentaries: Epistles of Paul The Apostle to the Romans and to the Thessalonians*, Edinburgh, 1972.

—— *Calvin's Commentaries: The First Epistle of Paul to the Corinthians*, Edinburgh, 1960.

—— *Calvin's Commentaries: The Epistles of Paul to the Galatians, Ephesians, Philippians and Colossians*, Edinburgh, 1965.

—— *Calvin's Commentaries: The Epistle of Paul The Apostle to the Hebrews and The First and Second Epistles of St. Peter*, Edinburgh, 1963.

—— *Concerning the Eternal Predestination of God*, 1961.

—— *Institutes of the Christian Religion*, Library of Christian Classics, 2 vols., 1975.

CALVIN, JOHN, *Sermons on the Epistle to the Ephesians*, Edinburgh, 1975.
—— *Sermons on Isaiah's Prophecy of the Death and Passion of Christ*, 1956.
—— *Sermons of M. John Calvin, on the Epistles of S. Paule to Timothie and Titus*, 1579.
CAPEL, RICHARD, *Tentations: their Nature, Danger, Cure*, 1632.
CARYL, JOSEPH, *An Exposition with Practicall Observations Continued Vpon the Eighth, Ninth, and Tenth Chapters of the Book of Job*, 1647.
CHADERTON, LAURENCE, *A Fruitful sermon*, 1584.
—— *An Excellent and godly sermon preached at Paules Crosse*, 1578.
CLARKE, SAMUEL, *General Martyrologie*, 1677.
—— *The Lives of two and twenty English Divines*, 1660.
—— *The Marrow of Ecclesiastical History*, 1675.
CLEAVER, ROBERT, *Bathshebaes Instrvctions to her Sonne Lemvel*, 1614.
—— *A Briefe Dialogve, concerning preparation for the worthy receiuing of the Lords Svpper*, 1627.
—— *A Briefe Explanation of the Whole Booke of the Proverbs of Salomon*, 1615.
—— *A Declaration of the Christian Sabbath*, 1630.
—— *Fovre Sermons*, 1613.
—— *A Plaine and Familiar Exposition of the First and Second Chapters of the Prouerbes of Salomon*, 1614.
—— *A Plaine and Familiar Exposition of the Ninth and Tenth Chapters of the Prouerbes of Salomon*, 1612.
—— *A Plaine and Familiar Exposition of the Eleuenth and Twelfth Chapters of the Prouerbes of Salomon*, 1607.
—— *A Plaine and Familiar Exposition of the Thirteenth and Fourteenth Chapters of the Prouerbs of Salomon*, 1609.
—— *A Plaine and Familiar Exposition of the Fifteenth, sixteenth, and seventeenth Chapters of the Prouerbs of Salomon*, 1609.
—— *A Plaine and Familiar Exposition: Of the Eighteenth, Nineteenth, and Twentieth Chapters of the Prouerbs of Salomon*, 1610.
—— *A Sermon Preached by Master Cleaver: on Psalme 51. verse 1*, 1610.
—— *Three Sermons vpon Marke, the ninth chapter. 22. 23. verses*, 1611.

Note. The above should be correlated with the explanation given on pp. 84 ff. Some of Cleaver's sermons are listed under John Dod.

COTTON, JOHN, *Christ the Fountaine of Life*, 1651.
—— *Gods Mercie mixed with his Ivstice*, 1641.
—— *Milk for Babes*, 1646.
—— *A Practical Commentary, or An Exposition with Observations, Reasons, and Vses pon The First Epistle Generall of John*, 1656.
—— *A Treatise of the Covenant of Grace*, 1659.
—— *A Treatise of Mr. Cottons. Clearing certaine Doubts concerning Predestination*, 1646.
—— *The way of life*, 1641.

CRISP, TOBIAS, *Christ Alone Exalted; in seventeene Sermons*, 1643.

CULVERWELL, EZEKIEL, *A Treatise of Faith*, 1630.

DENNE, HENRY, *A Conference Between a sick man and a Minister, shewing the nature of Presumption, Despair, and the true living Faith*, 1643.

—— *The Doctrine and Conversation of John Baptist*, 1643.

DOD, JOHN, *Fovre Godlie and Frvitfvl sermons*, 1611.

—— *A Plaine and Familiar Exposition of the Tenne Commandements*, 1617.

—— *A Plaine and Familiar Exposition on the Lords Prayer*, 1635.

—— *A Remedy against Privat Contentions*, 1610.

—— *Seven Godlie and Frvitfvll Sermons*, 1614.

—— *Ten Sermons tending chiefely to the fitting of men for the worthy receiuing of the Lords Supper*, 1611.

—— *Three Godlie and Frvitfvll Sermons*, 1610.

—— *Two Sermons on the Third of the Lamentations*, 1610.

Note. The above should be correlated with the explanation given on pp. 84 ff. Some of Cleaver's sermons are listed under John Dod.

EATON, JOHN, *The Discovery of the most dangerous Dead Faith*, 1641.

—— *The Honey-combe of Free Justification by Christ Alone*, 1642.

F., E. (FISHER, EDWARD), *The Marrow of Modern Divinity*, 1645.

—— *The Marrow of Modern Divinity*, 1646.

FENNER, DUDLEY, *Sacta Theologia*, 1586(?).

FIRMAN, GILES, *The Real Christian*, 1670.

FULLER, THOMAS, *Abel Redevivus*, 1651.

—— *The Church History of Britain*, 6 vols., Oxford, 1845.

—— *A History of the University of Cambridge*, 1840.

—— *The History of the Worthies of England*, 1811.

—— *The Holy State*, 1848.

GATAKER, THOMAS, *A Mistake, or Misconstrvction, Removed*, 1646.

—— *Shadowes without Substance*, 1646.

GILLESPIE, GEORGE, *Notes of Debates and Proceedings of the Assembly of Divines and other Commissioners at Westminster*, Edinburgh, 1846.

GOODWIN, THOMAS, *A Child of Light Walking in Darknes*, 1643.

—— *The Works of Thomas Goodwin*, 7 vols., 1861.

GREENHAM, RICHARD, *The Workes of Richard Greenham*, 1612.

H., D., *An Antidote against Antinomianisme*, 1643.

HALL, DAVID (ed.), *The Antinomian Controversy, 1636, 1638: A Documentary History*, Middletown, Conn., 1968.

HEARTWELL, JASPER(?), *Trodden down Strength, by the God of Strength, or, Mrs. Drake Revived*, 1647. (G. H. Williams, 'Called by Thy Name', *Harvard Library Bulletin* (1968), 278 ff., argues that the author is Heartwell.)

HILDERSAM, ARTHUR, *The Doctrine of Communicating Worthily in the Lords Svpper*, 1630.

—— *Lectvres upon the Fovrth of John*, 1629.

HILDERSAM, ARTHUR, *CLII Lectvres upon Psalme LI*, 1635.
HOOKER, THOMAS, *The Covenant of Grace Opened*, 1649.
—— *The Faithful Covenanter*, 1644.
—— *Fovre Learned and Godly Treatises*, 1638.
—— *The Patterne of Perfection*, 1640.
—— 'The Poor Doubting Christian Drawn to Christ', in *Thomas Hooker*, Harvard Theological Studies, xxviii, Cambridge, Mass., 1975.
—— *The Sinners Salvation*, 1638.
—— *The Sovles Exaltation*, 1638.
—— *The Sovles Hvmiliation*, 1638.
—— *The Soules Implantation*, 1637.
—— *The Sovles Ingrafting into Christ*, 1637.
—— *The Sovles Possession of Cnrist*, 1638.
—— *The Sovles Preparation for Christ*, 1632.
—— *The Sovles Vocation*, 1638.
—— *The Vnbeleevers Preparing for Christ*, 1638.
The Journals of the House of Commons, vol. ii, 1803.
Journals of the House of Lords, vol. vi, n.d.
LIGHTFOOT, JOHN, *The Journal of the Proceedings of the Assembly of Divines*. This is vol. xiii of *The Whole Works of the Rev. John Lightfoot, D.D.*, 1824.
LUTHER, MARTIN, *Luther: Lectures on Romans*, Library of Christian Classics, 1961.
—— *Luther's Works*, vol. xxvi, St. Louis, 1963.
MARTYR, PETER, *The Common Places of the most famous and renowned Divine Doctor Peter Martyr*, 1583.
MATHER, COTTON, *Magnalia Christi Americana*, 2 vols., Hartford, Conn., 1853.
MITCHELL, A. F., and STRUTHERS, JOHN (eds.), *Minutes of the Sessions of the Westminster Divines*, 1874.
MOSSE, MILES, *Justifying and Saving Faith*, 1614.
MUSCULUS, WOLFGANG, *Common places of Christian Religion*, 1563.
NORTON, JOHN, *Abel being Dead yet speaketh; or, the Life & Death of . . . Mr. John Cotton*, 1658.
OLEVIANUS, GASPER, *An Exposition of the Symbole of the Apostles, or rather of the Articles of Faith*, 1581.
PERKINS, WILLIAM, *The Workes of that Famovs and VVorthy minister of Christ in the Vniversitie of Cambridge, Mr. William Perkins*, 3 vols., Cambridge, 1608, 1609.
PRESTON, JOHN, *The Breast-Plate of Faith and Love*, 1630.
—— *The Deformed Forme of a Formall Profession*, 1632.
—— *The Doctrine of the Saints Infirmities*, 1638.
—— *Fovre Godly and Learned Treatises*, 1636.
—— *The Golden Scepter held forth to the Humble*, 1638.
—— *The Law ovt Lavved*, Edinburgh, 1633.
—— *The Nevv Covenant, or The Saints Portion*, 1630.

—— *The New Creatvre: or a Treatise of Sanctification*, 1633.
—— *Remaines of that Reverend and Learned Divine, John Preston*, 1637.
—— *The Saints Qvalification*, 1633.
—— *Sermons preached before his Maiestie*, 1630.
ROGERS, JOHN, *The Doctrine of Faith*, 1629.
ROGERS, RICHARD, *Certaine Sermons*, 1612.
—— *A Commentary upon the whole booke of Judges*, 1615.
—— *A Garden of Spirituall Flovvers*, 1638.
—— *Seven Treatises leading and guiding to true happiness*, 1603.
RUTHERFORD, SAMUEL, *Christ Dying and Drawing Sinners to Himself*, 1647.
—— *A Survey of the Spirituall Antichrist*, 1648.
—— *The Tryall & Trivmpth of Faith*, 1645.
SALTMARSH, JOHN, *Free-Grace: or, the Flowings of Christ's Blood Freely to sinners*, 1647.
SCHAFF, PHILIP (ed.), *The Creeds of the Evangelical Protestant Churches*, 1877.
SEDGWICK, JOHN, *Antinomianisme Anatomized or, A Glasse for The Lawlesse*, 1643.
SHEPARD, THOMAS, *Autobiography*, Boston, 1832.
—— *The Sound Beleever*, 1645.
SIBBES, RICHARD, *The Complete Works of Richard Sibbes*, 7 vols., Edinburgh, 1862-4.
SMITH, HENRY, *The Sermons of Mr. Henry Smith*, 2 vols., 1866.
SMITH, JOHN, *An Exposition of the Creed*, 1632.
STAUPITZ, JOHN, 'Eternal Predestination and Its Execution in Time', in *Forerunners of the Reformation*, ed. Heiko Augustinus Oberman, 1967.
TYNDALE, WILLIAM, *Doctrinal Treatises*, Parker Society, 1847.
—— *Expositions*, Parker Society, 1853.
URSINUS, ZACHARIAS, *The summe of christian religion*, 1633.
USSHER, JAMES, *The Whole Works of the Most Rev. James Ussher, D.D.*, 18 vols., 1847.
VOETIUS, GISBERTUS, *Selectarum Disputationum*, 5 vols., Utrecht, 1648-69.
WEBBE, GEORGE, *Briefe Exposition of the Principles of Christian Religion*, 1612.
—— *A Posie of Spirituall Flowers*, 1610.
—— *The Practice of Quietnes*, 1615.
WESTMINSTER ASSEMBLY DOCUMENTS:
A Copy of the Petition of the Divines of the Assembly, Delivered to both Houses of Parliament, July 19, 1643, 1643.
The humble Advice of the Assembly of Divines, Now by Authority of Parliament sitting at Westminster, Concerning a Confession of Faith, with the Quotations and Texts of Scripture annexed, 1647.
The humble Advice of the Assembly of Divines, Now by Authority of Parliament sitting at Westminster, Concerning a Larger Catechisme, Presented by them lately to both Houses of Parliament, 1647.

Westminster Assembly Documents (*cont.*):
The humble Advice of the Assembly of Divines, Now by Authority of Parliament sitting at Westminster, Concerning a Shorter Catechisme, Presented by them lately to both Houses of Parliament, 1647.
WINTHROP, JOHN, *A History of New England*, 2 vols., Boston, 1825.
—— *Journal*, 2 vols., New York, 1908.
YOUNG, ALEXANDER, *Chronicles of the First Planters of the Colony of Massachusetts Bay*, Boston, 1846.
ZANCHIUS, GIROLOMO, *H. Zanchius His Confession of Christian Religion*, 1585.

SECONDARY SOURCES

ALLISON, C. F., *The Rise of Moralism*, 1966.
ARMSTRONG, BRIAN G., *Calvinism and the Amyraut Heresy: Protestant Scholasticism and Humanism in Seventeenth-Century France*, Madison, 1969.
BANGS, CARL, *Arminius*, Nashville, 1971.
BARTH, KARL, *Church Dogmatics* (ii. 2), 1957.
BAVINCK, HERMAN, 'Calvin and Common Grace', *Calvin and the Reformation*, New York, 1909.
BEVERIDGE, W., *A Short History of the Westminster Assembly*, Edinburgh, 1904.
BREWARD, IAN (ed.), *The Work of William Perkins*, Abingdon, 1970.
BRIGGS, C. A., 'The Documentary History of the Westminster Assembly', *Presbyterian Review*, New York, 1880.
BROMILEY, G. W., *Thomas Cranmer Theologian*, 1956.
BRONKEMA, RALPH, *The Essence of Puritanism*, Goes, Holland, 1929.
BROOK, BENJAMIN, *The Lives of the Puritans*, 3 vols., 1813.
BROWN, J., *The English Puritans*, Cambridge, 1912.
BURRAGE, CHAMPLIN, *The Earliest English Dissenters*, 2 vols., 1912.
BUSH, JR., SARGENT, 'Establishing the Hooker Canon', in *Thomas Hooker*, Harvard Theological Studies, xxviii, Cambridge, Mass., 1975.
CAMPBELL, W. E., *Erasmus, Tyndale and More*, 1949.
CARRUTHERS, S. W., *The Everyday Work of the Westminster Assembly*, Philadelphia, 1943.
—— *The Westminster Assembly: What it was & What it did*, 1943.
—— *The Westminster Confession of Faith*, Manchester, 1937(?).
CARRUTHERS, WILLIAM, *The Shorter Catechism of the Westminster Assembly of Divines*, 1897.
CLARK, G. K., *The English Inheritance*, 1950.
CLEBSCH, WILLIAM, *England's Earliest Protestants 1520-1535*, 1964.
COLLINSON, PATRICK, *The Elizabethan Puritan Movement*, 1967.
COOLIDGE, JOHN S., *The Pauline Renaissance in England*, Oxford, 1970.
CREMEANS, C. D., 'The Reception of Calvinistic Thought in England', *Illinois Studies in the Social Sciences*, Urbana, 1949.

CUNNINGHAM, WILLIAM, *Historical Theology*, 2 vols., 1862.
—— *The Reformers and the Theology of the Reformation*, 1862.
DAKIN, A., *Calvinism*, 1940.
DAVIES, HORTON, *The Worship of the English Puritans*, Glasgow, 1948.
—— *Worship and Theology in England*, 1970.
DEJONG, PETER Y. (ed.), *Crisis in the Reformed Churches: Essays in commencement of the great Synod of Dort, 1618-1619*, Grand Rapids, 1968.
DICKENS, A. G., *The English Reformation*, 1964.
Dictionary of National Biography, 21 vols., Oxford, 1917.
DOWEY, E. A., *The Knowledge of God in Calvin's Theology*, New York, 1965.
DUFFIELD, G. E. (ed.), *The Work of William Tyndale*, Abingdon, 1964.
EMERSON, E. H., 'Calvin and Covenant Theology', *Church History*, New York, 1953.
—— *John Cotton*, New York, 1965.
FORSTMAN, H. J., *Word and Spirit*, Stanford, 1962.
FOSTER, H. D., 'Liberal Calvinism; The Remonstrants at the Synod of Dort in 1618', *Harvard Theological Review*, Cambridge, Mass., 1923.
FOSTER, J., *Alumni Oxonienses 1500-1714*, 4 vols., Oxford, 1891-2.
GARRETT, C. H., *The Marian Exiles*, 1938.
GEORGE, G. H. and K., *The Protestant Mind of the English Reformation*, Princeton, 1961.
GERRISH, B. A., *Grace and Reason: a Study in the Theology of Luther*, Oxford, 1962.
GIBSON, E. C. D., *The Thirty-nine Articles of the Church of England*, 1898.
GREENSLADE, S. L., *The Cambridge History of the Bible*, Cambridge, 1963.
—— *The English Reformers and the Fathers of the Church*, Oxford, 1960.
GROSART, A. B., 'Memoir of Richard Sibbes, D.D.', in *The Complete Works of Richard Sibbes*, vol. i., Edinburgh, 1862.
GROTE, GEORGE, *Aristotle*, 2 vols., 1872.
HALL, BASIL, 'Calvin against the Calvinists', in *John Calvin*, ed. G. E. Duffield, Abingdon, 1966.
—— 'The Calvin Legend', ibid.
—— 'Puritanism: the Problem of Definition', *Studies in Church History*, vol. ii, 1965.
HALL, DAVID, 'Introduction', *The Antinomian Controversy, 1636-1638: A Documentary History*, Middletown, Conn., 1968.
HALLER, WILLIAM, *The Rise of Puritanism*, New York, 1957.
HARGRAVE, O. T., 'The Freewillers in the English Reformation', *Church History*, New York, 1968.
HARRISON, A. W., *The Beginnings of Arminianism*, 1926.
HENDRY, GEORGE S., *The Westminster Confession for Today*, 1960.
HETHERINGTON, W. M., *History of the Westminster Assembly of Divines*, 1834.

HILL, CHRISTOPHER, *Intellectual Origins of the English Revolution*, 1960.
—— *Puritanism and Revolution*, 1969.
—— *Society and Puritanism in Pre-Revolutionary England*, 1969.
HODGE, A. A., *The Atonement*, London, 1868.
—— *A Commentary on the Confession of Faith*, 1870.
HODGE, CHARLES, *Systematic Theology*, 3 vols., 1873.
HOLWERDA, DAVID E. (ed.), *Exploring the Heritage of John Calvin*, Grand Rapids, 1976.
HOOGLAND, M. P., *Calvin's Perspective on the Exaltation of Christ*, Kampden, Holland, 1966.
HORTON, DOUGLAS (ed. and trans.), *William Ames*. Three works on Ames by Matthew Nethenus, Hugo Visscher, and Karl Reuter. Harvard Divinity School Library, Cambridge, Mass., 1965.
HOWELL, W. S., *Logic and Rhetoric in England, 1500-1700*, Princeton, 1956.
HUEHNS, GERTRUDE, *Antinomianism in English History with special reference to the period 1640-1660*, 1951.
HUNTER, A. M., *The Teaching of Calvin*, Glasgow, 1920.
JANSEN, J. F., *Calvin's Doctrine of the Work of Christ*, 1956.
KEVAN, ERNEST F., *The Grace of Law*, 1964.
KNAPPEN, M. M. (ed.), *Two Elizabethan Diaries*, 1933.
—— *Tudor Puritanism*, Chicago, 1970.
KNEALE, WILLIAM and MARTHA, *The Development of Logic*, Oxford, 1962.
KNOX, D. B., *The Doctrine of Faith in the Reign of Henry VIII*, 1961.
KNOX, R. B., *James Ussher Archbishop of Armagh*, Cardiff, 1967.
KNOX, S. J., *Walter Travers: Paragon of Elizabethan Puritanism*, 1962.
LAURENCE, RICHARD, *An Attempt to Illustrate those Articles of the Church of England, which the Calvinists Improperly Consider as Calvinistical*, Oxford, 1805.
LÉONARD, ÉMILE G., *A History of Protestantism*, 2 vols., 1967.
LEWIS, PETER, *The Genius of Puritanism*, Haywards Heath, 1975.
LITTEL, FRANKLIN H. (ed.), *Reformation Studies*, Richmond, 1962.
LUPTON, LEWIS, *A History of the Geneva Bible*, 5 vols., 1966.
McADOO, H. R., *The Structure of Caroline Moral Theology*, 1949.
McDONNELL, KILIAN, *John Calvin, The Church and The Eucharist*, 1974.
McDONOUGH, T. M., *The Law and the Gospel in Luther*, 1963.
McGRATH, PATRICK, *Papists and Puritans under Elizabeth I*, 1967.
MACKINNON, JAMES, *Calvin and the Reformation*, 1936.
McLELLAND, JOSEPH C., 'The Reformed Doctrine of Predestination', *Scottish Journal of Theology*, Edinburgh, 1955.
—— *The Visible Words of God*, Edinburgh, 1957.
McNEILL, J. T., *The History and Character of Calvinism*, New York, 1954.
MERRILL, T. F., *William Perkins*, Niewukoop, 1966.
MILLER, PERRY, 'The Marrow of Puritan Divinity', *Publications of the Colonial Society of Massachusetts*, Boston, 1937.
—— *The New England Mind: The Seventeenth Century*, New York, 1939.

MILLER, PERRY, *Orthodoxy in Massachusetts*, New York, 1970.
—— '"Preparation for Salvation" in Seventeenth-Century New England', *Journal of the History of Ideas*, New York, 1943.
MITCHELL, ALEXANDER F., *Catechisms of the Second Reformation*, 1886.
—— *The Westminster Assembly*, 1883.
—— *The Westminster Confession of Faith*, 1867.
MØLLER, JENS G., 'The Beginnings of Puritan Covenant Theology', *Journal of Ecclesiastical History*, 1963.
MORGAN, EDMUND P., *The Puritan Dilemma*, Boston, 1958.
—— *Visible Saints: The History of a Puritan Idea*, New York, 1963.
MORGAN, IRVONWY, *The Godly Preachers of the Elizabethan Church*, 1965.
—— *Prince Charles's Puritan Chaplain*, 1957.
—— *Puritan Spirituality*, 1973.
MORISON, SAMUEL ELIOT, *Harvard College in the Seventeenth Century*, Cambridge, Mass., 1936.
NEAL, DANIEL, *The History of the Puritans*, 5 vols., 1822.
NEALE, JOHN, *Elizabeth I and Her Parliaments*, 2 vols., 1953, 1957.
The New International Dictionary of the Christian Church, ed. J. D. Douglas, 1974.
NEW, J. F. H., *Anglicans and Puritans*, 1964.
NIESEL, WILHELM, *The Theology of Calvin*, 1956.
NUTTALL, G. F., *The Holy Spirit in Puritan Faith and Experience*, Oxford, 1947.
—— *Visible Saints*, 1957.
OVIATT, EDWIN, *The Beginnings of Yale (1701-1726)*, New Haven, 1916.
The Oxford Dictionary of the Christian Church, ed. F. L. Cross, 1975.
PACKER, J. I., 'Calvin the Theologian', in *John Calvin*, ed. G. E. Duffield, Abingdon, 1966.
PARKER, T. H. L., 'An Approach to Calvin', *Evangelical Quarterly*, 1944.
—— 'Calvin's Doctrine of Justification', Ibid. 1952.
—— *Calvin's New Testament Commentaries*, 1952.
—— *The Doctrine of the Knowledge of God*, 1952.
—— *John Calvin*, 1975.
PARKER, T. M., 'Arminianism and Laudianism in Seventeenth-Century England', *Studies in Church History*, 1964.
PEARSON, A. F. S., *Thomas Cartwright and Elizabethan Puritanism*, Cambridge, 1925.
PETTIT, NORMAN, *The Heart Prepared*, New Haven, 1966.
—— 'Hooker's Doctrine of Assurance: A Critical Phase in New England Spiritual Thought', *New England Quarterly*, Boston, 1974.
—— 'The Order of Salvation in Thomas Hooker's Thought', in *Thomas Hooker*, Harvard Theological Studies, xxviii, Cambridge, Mass., 1975.
PIERCE, WILLIAM, *An Historical Introduction to the Marprelate Tracts*, 1908.
PORTER, H. C. (ed.), *Puritanism in Tudor England*, 1970.
—— *Reformation and Reaction in Tudor Cambridge*, Cambridge, 1958.

REID, J. K. S., 'Editor's Introduction', John Calvin, *Concerning the Eternal Predestination of God*, 1961.

ROGERS, J. B., *Scripture in the Westminster Confession*, Kamden, 1966.

ROLSTON III, HOLMES, *John Calvin versus The Westminster Confession*, Richmond, 1972.

RUPP, GORDON, *The Righteousness of God*, 1953.

SASEK, L. A., *The Literary Temperament of the English Puritans*, Louisiana, 1961.

SCHAFF, PHILIP, *The Creeds of the Evangelical Protestant Churches*, 1877.

SHUCKBURGH, E. S., *Emmanuel College*, 1904.

SISSON, R. A., 'William Perkins, Apologist for the Elizabethan Church of England', *Modern Language Review*, 1952.

SOLT, LEO F., *Saints in Arms*, 1959.

SPRUNGER, KEITH L. 'Ames, Ramus, and the Method of Puritan Theology', *Harvard Theological Review*, Cambridge, Mass., 1966.

—— *The Learned Doctor William Ames*, 1972.

—— '*Technometria*: a Prologue to Puritan Theology', *Journal of the History of Ideas*, New York, 1968.

STOEFFLER, F. E., *The Rise of Evangelical Pietism*, Leyden, 1971.

TOON, PETER, *Puritans and Calvinism*, Swengel, Pa., 1973.

TORRANCE, T. F., *Calvin's Doctrine of Man*, 1952.

—— *The School of Faith*, 1959.

TREVELYAN, G. M., *England under the Stuarts*, 1965.

TRINTERUD, L. J., *Elizabethan Puritanism*, New York, 1971.

—— 'The Origins of Puritanism', *Church History*, New York, 1951.

—— 'A Reappraisal of William Tyndale's Debt to Martin Luther', ibid., New York, 1962.

TUTTLE, JULIUS H., 'Writings of John Cotton', *Biographical Essays: a Tribute to Wilberforce Eames*, Cambridge, Mass., 1924.

TYACKE, NICHOLAS, 'Puritanism, Arminianism, and Counter-Revolution', in *The Origins of the English Civil War*, ed. Conrad Russell, 1973.

TYLANDA, JOSEPH, 'Christ the Mediator: Calvin versus Stancaro', *Calvin Theological Journal*, Grand Rapids, 1973.

ULLMANN, STEPHEN, *Words and Their Use*, 1951.

USHER, R. G., *Reconstruction of the English Church*, 2 vols., 1900.

VAN BEEK, MARTINUS, *An Inquiry into Puritan Vocabulary*, Groningen, 1969.

VAN BUREN, PAUL, *Christ in our Place: the Substitutionary Character of Calvin's Doctrine of Reconciliation*, Edinburgh, 1957.

VENN, J., *Alumni Cantabrigienses (1500–1751)*, 4 vols., Cambridge, 1922–7.

VON RUHR, JOHN, 'Covenant and Assurance in Early English Puritanism', *Church History*, New York, 1965.

WAKEFIELD, G. F., *Puritan Devotion*, 1957.

WALLACE, RONALD S., *Calvin's Doctrine of the Christian Life*, Edinburgh, 1959.

WARFIELD, B. B., *Calvin and Calvinism*, 1931.

WARFIELD, B. B., *Studies in Theology*, 1932.

—— *The Westminster Assembly and its Work*, 1931.

WATKINS, OWEN C., *The Puritan Experience*, 1972.

WELSBY, PAUL A., *Lancelot Andrewes 1555-1626*, 1958.

WENDEL, FRANÇOIS, *Calvin*, 1969.

WHITE, B. R., *The English Separatist Tradition*, Oxford, 1971.

WILLIAMS, GEORGE H., 'Called by Thy Name, Leave us Not: The Case of Mrs. Joan Drake', *Harvard Library Bulletin*, Cambridge, Mass., 1968.

—— 'The Life of Thomas Hooker in England and Holland, 1586-1633', in *Thomas Hooker*, Harvard Theological Studies, xxviii, Cambridge, Mass., 1975.

WILLIS, E. D., *Calvin's Catholic Christology*, Leyden, 1966.

WOOD, A. A., *Athenae Oxonienses*, 4 vols., 1813-20.

—— *Fasti Oxonienses*, 1815.

WOOD, THOMAS, *English Casuistical Divinity During the Seventeenth Century*, 1952.

ZIFF, LARZER, *The Career of John Cotton*, Princeton, 1962.

THESES OR DISSERTATIONS

BANGS, CARL, 'Arminius and Reformed Theology', Ph.D. dissertation, University of Chicago, 1958.

BREWARD, IAN, 'The Life and Theology of William Perkins', Ph.D. thesis, Manchester, 1963.

CARTER, R. B., 'The Presbyterian-Independent Controversy with Special Reference to Dr. Thomas Goodwin and the Years 1640 to 1660', Ph.D. thesis, Edinburgh, 1961.

CHALKER, WILLIAM H., 'Calvin and Some Seventeenth Century English Calvinists: A Comparison of Their Thought Through an Examination of Their Doctrines of the Knowledge of God, Faith, and Assurance', Ph.D. dissertation, Duke University, 1961.

DAY, S. R., 'A Life of Archbishop Richard Bancroft', D.Phil. thesis, Oxford, 1956.

DEWAR, M. W., 'How Far is the Westminster Assembly of Divines an Expression of 17th Century Anglican Theology?', Ph.D. thesis, Queen's University, Belfast, 1960.

FARRELL, FRANK E., 'Richard Sibbes: a Study in Early Seventeenth Century English Puritanism', Ph.D. thesis, Edinburgh, 1955.

FULOP, R. E., 'John Frith (1503-1533) and His Relation to the Origin of the Reformation in England', Ph.D. thesis, Edinburgh, 1956.

HAGANS, J. M., *'The Marrow of Modern Divinity* and the Controversy Concerning it in Scotland', BD thesis, Trinity College, Dublin, 1966.

HASLER, R. A., 'Thomas Shepard: Pastor-Evangelist (1605-1649): a Study in New England Ministry', Ph.D. dissertation, The Hartford Seminary Foundation, 1964.

HUELIN, GORDON, 'Peter Martyr and the English Reformation', Ph.D. thesis, London, 1955.

IVES, ROBERT B., 'The Theology of Wolfgang Musculus', Ph.D. thesis, Manchester, 1965.

JOHNSTON, PHILIP F., 'The Life of John Bradford, the Manchester Martyr', B.Litt. thesis, Oxford, 1963.

KEEP, D. J., 'Henry Bullinger and the Elizabethan Church', Ph.D. thesis, Sheffield, 1970.

KLEMPA, WILLIAM J., 'The Obedience of Christ in the Theology of Calvin', Ph.D. thesis, Edinburgh, 1962.

KNOX, S. J., 'A Study of the English Genevan Exiles and Their Influence on the Rise of Nonconformity in England', B.Litt. thesis, Trinity College, Dublin, 1953.

POOLE, HARRY A., 'The Unsettled Mr. Cotton', Ph.D. dissertation, University of Illinois, 1956.

SHORT, K. R. M., 'The Educational Foundations of Elizabethan Puritanism: with Special Reference to Richard Greenham (1535?-1594)', Ed.D. dissertation, University of Rochester, 1970.

STRICKLAND, WILLIAM J., 'John Goodwin as seen through his Controversies of 1640-1660', Ph.D. dissertation, Vanderbilt University, 1967.

TIPSON, LYNN BAIRD, 'The Development of a Puritan Understanding of Conversion', Ph.D. dissertation, Yale University, 1972.

TUFFT, J. R., 'William Perkins (1558-1602), his Thought and Activity', Ph.D. thesis, Edinburgh, 1952.

TYACKE, N. R. N., 'Arminianism in England, in Religion and Politics, 1604-1640', D.Phil. thesis, Oxford, 1968.

WELLS, JUDITH B., 'John Cotton 1584-1652 Churchman and Theologian', Ph.D. thesis, Edinburgh, 1948.

INDEX OF SUBJECTS

INDEX OF NAMES

INDEX OF MODERN AUTHORS